GARDENLAND

Gardenland

NATURE, FANTASY, AND EVERYDAY PRACTICE

Jennifer Wren Atkinson

The University of Georgia Press
ATHENS

Paperback edition, 2020
Published by the University of Georgia Press
Athens, Georgia 30602
www.ugapress.org
© 2018 by Jennifer Wren Atkinson
All rights reserved
Designed by Erin Kirk New
Set in 10.5/13 Minion Pro by
Graphic Composition, Inc., Bogart, Georgia

Most University of Georgia Press titles are
available from popular e-book vendors.

Printed digitally

Library of Congress Cataloging-in-Publication Data

Names: Atkinson, Jennifer Wren, author
Title: Gardenland : nature, fantasy, and everyday practice / Jennifer Wren Atkinson.
Other titles: Nature, fantasy, and everyday practice
Description: Athens : The University of Georgia Press, [2018] |
Includes bibliographical references and index.
Identifiers: LCCN 2018011974| ISBN 9780820353197 (hardcover : alk. paper) |
ISBN 9780820353180 (ebook)
Subjects: LCSH: American literature—History and criticism. | Gardens in literature. |
Gardening in literature. | Agriculture in literature. | Environmentalism in literature.
| Agriculture—Social aspects. | Horticultural literature—United States—History. |
Environmental literature—United States—History and criticism.
Classification: LCC PS169.G37 A85 2018 | DDC 810.9/364—dc23
LC record available at https://lccn.loc.gov/2018011974

Paperback edition 978-0-8203-5874-1

For my parents, Dinah and Obbie,
who encouraged me to love all things green.

Contents

List of Illustrations ix
Acknowledgments xi

INTRODUCTION. "Gardens of the Mind": Planting the Seeds of an American Fantasy Genre   1

CHAPTER 1. American Garden Writing and the Reinvention of Work as Play   19

CHAPTER 2. Lost at Home: Mapping the Industrial-Era Garden and Farm   57

CHAPTER 3. Resensualizing the Garden: From Surface to Substance in Midcentury Food Writing   94

CHAPTER 4. Against the Grain: Reinventing the Garden in Contemporary Utopia   128

CHAPTER 5. Just Gardens: Uprooting and Recovery in the Postcolonial Garden   168

EPILOGUE. Garden Writing and the Phenomenology of Dirt   201

Notes   215
Bibliography   231
Index   249

Illustrations

1. Walker Evans, *Bud Fields Standing in Cotton Field, Hale County, Alabama* 11
2. Free vegetables 13
3. Thomas Cole, *The Course of Empire: The Arcadian or Pastoral State* 24
4. D. M. Dewey lithograph from *The Nurseryman's Specimen Book* 36
5. Illustrations from C. C. Coffin's "Dakota Wheat Fields" and Ray Stannard Baker's "The Movement of Wheat" 72
6. Map featured in Frank Norris's *The Octopus* 74
7. Tom Wesselmann, *Still Life #30* 101
8. The first Greenmarket 111
9. Map of Utopia by Ambrosius Holbein 133
10. Central Park cartoon by Frank Leslie 149
11. Ron Finley outside his home in South Central Los Angeles 157
12. Margaret Morton, *Bernard's Tree* 178
13. Ramiro Gomez and David Feldman, *Gardeners, Doheny Drive, West Hollywood*, and Ramiro Gomez, *A Lawn Being Mowed* 181

Acknowledgments

Many friends, colleagues, scholars, and garden writers made this book possible and are owed an immense debt of gratitude. While authors do not conventionally acknowledge people already quoted in their books, I wish to give special thanks to a handful of scholars whose writings were indispensable to this project. Perhaps the most influential work was William Conlogue's *Working the Garden: American Writers and the Industrialization of Agriculture*. Conlogue's analysis of industrial impacts on American farming and literature deeply shaped chapter 2 in this book and brought my attention to a number of important literary sources and passages discussed in that section. It is hardly a stretch to say that this chapter would not exist in its present form without his groundbreaking work. Warren Belasco's work in food studies was essential to my discussion of midcentury food politics and counterculture in chapter 3. I am especially indebted to his analysis of American representations of food in science fiction. I have also benefited tremendously from Rachel Azima's scholarship on Jamaica Kincaid, Lynne Feeley's work on the gardens of enslaved African Americans, and Patricia Klindienst and Pierrette Hondagneu-Sotelo's extensive research on immigrant gardeners in the United States. The influence and contributions of these six scholars are readily apparent in the pages that follow, and for this I wish to express my deep gratitude.

For bringing critical attention to Charles Dudley Warner's *My Summer in a Garden* after the book had been out of print for nearly 125 years, I thank Alan Gurganus, who not only played an important role in reissuing this book through the Modern Library Gardening series but also helped me understand Warner's profound influence on the genre of garden writing in his introduction to the 2002 edition.

It is a pleasure to acknowledge the kindness and intellectual support I received over the years from Lyman Tower Sargent, Lawrence Buell, Scott Slovic, Bill Brown, members of the Association for the Study of Literature and Environment, and participants in the 2013 "Earth Perfect?" symposium, particularly the organizers, Naomi Jacobs and Annette Giesecke. My research has also been supported by the librarians and staff at the University of Washington and University of Chicago libraries, with special thanks owed to Leslie Hurst, Dani Rowland, and Denise Hattwig.

Two chapters of this book revise versions of essays published earlier. Elements from the introduction were published originally in *Earth Perfect? Nature, Utopia and the Garden*, edited by Annette Giesecke and Naomi Jacobs (Black Dog, 2012). An earlier version of chapter 4 was first published as "Seeds of Change: The New Place of Gardens in Contemporary Utopia" in *Utopian Studies* 18, no. 2 (2007). I am grateful to the editors of these journals and collections for making it possible to publish revised versions of my work in the present book.

Many thanks go to my family and friends for their encouragement over the years. This book would have been impossible to write without their unwavering love and support.

Above all, I want to thank my mentor and friend, Lauren Berlant, for her intellectual, scholarly, and personal generosity. She has been a champion of this project for well over a decade and is, beyond any doubt, one of the most patient and visionary people I know. Lauren, you would make a fantastic gardener.

GARDENLAND

INTRODUCTION

"Gardens of the Mind"

Planting the Seeds of an American Fantasy Genre

> You might expect the winter solstice, by its absence of stimulus, to repair the moral ravages of the summer. . . . On the contrary, when the winds of January whip the windows, out come the flower catalogues, those glowing monuments of false promise. Forgetful of last season's failures, the gardener's eyes, feasting on pictured roses, grow bright with delirium. In hectic rhapsody he whispers enchanted names—Fiery Cross, Phantom Blue, Sunnybrook Earliana, Arabis Alpina, Beauty of Hebron.
> —Winifred Margaretta Kirkland (1916)

> For gardeners, this is the season of lists and callow hopefulness; hundreds of thousands of bewitched readers are poring over their catalogues, making lists for their seed and plant orders, and dreaming their dreams.
> —Katharine White (1958)

For those who aren't lucky enough to live in year-round gardening climates, winter is the high season of garden books. Trapped indoors for months at a time, armchair gardeners pass dark evenings poring over glossy publications and sketching new schemes, making wish lists from seed catalogs, reading how-to guides on pruning techniques, or visualizing the first ripe strawberry. Like any activity that transports the mind elsewhere—or else*when*—these winter reading rituals offer substitute pleasures in the absence of the "real thing," filling gardeners' imaginations with beds of fresh lettuce and ripe melons, planters overspilling with honeysuckle and hydrangea, the smell of tomato leaves, the flaming colors of autumn. Despite Henry Ward Beecher's nineteenth-century warning that gardeners not be "made wild by pompous catalogs from florists and seedsmen," growers often find the temptation impossible to resist. Katharine White, longtime editor for the *New Yorker* and a self-confessed "addict of gardening literature," once explained that "winter reading and winter daydreams of what might be—the gardens of the mind—

are as rewarding a part of gardening as the partial successes of a good summer of blooms" (21, 310). Czech author and garden-enthusiast Karel Čapek even claimed that he spent midwinter memorizing gardening catalogs until he could recite their openings like lines from the *Iliad*: "Acaena, Acantholimon, Acanthus, Achillea . . ." (19). In bookstores we may find these materials in the gardening section—but they might just as well be shelved under fantasy.

With spring's thaw, gardeners return to their plots, and daydreams fed by winter readings now take root in actual soil. But what if "real" gardening itself also serves as a kind of fantasy practice—a way of indulging desires for other states, places, activities, and times? What if the whole enterprise—from inner-city gardens, high-rise window boxes, and Martha Stewart to the laser-planed lawns of suburbia, Michelle Obama's White House garden, and those towering stacks of wintertime reading—tells a much bigger story about our hopes, fears, and anticipations?

Indeed, the reasons for gardening's popularity are not always self-evident. Practical considerations alone can rarely account for growers' extraordinary effort; as countless gardeners will attest, it is far easier to just buy that onion at the supermarket, bypassing the whole ordeal of back-straining work, unanticipated costs, muddy knees and dirty nails, the ruinous effects of bad weather and bugs—and, in the end, the uncertainty of success. Something infinitely more complex than onions and oleander surely drives this literature, fantasy, and everyday practice—something touching on our desires for connectivity, slowness, and sensuous contact with nature; for beauty, pride, and purpose in our work; for community, health, and home.

And yet to identify gardening as a "fantasy magnet" is not to say that the practice is somehow *unreal*, or to suggest that growers are indulging delusions in tending their plots. Rather, it is to suggest that like the publications themselves, which feed our imaginations with all the pleasures postponed by winter, gardening allows us to inhabit modes of thought and practice that may otherwise be suspended in daily life. As such, gardens have an uncanny ability to throw light on the broader structure of failure and frustration characterizing everyday experience in the office, factory, and home, in shopping centers, city streets, and cyberspace. This is precisely the mechanism that philosopher Ernst Bloch highlights in *The Principle of Hope*, reminding us that fantasy and utopian daydreaming are not simply acts of wishful thinking that point *elsewhere*; they are mirrors onto the present, drawing attention to the shortcomings of existing social structures. Perhaps, then, that image of the garden as a fantasy magnet is just the metaphor for guiding our discussion here: after all, any number of things may reveal their magnetic properties by shifting and turning when a lodestone is placed in their midst.

The insights offered by American garden writing are thus relevant beyond the domain of kale enthusiasts and compost geeks. Indeed, the genre's development from the nineteenth century to the present offers a unique angle of vision into some far-flung zones of U.S. history and culture: from the modernization of farming and mechanization of labor to the growth of modern cities, the rise of environmentalism, and everyday acts of resistance to the legacy of industrialization. Across these historical transformations, American writers and growers have turned to gardening practice to both manage anxieties and imagine alternatives, revealing a broader landscape of fantasy and longing for less alienated forms of labor, a sense of connection to place and the biological processes that sustain us, ways of imagining value beyond capitalist commodification, a more measured pace of daily life, and even hope for our planet's future.

In defining the garden as an idea, a place, and an action, landscape architects Mark Francis and Randolph Hester argue that "by making gardens, using or admiring them, and dreaming of them, we create our own idealized order of nature and culture" (2). Owing to the expansive terrain covered in this book, the "gardens" it explores take a diversity of forms that go beyond even Francis and Hester's broad framing. While personally maintained domestic spaces (food and ornamental plots) are the centerpiece of my discussion, I also examine cultivated sites like parks and lawns, community gardens and urban farms, orchards, landscape art, and more. Commercial farms appear throughout the story as well, often serving as a foil to the garden. Yet despite the outward variation in these forms, what unites the places and practices across the discussion is the simple act of encounter between people and living plants, and the understanding, as Isis Brook puts it, that "inherent in the idea of a garden is some kind of care or attention beyond the initial design." Thus, she elaborates, "gardening" at its most basic refers to efforts in which we act "to nurture plants, to shape and develop, or just to encourage what grows" (14).

Since these gardens take multiple forms and span vast arcs of time, their literary counterparts are highly variable as well. Writ large, "gardening literature" may refer to anything from instructional guides, seed catalogs, and reference books to glossy coffee-table publications with lavish images and minimal amounts of text. "Garden writing," on the other hand, carries a slightly more specialized meaning, often referring to a relatively stylized or "literary" mode where the writer's personal reflections and voice (which may range from formal to chatty) are more pronounced.¹ A certain "persona" thus emerges in much of this literature, connecting readers to garden writers we come to know as people, be they amateur home growers, botanists, or nursery specialists; humorists, novelists, artists, or critics; journalists, foragers, conversationalists, or philosophers. This range indicates the inherently hybrid and inclusive nature of the genre, in which a single text may embrace such elements as memoir, natural history, philosophy, local-color writing, DIY handbooks, and more.

Yet in exploring the many ways these real and represented gardens draw forth desires and fantasy elements in American literature and culture, I consider a wide range of texts reaching well beyond "garden writing" as such, including Thomas Jefferson's farm journals and Henry David Thoreau's whimsical reflections on his bean field in *Walden*; Progressive-era journalism and the agrarian novels of Willa Cather, Frank Norris, and John Steinbeck; postcolonial garden writing and the horticultural crime scenes depicted by Jamaica Kincaid, Leslie Marmon Silko, and Héctor Tobar; "guerilla gardening" manifestos, contemporary Hollywood film, and science fiction narratives by Kim Stanley Robinson, Ursula Le Guin, Octavia Butler, and Margaret Atwood. In fact, many of the cultural texts examined here do not consciously set out to talk about gardens at all; their explicit interest may lie with cities and public space, with matters of waste and value, with ways that people cope with historical trauma or merely survive the precarity of daily life. In the process, however, a surprising number end up drawing on the meanings and possibilities of cultivation and projecting into the garden's midst their desires for a better shot at the good life. In this way, encounters in the American garden open new vistas for literary and environmental studies along with other realms that initially seem remote from the world of leeks and hollyhocks.

I am hardly the first observer to note the fantasy elements in gardening. Yet until recently, both scholarly and popular discussions of this topic have often reduced the complexity and singularity of gardening practice by conflating it with a mere act of "escape," a technique for distancing ourselves from life's daily burdens and demands. Stanley Cohen and Laurie Taylor's influential 1978 sociological study, *Escape Attempts: The Theory and Practice of Resistance to Everyday Life*, provides a classic example of that traditional view in exploring daydreams, hobbies, games, and other "interludes" through a framework wherein fantasy is understood as disengagement as such. As Cohen and Taylor define it, fantasy "directs the flow of imagination and conjures up territories in an *alternative world*," making it "not just a matter of monitoring or distancing, but of projecting the activity or the self into something quite different" (73). Their example scenarios depict individuals largely absent from existing circumstances—even from their everyday identities: a child stuck at the dinner table imagines faraway adventures as a pioneer, a businessperson shuffling reports drifts away into sexual fantasies, a homemaker preparing dinner visualizes herself "as a member of royalty at a gala affair" (73).

Such characterizations also carry over when the discussion turns directly to gardening—which, interestingly, gets paired with stamp-collecting throughout *Escape Attempts*. Like the modeler or philatelist, Cohen and Taylor argue, the gardener "suspends self consciousness" through an activity that "is very high on routine and relatively low on monitoring or awareness." Indeed, the authors' rhetoric directly conflates gardening and utter banality: "is one really finding one's true self by sticking postage stamps in an album or growing large leeks?" they ask (98).

These statements are hardly surprising given our culture's long history of equating gardens with the apolitical and disengaged. The famous final lines of Voltaire's *Candide*, for example, express a resolution to return home and "cultivate our own gardens"—a remark many interpret as releasing the characters from reformist expenditures.[2] George Orwell's readers clearly understood this formula as well and sent angry letters to shame the author for keeping a rose garden, an activity, as one put it, that "encourages a sort of political quietism" (217). Moreover, there are plenty of contemporary gardeners who are themselves content to let this formulation stand: novelist Jamaica Kincaid recalls audience members in Charleston reproaching her for addressing race and politics during a keynote talk at a prestigious garden society ("Sowers" 41). Even climate change literature has seen fit to take a swipe at gardening. In her landmark book *This Changes Everything* (2014), Naomi Klein opens by previewing the social and ecological horror show just over the horizon—cities under water, collapsing life-support systems, climate refugees, and more—just before asserting it will take no effort at all to bring about this terrifying future: all that is needed is for us to "continue to do what we are doing now, whether it's counting on a techno-fix or tending to our gardens" (4). Browsing through any selection of American or British literature, from horticultural journals and advertisements to works of fiction in which gardens make brief cameos, the apolitical and escapist associations seem ubiquitous enough to warrant their own archive. And sure enough, if readers flip through the index of Martin Hoyles's horticultural history, *The Story of Gardening*, they will come upon the following entry: "Politics, incompatible with gardening" (311).

And yet for all the fantasy elements this practice undoubtedly involves, these hasty conflations—especially as depicted in Taylor and Cohen's caricatures of gardeners teleporting *out* of existing circumstances—grossly distort the extent to which gardens are also fundamentally about *presence*, engagement, immersion, the *now*. Moreover, to treat gardening as interchangeable with practices like stamp collecting or model-train building—as if any old hobby will do here—effectively strips the practice of its irreducible connectivity: its ability to enfold us in a dynamic biological process, to engage us in intimate, embodied, reciprocal encounters with the living world, and to reveal our embeddedness in networks of natural, literary, and social histories that bind all these relations at once. The garden, in short, is never some nonfunctional detail we might arbitrarily swap with some other hobby that happens to bring pleasure, any more than nature's process of growth and renewal could be exchanged for some other inanimate item on a list.

Moreover, as I emphasize throughout this book, fantasy and escapism can themselves carry a subversive potential. Indeed, even Cohen and Taylor acknowledge this in highlighting society's need to "carefully regulat[e] and patro[l]" fantasy zones, since it is here where "reality may slip away too far, providing glimpses of alternative realities" that can expose the injustices and inadequacies of actually existing conditions (95–96). Ernst Bloch notes a similar potential in his analysis of daydreams, travel, leisure activities, humanistic fantasies, and other indulgences when he shows the seemingly whimsical and frivolous as a manifestation of precisely that which is missing or deficient in actual life. As such, utopian scholar Ruth Levitas argues that these fantasy realms simultaneously engage both the absent and potentially present, desire and possible fulfillment, an imagined elsewhere and the real soil right beneath our feet and under our nails. In fact, she writes, it is precisely those tensions that express Bloch's understanding that it is "difficult to experience a lack and impossible to articulate it without some sense of what is lacked, the satisfaction that would meet the need. All wishful thinking," she writes, "thus draws attention to the shortcomings of reality, a necessary step on the way to change" (*Concept* 88).

"Comedies of Surplus"

While all this may strike readers as an overblown way to approach the meaning and possibility embedded in some patch of dirt with plants, even a single test case can illustrate the extraordinary versatility and appeal of the garden trope in American literature. Consider, for example, how the simple process of botanical increase is used to imagine alternatives to capitalism's environmental and social destructiveness, to commodity value and waste. From the novels of Richard Powers and Barbara Kingsolver to John McPhee's creative nonfiction and essays by popular garden writers like Michael Pollan and Ruth Stout, the "free gifts" of the soil are repeatedly juxtaposed with the conventional laws of capitalism that otherwise appear as the natural order of our world. Our daily experience, after all, is largely structured by arrangements where some form of subtraction must accompany a parallel act of increase: where the wealth and privilege of one class is secured through the reciprocal impoverishment of another; where more industrial production creates less biodiversity and every uptick in consumption exacts a corresponding environmental price; where "cheap" energy translates into tremendous costs for our atmosphere, forests, oceans, and one another.

Against these "zero-sum" arrangements, gardening practices are regularly imagined as a unique instance of the "net gain" in contemporary life, generating new value without depleting it from somewhere else. In short, gardens disrupt the seeming inevitability of capitalism's subtraction-based accounting. And in so doing, this figure allows writers, artists, and activists to pry open the doors to a wider realm of fantasy and utopian counter-imagining, one positioned squarely in the midst of everyday life.

Richard Powers's novel *Gain* (1999) provides a useful example here, situating a garden-based version of increase against the very legacy of American industrialization and economic growth. This zero-sum dialectic operates at the structural level of the novel through a double-helix narrative that alternates between two stories: on one hand, the spectacular two-hundred-year rise of Clare Chemical Company, which comes to dominate the global chemical industry, and on the other hand, the present-day demise of Laura Bodey, a single mother and small-town real estate agent who develops cancer in her forties. While the two accounts are largely separated in time, we ultimately see them to be fatally intertwined: not only does Laura live in the shadow of one of Clare's chemical plants, but she also fills her life with a vast array of consumer products that are the legacy of the chemical industry itself—household cleaners and bath soap, insecticides, skin creams, home perms, and more. As the braided stories call attention to the "costs" or "externalities" accompanying capitalist development, characters fatalistically assume the sacrifice of human lives and nature's well-being as necessary to the very logic of economic growth—from the founding days of Clare Chemical, when nineteenth-century industrialists escaped prosecution for fatal factory explosions "on the grounds that their works had done more cumulative good than harm" (68), to Laura's present-day attempt to reconcile herself to her impending death by focusing on the blessings that have accrued from the very industrialization that likely caused her cancer (320). As she is ravaged by the disease, Laura feebly reminds herself that one must ultimately "pay the check for the meal you've eaten" (40).[3]

Yet while the economic gains in the capitalist narrative feed off the human life at the center of Laura's story, the protagonist's garden emerges as the great counterfigure to this zero-sum model. That present-day narrative opens with an image of the sun, which philosopher Georges Bataille has described as an embodiment of "ceaseless prodigality," dispensing "energy—wealth—without any return" (28). And as we zoom down to Earth and then to Laura's backyard, the protagonist pauses to marvel at its ability to "lift new growth from out of nothing": to draw value from this solar economy, she has only to coax each plant in her garden to "catch a teacupful of the two calories per cubic centimeter that the sun, in its improvident abundance, spills forever on the earth for no good reason except that it knew we were coming" (Powers 3, 7). And so in the midst of a life-depleting (yet wildly profitable) corporate-capitalist world, Laura's solar-powered garden presents a unique exception to the gain-loss relations structuring the rest of the story.

The genre of nonfiction garden writing commonly seizes on this dynamic as well, depicting growers whose customary notions of cost/gain mechanics are overturned by the experience of working in the soil. In *Second Nature* (1991), garden writer Michael Pollan finds himself brooding over the closing moments of the twentieth century, burdened by a sense that we live in an unreplenishable, entropic world, until one day he stumbles across a botanical version of the "net gain" in the humble form of a squash. Concealed beneath a tangle of vines and leaves all summer, the undetected vegetable has quietly morphed into a thirty-pound colossus, leaving Pollan to wonder,

> Where did this thing, this great quantity of squash flesh come from? From earth, we say, but not *really*; there's no less earth here now than there was in May when I planted it; none's been used up in its making. By all rights creating something this fat should require so great an expense of matter that you'd expect to find Sibley squashes perched on the lips of fresh craters. That they're not, it seems to me, should be counted as something of a miracle. (171)

Prior to this moment, Pollan had reflexively imagined gardening to be like any other form of production in a world ruled by capitalist dynamics, where enrichment seems to require some form of subtraction. Yet in his garden, only a negligible amount of value (in the form of minerals) is used to produce this massive quantity of matter. Moreover, as Pollan explains, were he to leave his squash to decay where he finds it, "there would actually be a surplus in the garden's accounts; the soil would be both richer in nutrients and greater in total mass than it was before I planted it." Admittedly, much of the increase generated here comes from water; and yet as Pollan reflects, "considered from the vantage of the entire planet's economy of matter, [the squash] represents a net gain. It is, in other words, a gift" (172).

The strange alchemy in Pollan's and Powers's gardens may seem wondrous enough in its own right, and yet I argue that the real force of gardening's appeal cannot be fully understood without simultaneously considering its great counterfigure in industrial agribusiness. While the garden enthusiasts above celebrate their activity as the wellspring of exponential increase, much historical criticism of industrial farming zeroes in on its complicity with the subtraction-based accounting of capitalism—an enterprise that nurtures the growth of predatory market systems rather than life itself. Karl Marx roundly condemned farming models that profit only by "exploit[ing] and ... squandering ... the powers of the earth" and "the vitality of the soil." Conversely, his depiction of capitalism writ large resembled a sketch of imprudent farming, noting in a frequently quoted remark how the system develops "only by sapping the original sources of all wealth—the soil and the laborer" (*Capital III* 948–49; *Capital I* 475). Novelist John Steinbeck and journalist James Agee expand on this critique in a twentieth-century context, portraying the tragic consequences of cross-breeding industrial capitalism with nature's productive cycles. When crop prices fall in *The Grapes of Wrath*, landowners destroy the season's surplus to boost their market value, and in one of the novel's most iconic scenes, growers spray kerosene over a mountain of perfect oranges while hungry workers look on. Agribusiness thus stands for the madness and waste of capitalism itself: as Steinbeck writes, "Men who have created fruits in the world cannot create a system whereby their fruits may be eaten," a failure that culminates in the absurd arrangement where children die of pellagra "because a profit cannot be taken from an orange" (385).

While Steinbeck's sketch of capitalist agriculture focuses on starvation amid surplus, James Agee depicts humans consumed by crops and dehumanized laborers serving the needs of deified commodities. In *Let Us Now Praise Famous Men* (1941), the classic Depression-era portrait of southern cotton cultivation, a plant that sharecroppers "cannot eat" nonetheless demands the "greatest expense of strength and spirit" from growers, assuming a total power over human life that is the inverse of plants' life-giving powers. Rather than giving sustenance, this vampire-like crop drains the life force directly from its growers, and in the process, cotton cultivation comes to embody the very "doubleness" characterizing "all jobs ... by which one stays alive and in which one's life is made a cheated ruin" (325–26).

This is the story of American farming as Agee and Steinbeck tell it. Capitalist agriculture develops the natural conditions of production precisely as

Marx describes it: by "tearing them away from the individual independent labourer." The forces of nature, technology and innovation, the social character of labor, and the products of all those collaborations now return to "confront the individual labourers . . . as something *extraneous* and *objective*," as forces that are "independent of them and control them" (*Theories* 390–92). Within Agee's own account, such an arrangement creates a class of growers who must feel toward "each plant" in that cotton crop, and "toward all that work, . . . a particular automatism, a quiet, apathetic, and inarticulate yet deeply vindictive hatred, and at the same time utter hopelessness, and the deepest of their anxieties and of their hopes: as if the plant stood enormous in the unsteady sky fastened above them in all they do like the eyes of an overseer" (326–27).

These paradoxical scenes of starvation amidst surplus and humans enslaved to the very commodities they produce are key to understanding why gardening's mechanisms of increase have assumed such extraordinary traction in American literature and culture. As progressive critiques of farming reveal the waste and contradiction inherent in a system designed solely to produce exchange value, they create an opening for gardeners to reappropriate and entirely reimagine concepts like "crises of overproduction." Within the popular horticultural sphere, agribusiness's tragedy of waste becomes the gardener's "comedy of surplus"; here in the garden plot, where market values do not trump all other values and considerations, the grower's dilemma commonly revolves around schemes to *distribute* some outrageous surplus among others.

Gardening books like Ruth Stout's *How to Have a Green Thumb* (1955)—a best-selling midcentury work that is both instructional manual and comedic memoir—typify the genre's widespread preoccupation with managing excess. In marked contrast to Steinbeck's landowners, who battle nature's surfeit with kerosene, Stout launches a campaign to *integrate* the surplus of her garden into the collective metabolism of friends and neighbors. In one of her more colorful anecdotes, she recalls a summer that brings a windfall of tomatoes: when her own blistered-lipped family refuses to go on eating one more tomato, Stout turns to friends and strangers to accept a surplus otherwise doomed to rot. To her dismay, however, Stout discovers that everyone else is facing the same predicament at this frenzied and prolific time of year. Finally, after several failed attempts and a dedicated telephone campaign, Stout reports that she "located the neighbor of a friend who reluctantly consented to accept them *if* we would deliver them. She would make some catsup with them, although she [had] already made more than she wanted" (42).

Summer squash, in particular, appears in these mock-crises of overproduction with a unique frequency and humor. Radio personality Garrison Keillor

FIGURE 1. Walker Evans, *Bud Fields Standing in Cotton Field, Hale County, Alabama* (1936). The Metropolitan Museum of Art, Walker Evans Archive (1994.258.410) © Walker Evans Archive, The Metropolitan Museum of Art.

has quipped that summer is the only time country people lock their cars in church parking lots, a measure they must take to prevent gardeners from leaving zucchinis on the seats. In *Animal, Vegetable, Miracle* (2007), Barbara Kingsolver's memoir of her one-year "locavore" experiment, the family resorts to customizing midsummer dinner party invitations based on guests who will not only eat but also take home their zucchinis and other garden surplus (needless to say, folks without their own gardens). This stratagem echoes the fictional dilemma of characters in her novel *Prodigal Summer* (2000): faced with a cucumber surplus in August, the protagonist reflects that her garden "was like a baby bird in reverse, calling to her relentlessly, opening its maw and giving, giving. . . . She has put up thirty pints of kosher dills and still has so many cucumbers that she was having desperate thoughts. Here was one: she could put them in plastic grocery sacks and drive down the road hanging them on people's mailboxes like they did with the free samples of fabric softener." As she tells her friends, "People down the road run the other way when they see me coming" (400–401).

Yet garden writing's comedies of surplus are not just ways of imagining *alternatives* to dominant and unsustainable structures (whether Powers's chemical corporation, Steinbeck's agricultural empire, or the environmental costs of capitalism more generally). More importantly, these literary moments reposition nature's process as *the* fundamental structure of production and capitalism as the great exception and aberration. Suggestive here is Georges Bataille's work in *The Accursed Share* (1949), which challenges the basic tenets of conventional (or "restricted") economic theory: in its place Bataille proposes a more comprehensive understanding of "economy" that proceeds from the single, universal fact that "[o]n the surface of the globe, for *living matter in general*, energy is always in excess," and as such, "the question is always posed in terms of extravagance" (23). In other words, within the total balance of life's activity, the norm actually tends toward "outrageous expenditure" (28) rather than modes of scarcity or conservation bound to conventional cycles of capitalist production. Granted, Bataille's analysis does not address gardening per se, yet his fantasies and reflections on surplus bear an uncanny resemblance to those found throughout garden writing. Both, ultimately, identify the source of our world's "indefinite exuberance" (28) as the sun, which irradiates earth's surface with an energetic superabundance exceeding life's ability to absorb it. This not only generates the natural proliferations we see in garden reports from high summer but also gives rise to countless forms of social excess, epitomized for Bataille in the lavish gift-giving practice of the Native American potlatch—a practice bearing no small resemblance to the episodes depicted throughout our gardening accounts, where Kingsolver's

FIGURE 2. Free vegetables. Photo by Justine Sands, Bothell, Wash. (2017).

neighbors try to out-zucchini each other, and where Stout, worked into a state of panic, spends her days "dashing about trying to find someone to give [the surplus] to" (46). Thus, when we expand out from restricted models of economic theory to think of "economy" in its totality on Earth, Bataille shows that living organisms generally receive more energy than required for maintaining life, and whatever "energetic remainder" is not used for growth must necessarily be spent. The choice, he concludes, "is limited to how the wealth is to be squandered" (23): it will either be released luxuriously and deliberately, as depicted by our garden writers, or, as we see in capitalist regimes based on accumulation, that excess will periodically erupt in conflagrations of waste and war, as epitomized by Steinbeck's landowners burning mountains of produce.

Moreover, those writers who become seriously engaged with gardening also imagine this enterprise as an opportunity to convert *negative* to *positive* value (beyond just creating *new* value in the world). In other words, gardening not only transcends the need to generate value by subtracting it from some other social or environmental sphere; it may also *reverse* the customary dynamic altogether, converting the noxious and useless back into the useful and wholesome. Indeed, an extended lineage of American writers have imagined the garden as an icon of what Richard Powers calls "waste turned inside out" (34). Ruth Stout, for instance, challenges the negative implications in standard definitions of "refuse" after her own gardening experience reveals the concept of waste as "something valuable instead of as something worthless" (61), while garden writer Eleanor Perenyi inventories a multitude of things routinely tossed out, all of which her compost heap "devour[s] . . . and return[s] in a form that is priceless while costing nothing" (39). Nineteenth-century author Charles Dudley Warner similarly marvels at our practice of burying "decay in the earth" and feeding it with "offensive refuse," only to discover that "nothing grows out of it that is not clean; it gives us back life and beauty for our rubbish" (99). And prefiguring all of these, Walt Whitman's poem "This Compost" (1855) recognizes soil as a medium that "grows such sweet things out of such corruptions." After Whitman calculates the negative values "deposited" into the earth—rot, excrement, and whole generations of "distemper'd corpses"—he demands a fuller accounting of the bio-economy at work here. "How can it be that the ground itself does not sicken?" he asks. "What chemistry!" he exclaims,

> That all is clean forever and forever,
> That the cool drink from the well tastes so good,
> That blackberries are so flavorous and juicy,
> That the fruits of the apple-orchard and the orange-orchard, that melons, grapes,
> peaches, plums, will none of them poison me,
> That when I recline on the grass I do not catch any disease,
> Though probably every spear of grass rises out of what was once catching disease. (lines 36–41)[4]

At a historical moment when waste seems less like that which we banish to the margins than something constituting the very fabric and substance of daily life—a time when garbage haunts the collective unconscious with unprecedented intensity—we can hardly wonder at the resonance surrounding ideas of the garden as an agent of waste's undoing. Indeed, the very scale of anxieties surrounding waste has helped garden writing proliferate far beyond traditional manifestations in the backyard plots like those Stout and Perenyi depict. Today, both guerrilla gardening and mainstream growing programs expand on the garbage-to-gardens trope as they reclaim waste spaces (generally abandoned or unwanted lots in low-income neighborhoods) for growing flowers and food.[5] These plots may even be created out of the toxic soils of former industrial sites, with one community garden in San Francisco literalizing this idea of the transmutation of trash by installing a replica of the

Hanging Gardens of Babylon—made from dumpsters (Rosenberg). This notion pervades contemporary fiction and film as well: the scavenger-gardeners in Margaret Atwood's 2009 dystopia, *The Year of the Flood*, live by the creed that there is "no such thing as garbage, trash, or dirt, only matter that hadn't been put to a proper use" (69). Making this convention even more explicit, Pixar's 2008 film *WALL-E* opens in a planetary garbage dump (Earth itself eight centuries from now) and features a hero in the form of an animated trash compactor who discovers a single plant, pots it in an old shoe, and in so doing sets the film's entire plot into motion. Once the trash compactor leads humans home from exile on a faraway space station, the credit sequence depicts the renewal of human civilization, with our species rediscovering the lost art of cultivation and adopting a new role as Earth's gardeners. The waste-reversal trope has even prompted garden writers like Michael Pollan to make the profoundly hopeful gesture of hailing that humble Sibley squash as an instance of "entropy undone"—providing a culture conditioned by zero-sum ideologies with "reason enough to garden." "Living as we do in the autumn of a millennium," Pollan reflects, "and feeling somehow that we've come very late into this world, this strikes me as the harvest's most salutary teaching. . . . Here in my garden the second law of thermodynamics is repealed" (*Second* 173).

The Book in Outline

Ultimately, however, these meditations on waste, surplus, and value are but a single dimension within the vast and varied realm of American garden fantasy. And in this regard, both gardening and literary analysis share more than we might initially expect in their distinct ability to open endless new lines of inquiry and discovery for those who will look: wherever we invest our efforts here, we are sure to find a new shoot, an unnoticed intricacy, an unexpected or unlikely comeback.

Gardenland: Nature, Fantasy and Everyday Practice thus moves across a series of historical moments in American literature and culture, exploring the garden-based fantasies that emerge from each period's respective transformations, challenges, and opportunities. Our story here begins with nineteenth-century industrialism and urbanization; then moves through the twentieth-century rise of mass consumerism, factory farming, suburban sprawl, and environmental advocacy; and finally arrives at our present moment in the Anthropocene, where the garden has emerged as a flashpoint within debates about climate change, social justice, food production, and even the future of humanity's place on Earth.

In chapter 1 we return to the origins of American garden writing in the nineteenth century, which established the genre we recognize today by reinventing work as play. In its effort to bridge this basic gap within everyday experience, early gardening literature—most notably Charles Dudley Warner's *My Summer in a Garden* (1870)—sheds light on a much larger story about class and other ideological contradictions in the United States along with social desires to dismantle divisions between work and leisure, mental and manual activity, beauty and utility, the productive and the pleasing. Departing from the traditional bifurcations between instructional gardening literature and ornamental publications aimed solely at consumers, Warner's book celebrates the garden as an arena of practical activity that simultaneously reconnects us with simple pleasures like playing in the dirt—an activity that "gratifies one of our first and best instincts"—and thus establishes the integrated literary approach that has since become a standard feature of the genre.

Chapter 2 examines garden representation within late nineteenth- and early twentieth-century fiction, journalism, and horticultural literature just as industrialization was radically transforming the character of labor and the geography of farming in North America. Period writers responded by imagining the domestic garden as a foil to industrial agriculture, emphasizing its miniature scale over and against the exploded dimensions of "bonanza" farms and celebrating the meticulous handwork in domestic plots in contrast to mechanized and specialized labor on factory farms. In particular, scenes of mapping the landscape in garden literature indicate a lost sense of place-awareness and a strategy for turn-of-the-century Americans to manage anxieties about those social transformations. Yet these fantasies and longings for familiar, easy-to-navigate garden spaces not only reveal tendencies among Progressive-era writers; they also offer a backstory to developments in our own moment, when renewed interest in food production and local gardening practices have steadily grown in proportion to concerns over genetic modification, chemical toxins, seed patenting, and an increasingly globalized, corporate food system. At a moment when some of our most intimate relations to nature—agriculture and eating—have become nearly impossible to conceptualize or represent, we see gardening emerge as a node of desire for transparency and localized control in the circuits of food production, a practice that might allow us practically and imaginatively to close the gap between our daily lived experience and the source of our own biological sustenance.

Chapter 3 looks at desires and fantasies surrounding mid-twentieth-century farmers' and gardeners' markets in cities like New York as they reemerged after nearly half a century of dormancy. In an age of proliferating supermarkets and mass-produced, pseudosynthetic convenience foods, the postwar counterculture increasingly turned to rural communes, food cooperatives, organic methods, and many other practices that have culminated in today's "alternative" food movements. Yet period representations of market gardening programs involve more than just a rejection of the food and agriculture "establishment"; these writings also reveal a kind of revolt of the senses, a desire for intimate physical contact with our material landscapes, a longing to touch, taste, smell and consume the world of plant crops and soil-based life. As such, they highlight the complex affective and sensory structure of traditional food cultures and production practices while critiquing a consumer society that had devitalized food's potency as a repository of meaning, memory, and identity. In analyzing the writings of midcentury gardeners, food critics, agrarian activists, and literary figures like John McPhee, I argue that what may look like simple commentaries about fruits and produce can be read as a more complex story about pervasive social longing to restore the affective, narrative, and sensory intensity in everyday objects we encounter and consume. Moreover, this midcentury literature indicates how realms associated with the garden—even paved and crowded urban spaces marked by the mere presence of fruits and foliage—reanimated sensory experiences that had receded in other spheres of midcentury consumer culture.

Chapter 4 explores garden representation and fantasy in science fiction and utopian literature since the 1990s, along with recent guerilla gardening practices in U.S. cities. From the postapocalyptic gardens established by Octavia Butler's rebel Earthseed coalition in the *Parable* series to gardener-led insurgencies in Kim Stanley Robinson's *Mars* trilogy and Margaret Atwood's *Year of the Flood*, the garden's traditional reputation as innocent and apolitical has taken a decidedly rebellious turn. Rather than serving as a sanctuary from historical or political change as such (as imagined in Thomas More's original *Utopia* and many religious accounts featuring the garden as paradise or Eden), today's gardens are increasingly paired with figures of radical social struggle, redeploying what might be thought of as nostalgic to interfere with the future. This figurative reversal has also led contemporary literature to reimagine our relation to the city, where urban gardening practices like those of New York's "guerrilla gardeners" or the "gangster gardeners" of South Central LA recast passive users into the creators, architects, and cultivators of environments they inhabit, transforming the city itself in a more participatory and open-ended spatial "process"—one inclusive of both human and nonhuman communities.

Yet despite the fantasy and allure of much contemporary and historical garden representation, gardening in America hasn't always been a wholesome affair. Chapter 5 examines the garden-as-crime-scene in works of postcolonial literature like Jamaica Kincaid's *My Garden (Book)*, Leslie Marmon Silko's *Gardens in the Dunes*, and Héctor Tobar's *The Barbarian Nurseries*. Here, histories of violence, exploitation, and dispossession lurk just beneath the seemingly innocent surface of cherished domestic gardens. Yet despite these gardens' complicity in concealing historical crimes and inducing forgetfulness, postcolonial garden writers also present them as spaces for remembering—and redeeming—relations between historically oppressed peoples and the land. To this end, their accounts invent forms of "oppositional gardening" that foreground the often invisible contributions of those who create and maintain everyday landscapes and recover traditional storytelling practices that acknowledge the rich layering of collaborative, multigenerational, human, and nonhuman histories making up the shared geography of our North American soil.

Finally, the epilogue reflects on what the past century and a half of American garden writing—and the various fantasies it magnetizes—might tell us about humanity's changing place in nature. While much traditional nature writing has emphasized visual aspects of our experience, gardening literature is shaped by immersive, multisensory practice. These embodied encounters have important ethical implications insofar as they highlight sense experiences we share with other forms of life, and they facilitate felt and imagined connections that are a precondition for extending moral consideration beyond our own selves and species. Thus the past, present, and future of our relationship to nature looks different through the lens of the garden. Not only do its sensuous, embodied relations compel us to reconsider the historical role of gardening in American environmental thought and nature writing (a canon that has largely excluded garden experience, at least until very recently); looking forward, the proliferation of everyday encounters in the soil may also help us better acknowledge our membership in a more-than-human world as well as our obligations to the soil- and plant-based communities that sustain us.

CHAPTER 1

American Garden Writing and the Reinvention of Work as Play

> It seemed to me a very simple thing,
> this gardening; but it opens up astonishingly.
> —Charles Dudley Warner (1870)

One hardly need be a gardener, or a reader of garden books, to know that a good part of life is spent at work. There are the fortunate few, of course, who find their chief gratification at the office, factory, or farm; but for the rest of us, much of the workday is spent anticipating pleasures that come *after* clocking out. And it is precisely this arrangement that tends to split our identities and expectations between the demands of the workplace, on one hand, and the rewards of our "spare" time on the other—that alternative realm of leisure, rest, satisfaction, and play.

Within modern capitalist societies, this division between "work" and "life" is often regarded less as a specific economic and historical arrangement than an inevitable condition of our lives. Yet what if this were otherwise? What if labor and productive activity served as our primary source of purpose, pride, and gratification—even tempting us to invest our energy here *voluntarily*, barring any obligation to do so? What if, like "elective" or leisure-time pursuits themselves, work served as the antidote rather than source of monotony, alienation, brutality, and indifference in everyday life? In short, what if work itself was experienced as a practical mode of play?

Such a fantasy, it turns out, has been one of the signature features of American garden writing and practice from the late nineteenth century to the present. In the garden, growers discover opportunities for labor that are both joyful and useful. Celebrated garden writers like Ruth Stout have even characterized gardening without pleasure as a kind of category mistake, leading her to forswear the use of hired help in her garden. "I wanted no one lifting a finger in that garden unless he loved doing it," Stout once declared. "What if we had hired a man to dig those trenches and it had turned out that he didn't love to dig? Who could eat that kind of asparagus?" (20). Such sentiments are hardly limited to practical and instructional literature; they pervade fictional garden representations as well, from Progressive-era frontier romances to utopian literature to novels of everyday suburban life like Richard Powers's *Gain* (1998), where the activity of digging and planting is an emblem for labor experienced, not as wasted time, but rather as an end and a pleasure in itself. As Powers describes his protagonist's relation to this backyard ritual, "The work is play; the labor, love. This is the afternoon she slaves all week for," the one fulfilling pursuit to "complement the way she makes a living" on weekdays (7).

Yet like many of the green things growing in our gardens, this convention is hardly self-propagated; indeed, it traces back to seeds planted at an earlier moment in U.S. literature. And if American garden writing is understood, in part, as the fantasy of reinventing work as play, then our story must begin with Charles Dudley Warner's *My Summer in a Garden* (1870), a book that deserves much credit for establishing the genre as we know it today.

While Warner is surely better known for coauthoring *The Gilded Age* with Mark Twain than for his essays on dahlias and radishes, it is his folksy gardening memoir that surely has made the most lasting impact on American culture. Indeed, *My Summer* may be seen as the forerunner to Martha Stewart's empire, the best-selling books of Michael Pollan, the cult-like status of Slow Food, and countless other garden publications, products, and practices comprising today's DIY gardening craze. Within *My Summer*, the desire to bridge production and pleasure is established as one of the signature marks of the genre: from his opening lines, Warner celebrates the sheer joy of working in the soil, an activity simultaneously identified as play ("the commonest delight of the race") from childhood through old age, *and* as an activity essential to the very business of survival, inviting gardeners to count themselves among "the producers"—those who have "done something for the good of the world" in the daily round of their activities (5–6).

Such remarks may already seem familiar to contemporary readers. And yet this blended approach was a radical and pronounced departure from prevailing conventions in Warner's day. In fact, during much of the nineteenth century, U.S. gardening publications were overwhelmingly divided into two diametrically opposing camps—reflecting and reinforcing the very work/leisure split that Warner sought to bridge. Shelved on one side of this generic divide sat the instructional or "how-to" books, including almanacs, primers, and practical gardening manuals. On the opposite side of the aisle, readers would have found ornamental or "fine gardening" literature for connoisseurs—books primarily concerned with the pleasures of landscape aesthetics. In effect, that literary split set forth two very different versions of the garden: for some, this was an arena for engaged, hands-on *activity* and food production; for others it was primarily a *product*, a class-coded marker of taste to be consumed as a visual object. In fact, that split extended well beyond the genre of garden writing itself, also appearing in nineteenth-century writings from Thomas Jefferson, Henry David Thoreau, and Henry Ward Beecher to emerging journals on landscape aesthetics, the design of New York's Central Park, and thousands of landscape imitations that followed it. Even works of fiction—most notably Nathaniel Hawthorne's *The Blithedale Romance* (1852)—feature scenes where "opposing" versions of cultivation are pitted against each other: farms and allotments against scenic landscapes, subsistence plots against ornamental gardens.

These contradictions may seem of little relevance beyond a small cohort of gardening fanatics, but at stake here is more than just the distinction between working people's spinach beds and the lavish topiaries of millionaires. Read more broadly, this bifurcated literary practice reveals a larger structure of nineteenth-century class and ideological divisions—divisions between production and consumption, utility and beauty, aesthetic and commercial value, and mental and manual activity. Such binaries, moreover, extend well beyond the nineteenth century, having shaped worldviews within Western culture for millennia. Indeed, as political theorist Herbert Marcuse has pointed out, those divisions run all the way back to Classical philosophy, which established an "ontological cleavage of ideal from material value" as well as a bias against all activity relating to "the material provision of life"—that is, work—which was branded "in its essence [as] untrue, bad, and ugly" (93). Ever since, Western modes of thought and culture have subscribed to a hierarchy of value "whose nadir is functional acquaintance with the necessities of everyday life and whose zenith is philosophical knowledge": the realm of happiness, beauty, enjoyment, and "culture" (88).

When viewed in this light, American garden writing can be seen as both reinforcing those established hierarchies in the realm of everyday domestic activity but also, beginning with Charles Dudley Warner, fundamentally challenging them by transforming the garden into an iconic site for integrating production, pleasure, and play. *My Summer* bridged other chasms as well, synthesizing elements from disparate realms like philosophy, biography, natural history, and local-color writing into a single narrative that comprises most everything we associate with the gardening genre today. Warner's account reflects on aesthetic production and contemplation, physical exertion in the outdoors, encounters with nonhuman creatures, the satisfaction of producing one's own food, the wonders of nature's renewal, the delights of sharing surplus with neighbors, and above all, the sheer pleasure of playing in the dirt, a pursuit that "gratif[ies] one of our first and best instincts" (5). Ultimately, in moving beyond the split structure of previous literary practice, Warner relocated the pleasures and meaning of "garden" into the verb, opening a space for the genre to better imagine our active "communion with the vegetable life" and the dynamic character of nonhuman nature itself, which came to emerge more fully as a character, an event, and a presence (54).

Gardens without Work

> Labor is the curse of this world, and nobody can meddle with it, without becoming proportionably brutified. Dost thou think it a praiseworthy matter, that I spent five golden months in providing food for cows and horses?
> —Nathaniel Hawthorne to Sophia Peabody, Brook Farm (1841)

To understand the significance of Warner's transformation of American garden writing, it is instructive to revisit some key garden scenes in earlier works of nineteenth-century American literature. Nathaniel Hawthorne might be surprised to find himself included in a discussion of garden writing, but as it turns out, his fiction offers a classic example of the fantasies, divisions, and exclusions characterizing the genre in this period. In one of his best-known novels, *The Blithedale Romance* (1852), Hawthorne depicts the misadventures of a band of utopianists who seek to "begi[n] the life of Paradise anew" (9) on a farm commune in rural Massachusetts—an experiment loosely based on the author's own seven-month sojourn at the real agricultural commune of Brook Farm in 1841. The story begins with the aspiring pastoral poet, Miles Coverdale, setting out for a real pastoral adventure at Blithedale, a place he whimsically imagines as some "green garden blossoming with many-colored delights." Yet as the summer matures, Coverdale's fantasies are spoiled by the realities of hard labor. Prospects for finding the elusive good life here "amidst the accumulations of the barnyard" seem increasingly dim, and social tensions within the commune only add to Coverdale's misgivings. By August, the radiant idyll that initially colored his expectations has become "faded," while the pastures that once glowed in the narrator's imagination take on a "sunburnt and arid aspect" (128). Yet it is Coverdale's fellow communard, Zenobia, who delivers the most decisive blow to this initial vision of splendor in the grass. As the poet grows increasingly work-weary, Zenobia invents a grim horoscope with which to taunt him. According to her prognosis, Coverdale's joints will rust, his manners will grow rough, and in due course he will take to speaking through his nose and using "vile" tobacco. His mind, too, will inevitably follow suit: "Your literature," Zenobia predicts, "will be the 'Farmer's Almanac'" (62).

Like a reeking heap of manure dumped squarely on this pastoral tableau, the very mention of farm literature serves as the ultimate rebuke to Coverdale's fantasies of the beautiful, the poetic, and the ideal. Yet Zenobia's quip does more than just brand the *Almanac* as a menace to cultivated literary taste (a personal distinction Coverdale seeks with great fervor). At heart, her remark also reiterates a fundamental ideological split that had come to govern mid-nineteenth-century cultivation writing, which treated the practical activity of farmwork (along with its almanacs and how-to books) and the rarefied domain of the garden (represented by pastoral literature and publications on landscape design) as both spatial *and* literary adversaries. It is this broader division, then, that elevates Zenobia's otherwise playful quip into a full-blown detraction.

Of course, the opposition between material and ideal values in this exchange had existed long before Hawthorne's pastoralists set out on their rural experiment. As Marcuse notes in "The Affirmative Character of Culture," Aristotle shaped a good deal of Western philosophy in making "a specific historical form of division of labor and of social stratification tak[e] on the eternal, metaphysical form of the relationship of necessity and beauty, of matter and Idea" (93). This binary schema has had pronounced social and historical consequences ever since, effectively justifying a state of affairs where most people spend their lives "in the cheerless business of providing for the necessities of life," while enjoyment of "the true, the good, and the beautiful is reserved for a small elite" (92). Granted, when the modern concept of "culture" emerged in the bourgeois era, such elevated pursuits were no longer regarded as the exclusive birthright of a privileged social stratum but now deemed as *universal* values to which all classes might aspire. Yet even in its bid to make the beautiful, good, and true more socially inclusive, Marcuse explains, bourgeois ideology ultimately served to reinforce the underlying divisions of the classical era, "play[ing] off the spiritual world against the material world by holding up culture as the realm of authentic values and self-contained ends in opposition to the world of social utility and means." Thus emerged a concept that Marcuse calls "affirmative culture": an aspirational realm of music, art, literature—and later landscape gardening—whose decisive characteristic is the embodiment of a world "essentially different from the factual world of the daily struggle for existence, yet realizable by every individual for himself 'from within'" (93, 91, 95).

Marcuse goes on to state that experience of such privileged cultural activities is limited by "temporal restriction to special occasions," but he might well

FIGURE 3. Thomas Cole, *The Course of Empire: The Arcadian or Pastoral State* (1834).

have noted their spatial boundaries as well. After all, different geographies of cultivation—specifically the farm and the pleasure garden—have been used for thousands of years to demarcate lines between work and leisure, the necessary and beautiful, the material and ideal. Such an arrangement has perhaps its oldest and most pronounced literary expression in the dual conventions of pastoral and georgic, where pastoral's idealization of the shepherd's life in a gardenlike realm conceals the physical hardships of rural labor.[1] The georgic mode, on the other hand, has historically emphasized human work and production in the landscape, with Virgil's original *Georgics* providing farmers with practical instructions on cultivation and animal husbandry. As literary scholar Gail Finney thus notes, one of the fundamental binaries of these literary modes involves the division "between *otium* ('leisure, idleness') and its opposite, *negotium* ('business, labor'), [which is] excluded from the pastoral sphere" (10).

Yet American garden writers hardly needed to return to classical literature or philosophy for cues on how such hierarchies mapped onto different spatial forms; those formulas were already central to their own colonial mythology. Early European accounts of North America drew more heavily on pastoral's garden figures than the agrarian elements of georgic, repeatedly invoking garden imagery to idealize their mythical New World portraits.[2] The indigenous cultures celebrated by Michel de Montaigne, for example, were situated in a garden world that seemed to grow itself—a place filled with "wild fruits" that had not been cultivated by modern, civilized tastes and "artificial ways."[3] Such depictions offered a readily available vocabulary for American writers of subsequent generations as well. Robert Beverley's *History and Present State of Virginia* (1705) typifies an entire tradition of romanticizing Native American life as one of leisurely abundance, a tradition directly dependent on the idea of the garden to explain why people supposedly "idle" in their habits could live in a state of material plentitude. According to Beverley's account, New World cultures "seem'd to have escaped, or rather not to have been concern'd in the first Curse, *Of getting their Bread by the sweat of their Brows* . . . and only gather[ed] the Fruits of the Earth when ripe, or fit for use" (17, italics original). Meanwhile, when confronted with Native cultivation practices too obvious to ignore, Beverley simply dissociated them from organized agriculture as such, transforming their planting and harvesting into a leisurely form of play—that is, a form of gardening—pursued for "their Diversion alone, and not their Labour." Accordingly, Beverley maintained that "none of the Toils of Husbandry were exercised by this happy people; except the bare planting of a little Corn, and Melons, which took up only a few Days in the Summer" (156).[4] From there, apparently, nature did the work itself, as must necessarily be the case in any space deemed a "garden."

The idea of a garden without cultivation also served as a useful tool for slaveholders, allowing them to obscure the brutality of the American plantation system.[5] William Byrd II drew on this figure in much of his writing, including one of his most well-known descriptions of his 4,700-acre Virginia plantation. As he wrote of the property,

> We live here in Health and Plenty, and in Innocence and Security. . . . Our negroes are not so numerous or so enterprising as to give us any apprehension or uneasiness, *nor indeed is their Labour any other than Gardening* and less by far than what the poor People undergo in other countrys. (235; italics added)

Here, the garden euphemism is apparently powerful enough to rhetorically deactivate the impression of heavy toil that would otherwise accompany the very mention of plantation life and work.

Of course, no discussion of early American gardens and slavery would be complete without mention of Thomas Jefferson. Like other southern planters, Jefferson used the garden ideal to conceal the facts of labor, violence, and deprivation on his "plantation-paradise." Yet rather than disguising those violent relations by transforming his enslaved workers into "gardeners," as Byrd does, Jefferson seals off his garden zones from their utilitarian counterparts on Monticello and then erases the enslaved cultivators from those privileged realms within his writing. Collectively, these depictions create a portrait of Monticello that historian Lewis Simpson has called "a patrician domain of the mind over which African chattel slavery has no influence because it is simply excluded" (32). In fact, it is Jefferson who plays the star role as cultivator in the *Garden Book*—a position that is framed in overwhelmingly intellectual rather than subsistence terms.

One way in which Jefferson removed his gardens from the plantation fields below was through maintaining his *Garden Book* (an extensive collection of horticultural records and reflections spanning more than fifty years) separately from his farm records and other domestic accounts.[6] And while the *Garden Book* faithfully records daily weather conditions, hundreds of species, correspondence with nurserymen and botanists, soil quality from plot to plot, seed prices, and the arrival at table of nearly every vegetable planted in the gardens, Jefferson's slaves are largely absent from the pages—even though historical records show that they created and maintained the very plots at the center of all this activity and documentation (indeed, the one-thousand-foot-long terrace where Jefferson grew his kitchen garden was literally hewed from the mountainside by slave labor). The effort required to consistently omit these enslaved figures is especially noteworthy in passages documenting planting and harvesting—activities in which human hands obviously play a central role. Here, Jefferson constructs phrases that make the cultivator's agency more or less invisible: "Apr. 27. planted 11 Kentucky coffee seeds in the upper row of the nursery . . . Apr. 29. planted a sod of Peruvian grass," "Mar. 23 sowed 2 rows of Spanish onions," "July. 31. Cucumbers come to table" (366, 4, 6). Similarly, Jefferson's external correspondence about his garden often uses passive constructions and self-enclosed, solipsistic phrases that refer to features like "the undergrowth which I have not suffered to be touched" (323). His farm memorandum, on the other hand, *does* includes direct reference to his slaves. As Jamaica Kincaid has observed of this disparity, "each entry [in the *Garden Book*] reads as if it were a single line removed from a poem: something should come before, and something should come after"; those omissions turn up in the *Farm Book* "in the form of a list of names: Ursula, George, Jupiter, Davy, Minerva, Caesar, and Jamy; and the Hemings, Beverly, Betty, Peter, John and Sally" ("Sowers" 42).

Yet if Jefferson's carefully edited written accounts presented a one-sided portrait of Monticello's gardens, the actual landscape told a very different story. Like most other large plantations in the American South, Monticello was a patchwork of highly differentiated cultivation practices, including large tracts of specialized crops produced for market by gang labor, subsistence plots tended by enslaved people behind their own living quarters, kitchen gardens that produced food for the "Big House," and ornamental gardens for show. These formal "pleasure grounds" typically surrounded the mansion (often built on the highest ground to signify the planter's power and afford vistas of property below) and unfurled axially out from that center dwelling. While Jefferson adopted a more naturalistic aesthetic for Monticello, many southern plantations of the period featured French formal garden designs, which might include walkways and boxwood borders, parterre gardens laid out in symmetrical forms, color-coordinated flower beds, formal avenues lined with native trees through which visitors approached the grounds, and on the most extravagant estates, features like bowling greens, terraced grounds, fruit orchards and vineyards, fountains, sculptures, and other works of art.[7] As strategically designed visual displays meant to be "read" for a specific social meaning, these spaces are what architectural historian John Vlach calls "articulated": in the case of the plantation, the landscape announced racial and class hierarchy, the planter's wealth and power, connections to Old World luxury and taste, and of course the master's control over both nature and enslaved people. Moreover, the formality and geometric arrangements communicated links to European tradition as well as order imposed on the unruly New World wilderness (Martin).

Visitors who ventured to look in the spaces tucked away behind slave dwellings, however, would have found another set of gardens that did not fit so neatly within this official order. Many enslaved workers tended these improvised plots to supplement their meager diets with staple crops and sometimes earn cash from surplus produce. Often worked at night by the light of oil-drum fires with makeshift tools and seeds swapped between enslaved growers or smuggled out of the master's house, these slave gardens presented a marked contrast to the formal landscape that "performed" the plantation's official social order.[8] Indeed, as Lynne Feeley explains,

> Slaves' gardens . . . do not typically appear on site plans or sketches. If pleasure grounds were "articulated," slaves' gardens were "vernacular": developed within strict spatial and cultural limits, functionalized toward the needs of the enslaved community, and divested from the particular type of orderliness and ostentation exhibited in the pleasure grounds. To call slaves' gardens "vernacular" does not imply that they were less orderly or that they did not serve an aesthetic function. But it does signify that they developed improvisationally under the impossibly heavy weight of black plantation life, necessarily within a different set of cultural concerns, environmental resources, and aesthetic desires. (4–5)

The fact that these practices (and the enslaved gardeners themselves) are absent from the Monticello *Garden Book* is especially strange considering the direct role they played in supporting Jefferson's domestic affairs. As historians have learned from Jefferson's other memorandums and the domestic accounts of his granddaughter Anne Randolph, for many years the planter's household purchased provisions from these slave gardens on a regular basis. Such a practice might seem redundant considering the vast scale and diversity of Jefferson's own kitchen garden—a thousand-foot-long plot featuring over three hundred different plant varieties in any given season. Yet as Monticello historian Peter Hatch notes, while Jefferson's personal garden did include many food staples, its acreage was increasingly given over to experimental cultivars and natural observation.[9] Indeed, botany and horticulture were Jefferson's favorite sciences, and he avidly experimented with seeds collected from around the world as well as North American botanical "discoveries" brought back by the Lewis and Clark expedition (Tucker 51–54). Thus, the very slave gardens excluded from the *Garden Book* freed up the hilltop grounds to increasingly serve as a kind of botanical laboratory, a realm Jefferson could imagine and administer on intellectual, scientific, and aesthetic terms that transcended the sheer utility and metabolic need characterizing the zones below. As such, Jefferson's gardening and garden writing epitomize his own divided views on material versus ideal forms of production, reiterating the principles of affirmative culture where the "mental and spiritual world," as Marcuse writes, is segregated and preserved "as an independent realm of value" over and against the "realm of necessity [and] the material provision for life" (91).

Even today, this idealized treatment of the garden remains stubbornly persistent in representations of Jefferson's legacy. In *American Grown: The Story of the White House Kitchen Garden* (2012), First Lady Michelle Obama tells of her own family's visit to Monticello, where they are given seeds from Jefferson's garden. In creating her now-famous White House garden (the first food garden on its grounds since the Roosevelt administration in the 1930s), Obama planted the seeds in a special plot designated as "Thomas Jefferson's Bed" and included a plaque at the garden's entrance inscribed with one of Jefferson's many gardening quotes. Moreover, the Jefferson Bed was the only named plot at the White House, with all other sections simply labeled "collards," "cabbage," "blueberries," "onions." Yet once again, nowhere in either *American Grown* or the White House garden itself are the enslaved cultivators who supported Jefferson's enterprise mentioned.

If preserving the garden as an ideal space required writers to remove the facts of slavery from plantation accounts, it was the Yankee farmer who called for eviction from Hawthorne's *The Blithedale Romance*, where the realities of New England farm life "disenchant" romantics who come to live and work on this rural commune. Miles Coverdale, the story's narrator and aspiring pastoral poet, is clearly no enthusiast for manual labor, and so upon his arrival at the Massachusetts farm he reassures himself that "work" here will surely be pleasant, mild, and aesthetically suffused: like any enthusiastic hobby-gardener, he expects to "sleep dreamlessly after it, and awake at daybreak with only a little stiffness of the joints . . . usually quite gone by breakfast-time" (57, 60). Yet this imagined scenario is not just an indication of Coverdale's aversion to work; insofar as he considers himself part of the Boston *literati*, Coverdale also has professional motives for excluding the brutalizing aspects of farm labor from this pastoral reenactment. Indeed, by cloaking his experience in garden imagery and its historical associations, Coverdale valorizes his identification with a particular literary tradition and readership—"people of superior cultivation and refinement," as he puts it—a class that presumably excludes the almanac-reading farmers who work beside him at Blithedale (23).

Taking his cues from eighteenth-century associations between poetic production and a specialized landscape aesthetic, Coverdale aligns himself (and his summer-long pastoral experiment) with an elite literary heritage. A century earlier, English art historian and "man of letters" Horace Walpole had declared that "Poetry, Painting and Gardening, or the Science of Landscape, will forever by men of taste be deemed Three Sisters, or the Three New Graces who dress and adorn nature" (43). Such grandiose claims indicate how knowledge of landscape aesthetics in the period was placed alongside fluency in literary and visual arts as a marker of wealth, education, and taste. Some even promoted the correlation through elaborate analogies between gardens and their corresponding poetic forms, a schema that Joseph Addison once laid out in *The Spectator* (1766):

> There are as many kinds of gardening as of poetry: your makers of parterres and flower-gardens, are epigrammatists and sonneteers in this art; contrivers of bowers and grottos, Treillages and cascades, are romance writers. Wise and London are our heroick poets . . .[10]

And so the paired inventory continues (20). English landscape designers further invested gardens with literary associations by including carefully selected visual emblems in their grounds. Alexander Pope's garden at Twickenham, for example, evoked classical associations through architecture, inscriptions, and the busts of Virgil, Homer, and Horace, effectively linking the geography of Pope's own literary production with the Arcadian landscapes of the *Eclogues* and *Idylls*. And the English gardening style more generally carried its own poetic significance: as this "naturalistic" mode increasingly incorporated meandering walking paths, it invited its own narrative interpretation. One such example was the famous English garden at Stourhead, whose pedestrian circuit connected moments and objects into the threads of a plot. As visitors following the walkway sequentially encountered a well, grotto, a rustic cottage, the temples of Flora and Apollo, and a replica of the Pantheon, they experienced the unfolding story of Virgil's *Aeneid* (Moore et al. 137–41). Landscape historian Stephanie Ross points out that even less literal examples of this landscape mode invited their own acts of "reading" through strategically placed seats and benches, features that directed visitors' attention toward certain prospects while "impos[ing] a rhythm on the visitor's experience, suggesting moments of pause and reflection" (22).

Of course not just anyone could properly interpret these landscapes; they required a highly trained literary knowledge, as English landscape gardener and author Thomas Whatley noted in 1770. The various devices at Stowe, for example—whether "an allusion to a favourite or well-known subject of history, of poetry, or of tradition"—needed to be "examined, compared, perhaps explained, before the whole design is well understood" (155). For this reason, Miles Coverdale could hardly be expected to situate his own literary project in some cabbage patch at Blithedale: only an exclusive form of gardening could serve as the counterpart to belles lettres—a geography far removed from the kitchen gardens and plowed fields featured in those grubby almanacs Coverdale hoped never to read. Hence to secure his place within this more esteemed cultural genealogy, Coverdale adopts an iconic trope of contemplative life that emphatically links his own pursuit to elite modes from the previous century: he creates a hermitage.

As John Dixon Hunt argues in his study of the relations between English poetry and rural scenery, "No landscape garden of the eighteenth century was complete without its hermitage." These emblematic retreats were designed to announce "the idea of solitary meditation" and invoke "the austere regimen of the hermit fathers" (1). Pope's grotto at Twickenham is surely one of the century's most famous examples—a sanctuary that provided (in Pope's own words) a "Study for Virtuosi, and a Scene for Contemplation" (*Correspondence* 262). Indeed, Pope understood his hermitage and his poetic production as mutually fortifying each other; as he elaborated in the "Second Book of Horace":

> Soon as I enter at my Country door
> My Mind resumes the thread it dropt before
> Thought, which at Hyde-Park-Corner I forgot,

> Meet and rejoin me, in the pensive Grott.
> There all alone, and Compliments apart,
> I ask these sober questions of my Heart. (*Poems* 179)

The poetic associations of this eighteenth-century garden accessory carried well into the following century as well. As Hunt notes, the nineteenth-century hermitage

> offered [itself] to Wordsworth, for example, as a still familiar vocabulary for meditative poetry. His approach to Tintern Abbey and its visions of "something far more deeply interfused" are heralded by the smoke rising among the trees from "some hermit's cave, where by his fire / The hermit sits alone." (8)

Never one to miss an occasion for festooning his own activity in poetic convention, Coverdale thus creates his own hermitage in a treetop at Blithedale, describing the retreat as "a kind of leafy cave, high upward in the air." Like the scholars and poets before him, he retires here to contemplate the philosophical and utopian project to which he has committed himself, to "meditate an essay" or "make verses, tuning the rhythm to the breezy symphony that . . . stirred among the vine leaves." Yet the final item Coverdale mentions in this catalog of lofty pursuits is "the enjoyment of a cigar" (Hawthorne 91). Here, the numinous overtones of smoke rising from the ascetic's cave are comically inverted by an image of carnal indulgence. This particular joke, moreover, seems to have already enjoyed a long run before Hawthorne deployed it. In Richard Graves's poem "The Hermitage" (1776), the new proprietor of a country seat is asked

> Have you no temple, feat, or grotto?
> Or root-house, deck'd with classic motto?
> A *place* is now not worth a fardin,
> Without some gimcrack in your garden.

Therefore, in observance of the fashion, the landowner builds himself a hermit's hut:

> A place—for holy meditation,
> For solitude, and contemplation;
> Yet what himself will rarely use,
> Unless to conn his weekly news;
> Or with some jovial friends, to sit in,
> To take his glass, and smoke, and spit in. (261–62)

Within their irreverent portraits, both Graves and Hawthorne expose the hermitage (and the broader idea of the garden as sanctuary for soul-searching poets) as in fact a site of dissipation and self-indulgence. In one particularly suggestive scene, Hawthorne further underscores this joke by juxtaposing Coverdale's hermitage with the plowed fields and other agricultural operations underway beneath this elevated view: as Coverdale explains, his position in the hermitage "was lofty enough to serve as an observatory," allowing him to relax in the tree above while watching "a few of the brethren . . . digging peat for our winter's fuel," along with friends working "with a yoke of oxen hitched to a drag of stones" (93). This specialized landscape emblem thus provides both the physical and symbolic "cover" for our narrator to duck out of work on the farm below.

Coverdale's understanding and representation of the garden as a retreat from active exertions in nature reaches its culmination at the summer's end, after the elusive "good life" has failed to materialize for him at Blithedale. Frustrated in his attempt to find a "richer picturesqueness in the visible scene of earth and sky" (61), Coverdale abandons his work in the fields to rest up in an elegant inn back in Boston, spending much of this interlude voyeuristically gazing at private gardens and "fashionable dwellings" below his window. And in so doing, he explicitly affirms his preference for experiencing horticulture as a spectator activity: gazing at the lavish urban gardens below, Coverdale reflects, "I had not seen a prettier bit of nature, in all my summer in the country, than they have shown me here in a rather stylish boarding-house" (140). At last, then, the narrator's mislaid idyll finally materializes in the form of fashionable private garden plots (maintained by other, unnamed people), where the fruit hanging on apple and pear trees strikes him as "singularly large, luxuriant, and abundant," the soil boasts a "more than natural fecundity," and "grape-vines clamber upon trellises, and [bear] clusters already purple, and promis[e] the richness of Malta or Madeira in their ripened juices." All of this, significantly, is literally framed like a picture by Coverdale's window, allowing the narrator to settle into a routine of watching these still-life gardens from a distance and in "the laziest manner possible," "legs and slippered feet horizontally disposed" (137–38). It is a perfectly staged admission that physical exertion would spoil enjoyment of the garden's pastoral pleasures, pleasures emphatically associated with detached (visual) consumption and class-coded tropes in this scene's arrangement.

Whether Hawthorne does so consciously or not, his novel's repeated juxtaposition of these two versions of cultivation effectively rehearses the very split that had come to characterize gardening publications in mid-nineteenth century North America. While the more established literature of subsistence gardening and farming continued to provide practical instruction for growers, an emerging generation of design books—just now produced for the first time within the United States—largely excluded discussion of the cultivation process as such. With those practical matters increasingly confined to "how-to" publications like the almanac, the literature for connoisseurs focused on landscape aesthetics, displays of taste, and the philosophical pleasures of contemplating nature. Thus, as we shall see in our next section, domestic gardens became an everyday arena for cultivating class-coded forms of discrimination, distinction, and taste, and they assumed new significance by announcing the true American gardener's relation to nature in terms of consumption and leisure, a life beyond subsistence.

The American Garden Comes of Age

> We have barely declared our horticultural independence of the Old World and are starting to create an American type of gardening literature.
> —Thomas McAdam (1905)

While it may have chanced that a late frost killed prize plantings in May, that fruit trees failed to yield, or that cutworms wiped out a season of work in the tomato beds, mid-nineteenth-century gardeners scarcely had reason to complain about shortages in horticultural writing itself. Nearly seventy agricultural periodicals launched in the United States before 1850, and a broad selection of additional gardening publications were available to readers hoping to enhance their green thumbs (Wood 165). Martha Logan began publishing the first gardening calendar in colonial America in 1752, and *The Old Farmer's Almanac* remained in continual publication beginning in 1792; Bernard McMahon's highly influential *American Gardener's Calendar* (1806) appeared in eleven editions, and Thomas Bridgeman's popular *The Young Gardener's Assistant* (1829) generated two spin-off editions, *The Florist's Guide* (1835) and *The Kitchen Gardener's Instructor* (1836). Meanwhile, printed materials from *The Cottage Garden of America* (1848) and the *Shaker Seed Catalogue* to periodicals like *Magazine of Horticulture*, *The Cultivator*, and *Farmer and Gardener* supplied professionals and amateurs alike with instructions for nearly every imaginable horticultural concern.[11] By any measure, there seemed to be a veritable bumper crop in gardening literature during this period.

Yet to some discriminating observers, this abundance of gardening literature had nonetheless failed to produce suitable off-page results in the American landscape. Thomas Jefferson characterized American cultivation as a lesser cousin to English modes, explaining to a correspondent, "Here, as you know, we are all farmers, but not in a pleasing style" (461). This was to be contrasted with the practices and scenery he documented on tours of the English countryside, which boasted some of the world's most elaborately cultivated gardens. Visiting Europeans further added to the charge of American horticultural inferiority, sometimes reporting on the "slovenly" character of U.S. landscapes and their failure to bear out earlier myths of the New World as garden. In 1824 English traveler William Blane maintained that "ornamental gardening is an art at present totally unknown or at least unpracticed, in the United States" (30), an assertion reiterated by Frances Trollope in accounts of her American travels three years later: "From the time I entered America," she wrote, "I had never seen the slightest approach to what we call pleasure-grounds; a few very worthless and scentless flowers were all the specimens of gardening I had seen in Ohio; no attempt at garden scenery was ever dreamed of" (160).

Some champions of taste blamed a literary deficiency itself for these aesthetic failures. Indeed, prior to the 1840s, *all* publications on landscape design came from Europe. Thus, when Jefferson made the obligatory journey through Europe in 1786 to plan his grounds at Monticello, he carried with him one of the day's most influential English garden books, Thomas Whately's *Observations on Modern Gardening*, and directed all inquiries on his tour toward the matter of "making and maintaining a garden in that style" (qtd. in Marranca 244).[12] There were, after all, no American books to guide such an undertaking.

Yet no one was more emphatic about this link between the "slovenly" national landscape and the absence of a specialized domestic literature than Andrew Jackson Downing. And like Jefferson, Downing felt that wherever one *did* find beautiful gardens on this side of the Atlantic, one also found readers of the right books: that is, individuals who had been "improved by the study of European authors" (*Treatise* 40). This view, of course, directly heightened the stakes of Downing's own literary contribution as well as his status as the founder of American landscape architecture.[13] As he pronounced in 1841, "[I]n North America, almost every thing is yet before us" in terms of "the literature and practice of Landscape Gardening as an art," a mode that would directly appeal to the "cultivated and refined mind" (*Treatise* 40; "Essay" 247).

Downing's *Treatise on the Theory and Practice of Landscape Gardening, Adapted to North America* (1841) thus emerged as the first U.S. publication devoted expressly and exclusively to ornamental gardening and landscape design.[14] And when his periodical *The Horticulturalist* launched five years later, Downing appended the tagline *"the journal of rural art and rural taste"* to explicitly dissociate it from the older publications concerned with food crops and productivity. Indeed, the new movement's professional class even discarded the customary trade name "gardener" in favor of "landscape architect" (Zoh 59). Only in this thoroughly altered context, then, could it cease to appear strange that Frederick Law Olmsted—Downing's own protégé and the century's most famous park designer—would identify his primary weakness as an ignorance of plants and gardening techniques (Simo 135). This work, after all, was now more concerned with the plotting of scenes rather than the potting of seeds.

Given Downing's fervent admiration for the "peculiar and distinguishing *luxury*" characterizing the English landscape tradition (*Rural* 548; italics original), his designs often seemed better suited to wealthy homeowners who could afford teams of hired landscapers to create those sylvan scenes. As architect Lewis Allen wrote in 1852, the schemes were "too expensive for general use [among working-class mechanics and farmers]; they will do for what are termed gentlemen farmers, and mechanics, who work, if at all, in gloves" (73). Indeed, much of Downing's writing and designs were inspired by English estates that were themselves historical products of the laws of primogeniture, a process of land inheritance that he credited for "the continual improvement and embellishment of those vast landed estates which remain perpetually in the hands of the same family," each generation cumulatively adding to a cultivated perfection. As Downing reasoned, "[T]hese advantages in the hands of the most intelligent and the wealthiest aristocracy in the world" had made "an entire landscape garden of 'merry England'" (*Treatise* 37–38).

Yet as a savvy businessman, Downing also took care to assure readers that the new, distinctly "American" form of gardening and garden literature really was for everybody, observing "no barriers" of class and elevating everything from "the humblest cottage windowboxes" to the "large landed estates" of five hundred acres (*Treatise* ix–x). And middle-class audiences proved eager to read his books and emulate those gardens on whatever scale possible. As farms were increasingly converted to rural residences, villas, and cottages in the decades following the Civil War, Downing's designs gained wide appeal, spreading with increasing momentum as the American middle class "elevated the appearance of their properties from unkempt barnyards to domains of refinement" (Rogers 65)—and indeed supplanted the landed gentry as the primary market for such landscape gardens and literature. This trend had notable material effects across the geography of North America, from the increasingly split design distinguishing front-yard and backyard residential spaces to the naturalistic and explicitly "non-productive" scenery of the Greensward Plan for New York's Central Park, which ultimately became the template for thousands of urban parks to follow.

FIGURE 4. D. M. Dewey lithograph from *The Nurseryman's Specimen Book of American Horticulture and Floriculture, Fruits, Flowers, Ornamental Trees, Shrubs, Etc.* (1872). Courtesy of Historic Newton, Newton, Mass.

Yet where Jefferson and Coverdale suppressed the presence of enslaved gardeners and grubby farmers in their garden idylls, many of the new landscape publications (following Downing's call for the "removal or concealment of everything uncouth and discordant") began instructing homeowners to eliminate vegetables and edible cultivars themselves, along with other visual aspects evoking subsistence practices (*Treatise* 18). In *The Art of Beautifying Suburban Home Grounds of Small Extent* (1870), for example, Frank J. Scott includes a design template for suburban homes that "does not include orchards, pastures, or meadows, but is devoted to the development of sylvan beauty rather than pecuniary utilities, or farm conveniences" (176). His scheme does make an exception for gardeners who wished to grow their own strawberries, yet even here he recommended that these be planted deep within "young shrubbery plantings, where their presence will not be noticed" (178). Robert Copeland's *Country Life* (1866) even recommended that farmers themselves adopt these picturesque design principles, reasoning that

> Even if it is easier to plough up to a straight road or wall or row of trees, than to a curved line: what of that, if by planting trees in groups, and curving the roads, we can produce beautiful effects in form and color . . . ? The few dollars a year saved in the one case . . . are no compensation for the loss of the pleasant lessons which the beauties of nature must teach every willing mind. (4)

Such prescriptions inverted the priorities laid out earlier in publications like the *Genesee Farmer* (1845), which explicitly prioritized the function of middle-class gardens in descending order from generating profit (primary), then supplying a family's own material wants (secondary), and, lastly, providing an "innocent recreation" (67).

This divide visibly played out in gardening literature and flower publications explicitly produced by and for women as well.[15] In an 1864 series for the *Atlantic Monthly*—particularly in her essay on "The Lady Who Does Her Own Work"—Harriet Beecher Stowe had highlighted the vigorous activity involved in home and garden maintenance to push back against notions that women were too delicate to partake in strenuous forms of labor. A more explicit call to hands-on action in the soil was published by Anna Bartlett Warner in *Gardening by Myself* (1872) and *Miss Tiller's Vegetable Garden and the Money She Made by It* (1873), which fit in the tradition of American self-help treatises by drawing on Warner's own personal experience of earning a living through market-gardening after her family's fortune was lost in the Panic of 1837. And readers anxious that they might be unfit for the physical demands of gardening were reassured by Sophia Orne Johnson, whose instructional treatise, *Every Woman Her Own Flower Gardener* (1871), declared that women "live in-doors too much, and thus sacrifice their health and spirits." She urged hesitant readers to incrementally build from simpler to more strenuous tasks: "Garden by degrees, my friends, and cultivate your muscles, with your plants!" (7).[16] Yet toward the end of the century, periodicals like *The Ladies' Floral Cabinet* (1872–87) and the books of Celia Thaxter, Mabel Osgood Wright, Alice Morse Earle, and Neltje Blanchan tended to emphasize the domestic role of middle-class women as discriminating consumers rather than producers (Lovett 91), commonly omitting practical instruction for their suburban gardens. Indeed, this literature helped make the garden serve as "a new class ideal," a visual emblem whose proper design and upkeep, according to Beverley Seaton, became "as essential as any other material aspect of the family's lifestyle" (42). Celia Thaxter's *An Island Garden* (1894) devotes an entire chapter to floral arrangements, meticulously detailing everything from the variable lengths of stems, the compatibility of different flowers with particular vases and bowls, and the embroidered linens on which these might be placed—yet scarcely gives a word to the actual cultivation of these plants right outside her parlor window (84–96). Similarly, Mabel Osgood Wright documented elaborate flower-arranging regimens in her writing, and although she allocated a bit more discussion to the hands-on, soil-based practices behind those decorations, the author's role remained principally that of designer and manager of the grounds, while her hired garden laborer—whom Wright labeled an "animated shovel" in the *Garden of a Commuter's Wife* (1901)—was left to perform the manual work (47).[17] By the early twentieth century, the impracticality of these works had become something of a running joke. In Edmund Lester Pearson's satirical *The Librarian at Play* (1911), the narrator excitedly brings home a stylish book entitled *The Gardener's Guide, or a Vade Mecum of Useful Information for Amateur Gardeners, by Martha Matilda Bunkum*, but in searching its index for instructions on planting sunflowers, he and his wife Jane find that entries skip from "sunbonnet" and "sun-dial" to "sweet peas." Distracted by the sunbonnet listing, Jane flips to this section and learns that such an old-fashioned accessory is actually "not so bad" if one goes for pink. Once back on the hunt for sunflower instructions, the couple concludes that Mrs. Bunkum must be too sophisticated "to use such a vulgar name as sunflower" and probably listed the flower under its scientific name, which sends them off on another research detour to discover what that name may be. Their local librarian lends a hand by consulting Liberty Hyde Bailey's *Encyclopedia of American Horticulture* to determine the sunflower's Latin name (*helianthus*); yet rather than simply sticking with Bailey's work at that point, the couple returns to Mrs. Bunkum's book to learn only that the *helianthus* is "one of the most attractive and satisfactory of the perennials. Nothing so suitable to place against a wall, or to employ to cover a shed or any other unattractive feature of the landscape" (35). The quest ends with the narrator burying his copy of Mrs. Bunkum's book where he originally intended to plant the seeds. In a subsequent story from the collection, Pearson's narrator develops an inferiority complex in reading the paradoxically titled *The Simple Garden*, a book featuring lavish illustrations of imported marble benches and garden sculptures. After the book recommends that he plant sweet peas and notes they should be mulched, the remainder of the story turns to the narrator's attempts to find out what *mulch* means, which *The Simple Garden* never defines. After a fruitless quest, he finally decides that *mulch* means to attack the flowers savagely with a hoe, which he does while Jane's back is turned.

Writers of the older, practical gardening publications and almanacs, most of whom were in the nursery or seed businesses, responded with less good humor at the impractical slant of these new books. In *Gardening for Profit* (1867), Peter Henderson wholly dismissed the stylish publications now being peddled by "ex-editors, lawyers, mechanics, etc."—in short, people engaged in the gardening business merely "as a pastime" (vii). Even Henry Ward Beecher weighed in to criticize the impracticality of such literature. In his encyclopedic work *Plain and Pleasant Talk about Fruits, Flowers and Farming* (1859), he includes an entry on "Pleasure of Horticulture" that takes direct aim at the silly new craze for "*pastoral cant*" in garden literature and "so-called *fine writing* . . . about rural affairs," along with its "senseless gabble about dew, and zephyrs, and stars, and sunrises—about flowers, and green trees, golden grain and lowing herds," only to conclude his remonstration with an endorsement of the older, practical genre to which his own text presumably belongs (136; italics original). Authors of the subsistence and market-gardening books also pointed out how the new generation of design books misrepresented—or simply ignored—that most essential fact of embodied gardening practice: dirty hands and physical exertion. This omission seemed particularly audacious in Copeland's *Country Life* (1866), which not only sought to lure novices into gardening with promises of "pleasure [and] no more than a healthy amount of labor," but even went so far as to suggest that *farmers* themselves could also learn to appreciate the finer aspects of nature by studying its contents. Copeland opens by expressing the fanciful hope "that some who now earn their bread with the sweat of their brow, and look upon their calling as a treadmill of drudgery and endurance, may here learn that within the round of their daily duties they have every thing which can expand the mind and ennoble the soul" (title page). As a corrective, practical garden-writer Peter Henderson (emphasizing his "*working experience* in all departments of gardening") opened his own manual the following year with a sobering reminder to would-be gardeners: "I can safely say that we wor[k], on average, sixteen hours a day, winter and summer, with scarcely a day for recreation" (viii, 16; italics original).[18] As garden historian Thomas Mickey notes, when Henderson died in 1890, "his obituary referred to his garden books as being popular because they were 'eminently practical'" (94).

Yet in light of the rapidly increasing popularity of ornamental gardens and literature in the decades following the Civil War, most middle-class Americans seemed undeterred by the impracticalities and contradictions of the new design genres, which proliferated alongside growing garden audiences—which were themselves created by increased wealth, industrialization, demographic shifts toward suburban residence, and faster and more frequent travel to Europe, where Americans observed luxuriant models of ornamental landscape gardening. And so by 1905 when *Garden Magazine* contributor Thomas McAdam assessed the current state of American gardening literature, he applauded how far the genre had come since the previous generation. Readers could now purchase books like *The Garden of a Commuter's Wife* and *Elizabeth and Her German Garden*—books "worth having," McAdam claims, even though he admits the latter book "doesn't ring quite true, and of course there is nothing about gardening in it." He also recommends two remarkably pricey titles despite his observation that consumers shouldn't actually expect to learn anything about cultivation techniques from them: as he put it, "No one reads such books, but they are magnificent picture galleries, and make appropriate gifts for wealthy persons, architects and landscape gardeners." Across the review, McAdam contrasts this bright new generation with the older publications, which featured "scarcely a book . . . that a gentleman would care to have in his parlor." Admittedly, there had always been "plenty of sober, useful" works in the American gardening canon; but alas, these remained "hopelessly unbeautiful" and had that unfortunate "look of the barn about them":

> faded covers, cheap paper, small type, scanty margins and gruesome old woodcuts; they all abounded in realistic portraits of hairy caterpillars, apple scab, plum rot, and the like—all in heroic size—and no book was complete without a certain classical picture of the codling moth's offspring eating the heart out of an apple. (229–30)

In effect, McAdam's summary reveals that the real menace to fine garden writing and its associated fantasies had never been worms or apple blight but rather the specter of the farm itself. And as we have seen, he was hardly alone in voicing this bias. Miles Coverdale doubles down on this claim in identifying farming practices as *fatal* to self-cultivation and the development of elevated poetic sensibility, insisting that unlike the gardenist and the scholar, the "yeoman and the scholar—the yeoman and the man of finest moral culture... are two distinct individuals, and can never be melted or welded into one substance" (Hawthorne 61).

This conviction that practical agriculture was antithetical to the fantasy, leisure, and aesthetic gratification characteristic of ornamental publications thus took its most insidious form in the literature's ritualistic expulsion of the farmer. Such evictions abound in fiction and nonfiction alike, from Francis King's sympathetic response to garden enthusiasts who "do not want to meet the man with the hoe at every turn" on their grounds (*Well-Considered* 207) to Mabel Osgood Wright's account of wildflower-gathering excursions spoiled by the intrusion of pragmatic farmers too obtuse to fathom the pursuit of beauty for its own sake: one farmer assumes that Wright and her friends "must be getting things 'to make beer of'" or must be "gathering 'greens'" to eat as they pluck flowers from the roadside; another interrupts the outing (and the pleasure Wright and company take in experiencing nature in purely aesthetic terms) by "[telling] us what everything we had was 'good for.' We should never have rheumatism if we ate this. That was good for fever" (*Flowers* 195). Coverdale likewise tries to shield his lofty pastoral visions from the unromantic interjections of Silas Foster (Blithedale's only bona fide farmer) as he daydreams with his friends: as Coverdale complains during one of these disrupted reveries, "when[ever] Silas did speak, it was very much to some practical purpose," such as tending their hogs or weeding vegetable plots (19–20).

Yet as philosopher Simone de Beauvoir reminds us, a fundamental instability lurks at the heart of all such exclusive constructions: "no group ever sets itself up as the One without at once setting up the Other over against itself," leaving the identity and meaning of each term utterly dependent on the other—and thus open to dissolving when uncoupled from its counterpart. In short, for the fantasy of the ideal garden to have any real force, it must continually be set off against the forms and qualities that bedevil it. Inevitably, then, that excluded term comes seeping back onto the scene like the pastoralist's bad conscience—a return of the repressed that is vividly staged during Coverdale's homecoming tableau near the end of *The Blithedale Romance*. As our narrator sets off for his ultimate visit to Blithedale after his late-summer hiatus, all the "sunny freshness" of his early pastoral hope returns to brighten his homecoming stroll on this perfect September day: he passes colorful toadstools and autumn berries, "orchards of ruddy apples,... fields of ripening maize,... patches of woodland, and all such sweet rural scenery" (189). Finally, after having paid one last visit to his cherished hermitage, Coverdale's reverie is capped when he stumbles upon a dreamlike masquerade in the woods, a "fantastic rabble" composed of all his fellow communards presenting themselves as nymphs and "chimeras" (195). And yet, at this very moment, our narrator observes the single, ruinous effect of the farmer's presence amid this fantasy pageant:

> But Silas Foster, who leaned against a tree near by, in his customary blue frock, and smoking a short pipe, did more to disenchant the scene, with his look of shrewd, acrid, Yankee observation, than twenty witches and necromancers could have done, in the way of rendering it weird and fantastic. (194)

Of course, if figures of practical agriculture automatically "disenchant the scene" for romantic pastoralists like Coverdale, most real gardening practices were already doomed to fall short as a source of sensory and aesthetic pleasure. After all, "garden" is always at once both noun and verb, an activity requiring continual bodily exertion—activities like digging, planting, fertilizing, mulching, weeding, pruning, and more. Surely most American growers and readers would already have seen such exclusive schemes as profoundly misaligned with their own lived experience in gardens—spaces that were neither immutable, effortless ideals nor realms of sheer toil and discontent, but rather infinitely complex hybrids where people went about their daily business experimenting, playing, blessing the rain and cursing the aphids, competing with neighbors, following or flouting the trends, reducing grocery bills or blowing small fortunes, trading tips, roughing their hands, and staining their lips berry-blue. In this realm where work could be profoundly gratifying and pleasure exceedingly practical, the divided nature of nineteenth-century garden writing could not go unchallenged for long.

For "The Love of Dirt": Pleasure and Production in Warner's *My Summer in a Garden*

> The things I may do in my garden multiply on my vision.
> —Charles Dudley Warner (1870)

For late nineteenth-century Americans working in an increasingly specialized and industrialized economy—a system hardly designed to gratify desires for engaged, sensuous, or unalienated experience—the prospect of experiencing work as a kind of play was bound to appeal. And indeed, just two decades after Blithedale's communards failed to reconcile these disparate modes, Charles Dudley Warner's *My Summer in a Garden* (1870) reinvented the genre of garden writing not only by integrating production and pleasure but also by opening a space to bridge our divided notions of nature and culture, exertion and reflection, physical and philosophical activity, and more.[19]

As editor of the influential *Hartford Courant*, a popular author, and cofounder of the Nook Farm literary colony (along with Harriet Beecher Stowe and Mark Twain), Warner enjoyed considerable visibility during his lifetime (1829–1900). Much of his popularity came directly from *My Summer in a Garden*—Warner's first book—which proved an instant hit and sold out the first printing within three weeks of publication ("Brief Mention" 2). Fellow authors like Mark Twain called the book "perfectly magnificent," a "rich, delicious" work in which "every page glitters like a cluster-pin with many-sided gems of fancy" (294). A reviewer for *The Galaxy* seemed especially taken with the wide-ranging audiences *My Summer* embraced, devoting much of the review to listing off these potential readers: here was a book "for one skilled in horticulture, for one totally ignorant of it, for a man in low spirits, for a woman who is gay, for a hypochondriac, for the man in full health, and in short, for any other man" (309). Three years after its initial publication, a critic attributed *My Summer*'s success to "a freshness that delighted everyone, a charming out-door atmosphere, and much delicate and quiet humor" (Higginson 333). And when Warner died in 1900, an announcement of his passing in *Public Opinion* claimed that the author may have done "more pretentious things than 'My Summer in a Garden,' but never anything that was more gratifying to the public." Indeed, the announcement concluded, "we do not forget his editorial connection with the 'Hartford Courant,' nor his interest in prison reform; but the world knows him from 'My Summer in a Garden'" ("Charles Dudley Warner" 564).

Such acclaim may come as a surprise to today's readers, since Warner largely disappeared from the critical spotlight where many of his Nook Farm colleagues remained in subsequent years. Following its brief but significant period of popularity, *My Summer in a Garden* went out of print for nearly 125 years, during which time garden enthusiasts simply had to pass tattered old copies "perennially from hand to hand," as garden writer Alan Gurganus noted when the book was finally reissued in 2002 (xii). Perhaps Warner's work on *The Gilded Age* (1873)—a book that enjoyed the lasting star power of Mark Twain as coauthor and whose very title became a trademark for the historical period—simply eclipsed *My Summer* over the decades that followed. Whatever the reason for the book's long, shadowy interlude, it seems undeniable that were garden writing a more prominent genre in its own right, Warner surely would have maintained greater prominence over the past century and a half as one of its key architects. After all, his richly soiled fingerprints can still be seen nearly everywhere in the flourishing modern genre we recognize today.

Warner's background made him the right gardener for this job, allowing him to animate his account with literary elements largely missing from the existing canon: a subjective voice, a dynamic narrative arc, and above all, the gardener's persona itself. Indeed, it seems strange in hindsight that this subjective presence remained so dim in many earlier accounts; after all, what ultimately makes a given expanse of soil and plants a "garden" is the effort and intervention of the gardener as such.

Moreover, the narrator's distinct persona and playfully humorous tone help underscore the childlike delight that Warner takes in his work. Granted, the account frankly acknowledges the physical demands of gardening and extols the activity for its practical purpose and concrete results. Yet Warner consistently depicts a process that is also an end and pleasure in itself. Indeed, to miss that part of the equation, he suggests, would be to commit a category mistake. Gardening's underlying pleasure principle is handily summarized in an early passage where Warner questions the wisdom of conventional instructional literature, which "say[s] that trees shade the garden too much, and interfere with the growth of the vegetables." He concedes the technical accuracy of this point but notes a more fundamental truth that it omits: "when I go down the potato rows, ... the sweat pouring from my face, I should be grateful for shade. What is a garden for? The pleasure of man. I should take much more pleasure in a shady garden. Am I to be sacrificed, broiled, roasted for the sake of the increased vigor of a few vegetables? The thing is perfectly absurd" (21).

Such an understanding of gardening as a practical mode of play infuses every topic Warner takes up, from relations with neighbors to eating from his garden to the elemental act of digging and planting itself. Even when recounting setbacks like the endless raids on his garden by trespassing chickens, children, and songbirds, Warner stages his predicament like some extravagant game of capture-the-flag, enlisting an ever-expanding menagerie of characters to protect his strawberries and peas. After recruiting toads and cats to devour smaller adversaries, he wonders if the half-acre planting will soon morph into a "zoological garden" (19). For the larger two-legged foes who strip his pear trees and grapevines, Warner impishly imagines his garden transformed into a fortress of deterrence, daydreaming how easy it would be to keep kids away if only one could "grow a variety of grapes like ... bullets, that should explode in the stomach: the vine would make such a nice border for the garden—a masked battery of grape." Alternately, as an option infinitely more terrifying, he proposes universal Sunday school schemes to keep Hartford's children locked away during fruit season (69, 27).

My Summer maintains this tongue-in-cheek approach even in addressing more sacrosanct matters in American culture. Warner's characterization of gardening as "a kind of declaration of independence," for instance, plays off familiar fantasies of frontier-style self-sufficiency, imaginatively converting his suburban garden into a virtual homestead on the rustic fringe of society. Expanding on this horticultural "declaration of independence," Warner reflects:

> I know of nothing that makes one feel more complacent, in these July days, than his vegetables from his own garden.... The market-man shows me his peas and beets and tomatoes.... "No, I thank you," I say carelessly; "I am raising my own this year." ... To raise his own vegetables makes a person feel, somehow, more liberal. (49)

Yet then, like a child who insists on tasting his mud pie simply because he made it himself, Warner zealously chokes down a bumper crop of the very squash he has always found "contemptible"—a likely wink to readers in conceding the whimsical nature of any such back-to-the-land subsistence fantasies in our modern age—an impractical dream unless one is willing to adopt an all-kale diet during winter.

Still, such daydreaming conspicuously departs from the idle pleasures of Jefferson, Byrd, and other planters who enjoyed their garden paradise sitting indolently "under vines and fig trees." Indeed, Warner is emphatic with both readers and houseguests that *he* performs the work in this garden, noting with pride how visitors are commonly "surprised to learn that I had the sole care of it" (41). Not until Warner does this emphasis become a mainstay of gardening literature, with subsequent writers no longer feeling compelled to explain their reasoning in asserting, as prominent garden writer Hanna Rion does in 1912, that she would as soon consider having a secretary compose her book "as to permit a gardener to plant or dig among my flowers" (35).

Moreover, Warner's refrain about having the "sole care" of his garden ramifies out to inform a whole host of related fantasies and reflections about what gratifying productive activity could mean: in the space of the garden, not only is work transformed into a kind of play, but acts of leisure and indulgence are also elevated by virtue of the skill, patience, planning, and effort they involve—not to mention the incontestably practical results they yield. Warner thus marks a decided point of departure from older modes of garden writing by constructing labor as philosophical, and agency as always practical and embodied, in a way that none of his predecessors would have imagined. Proudly identifying with the manual laborer's experience, he declares that "[t]he man that has planted a garden feels he has done something for the good of the world. He belongs to the producers" (5). In fact, after meeting with great success in his vegetable plots, Warner marvels at a set of effects that he "had not expected":

> I have never read of any Roman supper that seemed to me equal to a dinner of my own vegetables; when every thing on the table is the product of my own labor[.] . . . It is strange what a taste you suddenly have for things you never liked before. The squash has always been to me a dish of contempt; but now I eat it as if it were my best friend. I never cared for the beet or the bean; but I fancy that now I could eat them, tops and all, so completely have they been transformed by the soil in which they grew. I think the squash is less squashy, and the beet has a deeper hue of rose, for my care of them. (50)

Apparently it is not just the beets and beans that have been "transformed by the soil" here but also the individual who grows them. Significantly, such a conversion stands in direct opposition to the effects of labor Coverdale famously characterized at Blithedale, where "[t]he clods of earth, which we so constantly belabored and turned over and over, were never etherealized into thought. Our thoughts, on the contrary, were fast becoming cloddish" (61). This formula, where "labor symbolize[s] nothing"—and indeed leaves Coverdale and company "mentally sluggish in the dusk of the evening"—directly reiterates the ideologies of affirmative culture, where values of "the good, the beautiful, and the true . . . permeate and transfigure 'from above' the realm of necessity, of the material provision for life" (Marcuse 91). Yet for Warner, value and virtue move in the opposite direction, proceeding from our embodied, physical, and affective expenditures in the soil. And this labor-based pleasure gives Warner a kind of insight that Coverdale (who had not contributed to the meal's production) proved incapable of grasping during his first supper at Blithedale. In this early scene, Coverdale sits amazed at the relish with which the head farmer, Silas Foster, enjoys his food, "gorg[ing]" himself and "gulping . . . down" everything before him; "cut[ting] slice after slice of ham; perpetuating terrible enormities with the butter-plate; and, in all other respects, behaving less like a civilized Christian than the worst kind of an ogre" (29). While Coverdale's unflattering depiction might have us believe Silas to be an unreflective brute, it seems reasonable to conclude the very opposite here: by virtue of his energetic investment in this food, Silas experiences the meal as intensely sensuous and gratifying; meanwhile, for Coverdale the dinner is little more than an opportunity to reestablish class identity through the observation of proper etiquette. It is this visiting poet, in fact, who remains insensible to the pleasures and complexities in eating and who narrowly fixates on the misuse of utensils and the quality of the plates and linens.[20]

Warner thus underscores a new phase in American garden writing by celebrating the sensual and aesthetic pleasures available not despite, but precisely *because* of, the intensive effort they demand in the garden. In fact, these tributes have become so ubiquitous in contemporary gardening as to seem an obligatory feature of the genre: eating and engaged physical exertion are elevated to the extent that they allow us to participate in nature's cycles at the most intimate level—the body itself. It is thus with a tone of pride rather than exasperation that Warner declares, "There is not a pea here that does not represent a drop of moisture wrung from my brow, not a beet that does not stand for a back-ache, not a squash that has not caused me untold anxiety" (51).

Such moments, however, also indicate how carefully Warner must tiptoe through the narrow rows of his garden narrative. While he aspires to provide a truthful account of the physical exertion this activity demands, too much emphasis on this "back-ache" and "anxiety" might inadvertently validate the disillusionment of hands-off garden elitists like Coverdale, for whom the realities of farm labor are unpleasant enough to warrant abandoning the enterprise altogether. Such a risk may explain Warner's persistent effort to preserve the pleasure element at every turn, even in the most farfetched scenarios. One day when Warner finds himself toiling beneath an unusually hot sun, he imagines covering the whole garden with an awning to make the task less onerous. Yet as this reflection develops, Warner hits on a less expensive solution, concocting a scheme where the gardener might hire others to "carry a sort of canopy over you as you hoed. And there might be a person at each end of the row with some cool and refreshing drink" (22). It is essential to note the fine print in this little fantasy exercise: rather than hiring this team to do the hoeing *for him* (as we initially expect he will propose), Warner imagines using those individuals in a way that merely enables him to complete the task *himself*. Their function, in other words, is to ensure that the gardener's tasks remain pleasurable, rather than to eliminate those tasks as such.

Such an arrangement indicates both an important distinction from the pleasure fantasies of earlier garden representation and a certain limit to Warner's success in moving beyond those inherited divisions. No sooner has he encountered an unpleasant fact than Warner reinvokes the two classical modes of cultivation to avoid it, dividing his activity in such a way that one class performs the onerous tasks precisely to preserve the garden as a pleasure arena for the other group. Pure drudgery, in other words, is not eliminated but rather outsourced in this scene. Accordingly, while Warner's project has reimagined gardening as symbolized physical activity in order to move beyond the split structure of the timeless picture garden (the domain of connoisseurs) and the plain-toil version of horticulture (the domain of laborers), Warner continually finds that middle ground itself to be somewhat unstable.

Moreover, it is not just July's oppressive heat that challenges *My Summer*'s vision of work-as-play in the garden. Warner also finds himself foiled by the very attempt to incorporate the two dominant modes of garden writing into his account. Specifically, his predicament arises from drawing from both the practical elements of the how-to literature and the pleasure elements of the design-oriented publications, while leaving those disparate categories themselves more or less intact. Indeed, this unsteady balancing act emerges in the opening lines of Warner's book: "The love of dirt is among the earliest of passions," it begins, and over the course of life one inevitably rediscovers "the love of digging in the ground (or of looking on while he pays another to dig)" (5). Here, Warner graciously invites audiences and actors from both garden traditions into his discussion; yet as this same remark reveals, simply *incorporating* these antagonistic subject-positions does not *reconcile* the contradictions they embody. In fact, the textual brackets plainly reinscribe the ideological brackets that separate the subjects who work and subjects who merely recreate in the garden. In a sense, then, one could argue that rather than discarding the barriers between these inherited modes, Warner merely alternates between them, occupying them separately and in turn. As such, the narrator often moves through his own account like a pendulum, leaving that which he swings between securely in its place.

Yet it is precisely this transitional quality, and Warner's sometimes divided persona, that make *My Summer* such a fascinating text. We become witness here to Warner's heavily conditioned literary sensibility, the garden's ongoing development, and the grower's self-adjusting reflections as they move through an experiment that surprises, disrupts, and often overturns the very conventions informing it. Encounters that begin with a certain set of inherited assumptions or imply allegiance to a particular vein in gardening "identity" continually veer off in new directions or yield entirely new, hybrid fruits.

Such shifts and reversals are perhaps most prominent in *My Summer*'s short chapter on the disputed economic value of gardening. Warner wavers endlessly on this topic, at one moment trying to determine if a garden "pays" for itself in market terms and at other times insisting that its value utterly defies quantification, even calling it "a sort of profanation" to "turn into merchandise the red strawberry" or "compute in figures" the delight gardening brings to our everyday routine (79). Nor is this contradiction diminished when Warner momentarily sets aside his regard for those more lofty, intangible values and "yield[s] to popular clamor [by] discuss[ing] the profit of my garden." Selecting his potato patch as a financial test case, Warner devises a table computing all inputs and outputs—a wink, quite likely, at a parallel scene in Henry David Thoreau's *Walden*, where the author calculates profits from the garden he grows outside his cabin in the woods. Yet this exercise ends up splitting our narrator in *My Summer* between the interest of the worker-persona and the landowner-persona: after all, with Warner simultaneously occupying both roles in this dramatization, the conflict between them is bound to emerge. As a property owner seeking to maximize profits, Warner initially decides to set the worker's wages at the lowest imaginable rate: he "figured it right down to European prices—seventeen cents a day for unskilled labor" (in comparison to standard wages from the period, this rate proves exceptionally low).[21] Yet since he also performs that work himself, Warner pauses midway through the scenario to admit he had "some difficulty in fixing the rate of my own wages." Thus, in assigning a final market price to the potatoes, Warner's figures appeal directly to his experience and physical expenditure as a manual laborer working in the summer heat: he insists that two cents per potato is a fair value, noting "this I should have considered dirt cheap last June, when I was going down the rows with the hoe. If any one thinks that two cents each is high, let him try to raise them" (80–81). Initially identifying with the propertied class that would hire others to do its gardening (Warner *is*, after all, the owner of this plot), Warner's embodied experience as a cultivator ultimately redirects his allegiance to the laboring classes and the priority owed to their claims for compensation.

And so Warner's conception of value continually leads back to the *grower's effort* on behalf of the garden, and to the way this process promotes an intimate exchange between human and nonhuman nature that yields a profit to both (as I will discuss more thoroughly in a moment). If one considers this emphasis alongside the garden writing of Thoreau (whose own bean-growing experiment in *Walden* appears to be reenacted in this scene), the broader significance of Warner's innovation becomes more apparent still. For Warner celebrates the garden's merit on terms that were never fully embraced by Thoreau. Indeed, Thoreau runs up against a philosophical impasse that Warner breezes right past, discovering gardening to be a minefield that jeopardizes two of the central priorities of his Walden project: to affirm the value of "wild" nature in noninstrumental terms, and to cultivate his own mind and spirit beyond the influence of social convention.

Thoreau's first conflict here (celebrating nature's intrinsic worth) becomes manifest in the opening passages of "The Bean Field" chapter. Across much of *Walden*, Thoreau has focused on celebrating the "wild" aspects of nature, the world of nonhuman things and processes that are not directly useful to human actors but that exist for themselves and flourish in their own ways (186). Yet while he notes that the sun itself can "loo[k] on our cultivated fields and on the prairies and forests without distinction," Thoreau, as a gardener, cannot. His obligation to protect his bean plants suddenly requires him to takes sides in nature, to make "invidious distinctions with [the] hoe, leveling whole ranks of one species, and sedulously cultivating another." And in doing so, Thoreau finds himself "ruthlessly" disturbing the weeds' "delicate organizations," while regarding worms and woodchucks as his "enemies" (152, 146). Much of this talk, admittedly, is staged in a deliberately playful manner.[22] And yet the antagonisms here (both between Thoreau and these undomesticated forces, and between the imperatives of production and *Walden*'s stated environmental ethic) are real enough that Thoreau closes the chapter by making reparations to all the wild species he has subdued on behalf of his beans: he shares his harvest with the woodchucks and celebrates "the abundance of the weeds whose seeds are the granary of the birds" (157). By late summer, Thoreau even seems relieved to abandon his gardening and watch the domesticated beans "cheerfully returning to their wild and primitive state" (149).

To the extent that Thoreau regards undomesticated wilderness as sacred and "pure" (a term he faithfully repeats across the account), it was likely inevitable that cultivation would come under fire. Indeed, Thoreau's critique of Concord farmers and their rampant materialism explicitly depicts domestic crops as a vandalism of nature. In rattling off a litany of complaints against his avaricious neighbors, each of Thoreau's charges grows more damning than the previous: he condemns farmers who "would carry the landscape . . . would carry his God, to market." As this diatribe reaches its crescendo, Thoreau finally throws down the gauntlet: "As if you were to raise your potatoes in the church yard!" (185–86). Thus, despite his efforts to balance the wild and domesticated elements of his bean field, such comments hardly show Thoreau's bias to be in the garden's favor.

Meanwhile, gardening binds Thoreau to patterns of repetition and convention that seem to compromise his second great priority in *Walden*: the cultivation of a radical self-reliance and individualism. Such a personal commitment, in Thoreau's view, is ideally pursued on the margins of society—an unsurprising conviction given his fondness for the old romantic formulas wherein humans were once carefree and independent hunters but eventually became slaves to domesticity, adopted agriculture to support the social enterprise, and woke up one day to find themselves "tools of their tools." As Thoreau summarizes the process, "The man who independently plucked the fruits when he was hungry is become a farmer; and he who stood under a tree for shelter, a housekeeper" (35). This noble-savage myth does little to elevate Thoreau's views on the garden, an antagonism that becomes even more explicit in *A Week on the Concord and Merrimack Rivers*. Here, Thoreau announces that "my genius dates from an older era than the agricultural." "Gardening," he reflects, "is civil and social, but it wants the vigor and freedom of the forest and the outlaw" (346). Predictably, Thoreau contrasts the "highly cultivated man" with the Native American, whose "intercourse with Nature is at least such as admits of the greatest independence of each. If he is somewhat of a stranger in her midst, the gardener is too much of a familiar. There is something vulgar and foul in the latter's closeness to his mistress, something noble and cleanly in the former's distance" (347–48).

Of course Thoreau cannot possibly believe in his own account of the pre-agricultural Native American in this passage. Elsewhere in his work he writes explicitly about unearthing Native farming artifacts, and in "The Bean Field" itself Thoreau folds in indigenous cultivation practices when critiquing fellow citizens who bind themselves to convention — a generation that "is very sure to plant corn and beans each new year precisely as the Indians did centuries ago and taught the first settler to do, as if there were a fate in it" (155). In any case, Thoreau's belief that husbandry is incompatible with radical individualism and self-cultivation pervades his account, and despite efforts to minimize this ideological compromise when entering the horticultural contract (Thoreau keeps only a "half-cultivated field," for example), the conventions of husbandry immediately begin to do their work structuring his behavior and thinking (149). In admitting his fondness of gardening, Thoreau states that he loved the bean field because it "attached me to the earth"; however, the syntax of his full remark betrays a somewhat different allegiance. Thoreau's first and primary identification is now with the uniformity and the ordered rows, while the plants themselves have become secondary: as he puts it, "I came to love my rows, my beans" (146). In the course of imposing a human order on nature, his own mind appears to have fallen prey to domestication as well.[23]

Yet while Thoreau's shadow may loom prominently over discussions of the garden's value in *My Summer*, Warner's own experiment ends on a markedly different note. Both writers see gardening as a process that attaches them to the earth (the myth of Antaeus is invoked at the outset of *Walden* and *My Summer* alike); similarly, both understand the way it binds them to social convention and repetition (indeed, Thoreau calls his bean field "the connecting link" between society and wild nature). The chief difference here is that Warner happily embraces this second set of terms. And perhaps Thoreau sees less merit in gardening's tendency to connect us to the social enterprise because for him, at least within "The Bean Field," sociality simply means custom, order, "rows" — rarely the company of friends and neighbors. His efforts in the garden, moreover, culminate in a sale, making the marketplace the principal mechanism through which his beans attach him to others: Thoreau has produced them to "exchang[e] them for rice" (152).[24] Warner, on the other hand, "trades in" his crop for the company of others. As he writes,

> There is no prettier sight, to my eye, than a gardener on a ladder in his grape-arbor, in these golden days, selecting the heavier clusters of grapes, and handing them down to one and another of a group of neighbors and friends, who stand under the shade of the leaves ... and cry, "How sweet!" "What nice ones!" and the like—remarks encouraging to the man on the ladder. It is a great pleasure to see other people eat grapes. (83)

As this passage makes plain, there is nothing reclusive about Warner's commitment to the natural world; indeed, his engagement with nature directly *enhances* his social attachments. And thus in reflecting back on the cultivation of his pear tree, Warner highlights how each realm mutually reinforces the pleasure of the other, alternating between his growing intimacy with the vegetable world *and* his neighbors: in gardening, "you recall your delight in conversing with the nurseryman"; you "hover about the healthy growing tree with your pruning-knife"; you "show it to your friends, reading to them the French name ... on the label"; you provide seasons of "long care" for the developing seedling (87–88). The upshot and merit of this inclusive approach is a collapsing of the realms of nature and culture into each other, to the ultimate profit of both: as the opportunity to share with friends enhances Warner's gardening, so do the natural mechanisms that underpin the garden, and in this way Warner finds himself doubly committed to working on behalf of nature's process. As he evaluates the activity of tending his pear tree, Warner explains that "you enrich the earth for it; you train and trim it, and vanquish the borer, and watch its slow growth." And in the course of that service, the tree reciprocates human care by allowing the grower to experience an activity in which "you feel that you somehow stand at the source of things, and have no unimportant share in the processes of Nature" (88–89). Thus, while Warner has not explicitly set out to develop any environmental ethic here, he ends up expressing one all the same, celebrating a mode of "communion with the vegetable life" that would pertain equally well to our relation with "wild" things as to their domesticated cousins (54).

The gardener's specific position here, standing "at the source of things," ultimately becomes a foundation for all other pleasures and virtues celebrated in *My Summer*, and Warner's preface culminates in a reverie about nature's vital processes—how they engage the human sensorium and remind us of our intimate participation in the circulation of things. As Warner reflects:

> There is life in the ground; it goes into the seeds; and it also, when it is stirred up, goes into the man who stirs it. The hot sun on his back as he bends to his shovel and hoe, or contemplatively rakes the warm and fragrant loam, is better than much medicine. The buds are coming out on the bushes round about; the blossoms of the fruit trees begin to show; the blood is running up the grapevines in streams; you can smell the Wild flowers on the near bank; and the birds are flying and glancing and singing everywhere. (6)

Yet just as significant as the content of such reflections is the fact that they are largely absent from Warner's writing when he begins his season in the garden (the preface containing the passage above was, as is the case with most prefaces, written for the final published account, which Warner completed long after the summer's end). This gradual shift in sensibility suggests the central importance played by the formal qualities of *My Summer:* indeed, I argue that the book's form itself not only redirects Warner's focus and commitments but also the focus of American garden writing at large. In revisiting the stated objective Warner lays out in his opening page—to leisurely "pursue no orderly system of agriculture or horticulture, but range from topic to topic, according to the weather and the progress of the weeds, which may drive me from one corner of the garden to the other" (9)—we immediately see that such an approach will require Warner to invent a new literary mode. After all, the existing forms of garden writing in 1870 offered a mutually exclusive choice between the instruction manual and the connoisseur book, neither of which could accommodate the topical improvisation and open-ended experimentation Warner proposes here. Generally adhering to an encyclopedic structure, practical guidebooks and primers of the time (the *Almanac, Gardener's Calendar, American Gardener's Assistant*) were designed for readers to flip directly to the appropriate page on grafting fruit trees or growing cabbages. On the other hand, the "hands-off" conventions of formal landscape and design publications would hardly do for Warner's purpose either; indeed, their focus on fixed scenes and formal features like borders and color groupings were directly at odds with the author's intent to document an evolving *process*—not to mention his love of activities like digging and playing in the dirt.

Accordingly, Warner adopted a format that both allowed more narrative liberty than those practical guides would have permitted, while animating the landscape and the labor process that often remained frozen within purely ornamental books. And as it turns out, Warner's most important formal innovation may well have been inadvertent: his writings originally appeared in the *Hartford Courant* in installments, which Warner later compiled into a single work at the urging of Henry Ward Beecher. Over the course of the summer named by this title, Warner wrote one essay for publication during each of nineteen consecutive weeks spent in his garden. The resulting product—*My Summer in a Garden*—thus serves as the historical record of an ongoing cultivation project, chronicling the self-adjusting reflections that accompanied the process.

What this "serial" approach ultimately makes possible for the writer—and visible to the reader—is an expanding awareness of nature's agency as it progressively shapes the gardener's lived experience from spring into fall. Warner's entry in the opening week of the project, for example, seems reflexively to reinscribe hierarchies that historically assigned greater value to philosophical and intellectual aspects of our relations to nature (as opposed to more physically intimate exchanges between the human body and nonhuman world, such as immersing one's hands in the soil and eating directly from it). As Warner declares in these early moments, "The principal value of a private garden is not to give the possessor vegetables and fruit" but rather "to teach [one] patience and philosophy, and the higher virtues" (9). Yet *My Summer*'s journal-like and season-bound format gradually exerts a gravitational effect of its own, progressively shifting the text's emphasis away from those abstract and disembodied aspects of garden fantasy and toward celebrations of living matter itself—the simple but always-surprising fact that "there is life in the ground." And given the chronological nature of these stylized field notes, one might even venture that there is something fitting in Warner's initial focus on gardening's abstract and rarefied properties, since these "pre-season" statements appear well before the advent of the midsummer garden's material abundance. After all, in early spring Warner's garden cannot yet be smelled, touched, or sampled: his corn remains more idea than substance, a mere two-inch nub in the dirt, while the profusions of fruit and vegetable growth are dim promises on the horizon (Warner can only imagine the taste of his newly planted raspberries and "how fine they will look on the table next year") (10, 15). At this stage, then, the existing garden seems commensurate with the abstract constructions Warner favors. Yet that premature and immaterial garden of "patience and philosophy," divested of its most sensual qualities, soon proves incapable of relating the lived experience and *process* of gardening that makes ever-increasing claims on Warner's energy and imagination over the summer. Indeed, as the account progresses, remarks about the garden's symbolic or spiritual qualities progressively taper off, and those that remain now seem wholly ineffectual and out of place alongside rich, sensuous passages that almost burst on the reader's taste buds. It is as if the rise and fall of the book's momentum is driven by the garden's seasonal rhythm itself.

Consequently, by the final few chapters, Warner's garden is hardly a frozen scene or mere symbol for moralizing; rather, it becomes a full-blown *event*, a high drama deserving its own thoroughly elaborated narrative. As Warner attempts to describe this landscape in the final days of a frenzied summer, he finds himself rapt in a kind of morning-after reverie, sitting spent but contented amidst the "evidences of a ripe year":

> But what a combat has gone on here! What vegetable passions have run the whole gamut of ambition, selfishness, greed of place, fruition, satiety, and now rest here in the truce of exhaustion! What a battle-field, if one may look upon it so! The corn has lost its ammunition, and stacked arms in a slovenly, militia sort of style. The ground vines are torn, trampled, and withered; and the ungathered cucumbers, worthless melons, and golden squashes lie about like the spent bombs and exploded shells of a battle-field. So the cannonballs lay on the sandy plain before Fort Fisher. So the great, grassy meadow at Munich, any morning during the October Fest, is strewn with empty beer mugs. (85)

Rendered in epic fashion and filled with intrigue, rivalry, revelry, and passion, Warner's language now bursts with highly uncharacteristic exclamatories, animating the garden's full agency as tropes of "combat" shift to a tone of carnival-like hilarity culminating in the celebrations of Oktoberfest.[25]

As an unfolding journal and installment piece, *My Summer*'s narrative form thus proved better able to capture the *process* and *activity* of gardening that otherwise remained frozen in many of the inherited modes. Yet as the tableau above also indicates, Warner's project goes even further by insisting that something necessarily reciprocal is happening here. In the midst of this battlefield/beer garden, we can see the gardener engaging and exchanging with another entity that does not exist simply to be acted upon. After arriving in the nineteenth and final week of his account, Warner even admits that he initially harbored "too vague expectations of what my garden would do of itself" (91). And lest he forget the exuberance of nature's own agenda after the two parties have retreated in a truce for the winter, Warner reminds himself that even in these frozen months, "the forces of chemistry will be mustering under the ground, repairing the losses, calling up the reserves . . . and making ready for the spring campaign"—with or without his management and intervention (97). As such, the book's latter chapters reveal the extent to which nonhuman agents have increasingly made their own claims on Warner, emerging more fully as bona fide characters in their own right.

In moving beyond the inherited conventions, Warner created a literary model that proved more responsive to the experiential aspects of garden practice, better suited to integrating both production and play, and more fully equipped to acknowledge what is startling, unique, and unruly about the enterprise. His technique went on to fertilize garden writing across the following century: indeed, distinct echoes of Warner's cavorting carnival-goers and exploding squash-bombs can be heard throughout books like *Second Nature* (Michael Pollan's debut garden book from 1991), where gardening is experienced as both high drama and comedy. In cultivating a "multicultural, transhistorical" collection of Sibley squashes developed by Native Americans, hollyhocks donated by Long Island friends, "frizzy heads" of Italian Lollo Rosso lettuce, local Jenny Lind melons and roses from Second Empire France—all of which bloom beneath a "skyline of tomato cages festooned with golden Mandarin Cross tomatoes"—Pollan wonders if gardening makes him something like a librarian assembling and preserving information from across the globe (264–65). But on second thought, he decides that librarian is not quite right,

> because what I'm making here is no mere catalog, not just an archive of the old but something that, in its juxtapositions and conjoinings, has no precedent: something new. No Dewey decimals around here, and don't come looking for the library's hush and order. This place come summer'll be more like a buzzing marketplace, a teeming, polyglot free port city where all manner of diverse and sundry characters—immigrants drawn from near and far, past and present, East and West, upstairs and down—will meet and mingle and fuse in heretofore unimaginable combinations. (267)

Along the way, it seems, something similar had happened in American garden writing itself, a process of "juxtapositions and conjoinings" that helped writers move past those older, single-vision accounts of the garden. Through integrating work and play, the physical and philosophical, and both human and nonhuman agency, Warner's book deserves much credit for forging a path beyond the early limitations and polarizations of the genre, and for planting the seeds out of which these once "unimaginable combinations" could all the better flourish.

CHAPTER 2

Lost at Home

Mapping the Industrial-Era Garden and Farm

> Close your eyes: visualize walking toward a simple farm fence; a
> meadowlark takes flight as you come near. See yourself on the edge
> of a fragrant mown pasture; look beyond to a ripening corn field,
> tasseled and green. Scan over to one side, to a neat farmhouse with
> barn and silo nearby.... Meld these together in your mind, slowly
> creating a picture. Think of the many, many times you have seen
> this familiar place. This is a countryside you have known in paintings
> and illustrations since childhood.
> —Sally Schauman (1998)

Nearly two and half centuries after it was penned on the eve of the Revolutionary War, Hector St. John de Crèvecoeur's *Letters from an American Farmer* (1782) remains one of those touchstones of early American literature and colonial life, taking up some of the central questions of an emerging national identity: slavery, frontier settlement, immigration, self-governance, and relations to the land. In perhaps the best-known section of the book, Crèvecoeur's narrator famously asks: "What, then, is the American, this new man?" Answering this question requires a varied and complex response, but on one point Crèvecoeur is unequivocal: "we are a race of cultivators," he declares (15).

Today, of course, with the U.S. farming population standing below 2 percent, Crèvecoeur's declaration seems about as anachronistic as the metric of horsepower. And yet despite the vocation's dramatic decline, the archetypes of agrarian life—above all the geography of the farmstead—remain stubbornly embedded in our cultural imagination. While average Americans may know nothing about the right soil chemistry for growing corn, almost any child can sing "Old MacDonald" and doodle a portrait of the classic barnyard scene. Publications for adult readers invoke these same mnemonic elements as well. Generations after Crèvecoeur, late twentieth-century critical studies of

American farming like Schauman's "The Garden and the Red Barn" and Freyfogle's *The New Agrarianism* still opened with inventories of the traditional barnyard ensemble in order, as they claim, to situate readers in "familiar settings": Freyfogle ritualistically names off "garden, orchard, kitchen, woodlot, toolshed, and yard" (xiv). Even today's staunchest urbanite could intuitively recite this list.

Yet if Crèvecoeur were to wander the aisles of our twenty-first-century bookstores, he would undoubtedly find something amiss in the latest generation of writing on food and farm production. Despite the farm's age-old status as a kind of shorthand for the familiar and prosaic, the vast bulk of these new publications take as their starting point a radical dislocation and disorientation. In fact, the genre's muckraking authors hardly linger in actual fields or barnyards long enough to muddy their boots, instead setting off to explore the immense distances and discontinuities of a globalized industrial food system, seeking to demystify what our food *is* and where it comes from, how it is engineered, homogenized, processed, disassembled, recombined, transported, and consumed across vast international networks and by means of a bewildering array of economic policies, trade structures, and corporate regimes. As Allison Carruth notes, contemporary food and farm literature after 9/11 joined the postmodern novel in becoming deeply invested in "mapping systems at all scales" (119). The first decade of the twenty-first century saw a marked surge in such publications, with 2006–7 standing as a kind of high-water mark: in those two years alone, *The Omnivore's Dilemma* (Pollan); *Organic Inc.* (Fromartz); *Animal, Vegetable, Miracle* (Kingsolver); *Grub* (Lappé and Terry); *The Revolution Will Not Be Microwaved* (Katz); *Don't Eat This Book* (Spurlock); *What to Eat* (Nestle); *The Way We Eat* (Singer and Mason); *Slow Food Revolution* (Petrini and Padovani); and *Real Food Revival* (Vinton and Espuelas), along with many others, all launched comparable expeditions into the tangled terrain of postmodern foodways.[1]

Michael Pollan's *The Omnivore's Dilemma*, the most prominent work in this 2006 cohort, conveniently summarizes the zeitgeist of these contemporary accounts. In his opening remarks, the author wonders how we arrived at a moment "where we need investigative journalists to tell us where our food comes from, and nutritionists to determine the dinner menu" (1). Ironically, tackling this question by returning to the farm itself—to the very root of the system and the provenance of our food—merely intensifies Pollan's sense of bewilderment. One of the most disorienting moments in his account unfolds in an Iowa cornfield, now a veritable moonscape from October till May, which blankets the whole state like some "great tarmac only slightly more hospitable to wildlife than asphalt" (36). Standing amid the American corn belt's 125,000-square-mile monoculture, Pollan tries to map this farm's dimensions by casting navigational feelers that stretch all the way down the Mississippi River to the Gulf of Mexico's poisoned waters, out to Monsanto's seed-genetics laboratories and Coca-Cola's boardrooms, and across the globe to distant oilfields supplying energy to produce all this stuff—creating a narrative that reads more like some dizzying navigational piece than any classic barnyard account. And while Crèvecoeur would hardly miss the irony of a so-called race of cultivators now requiring professionally guided tours through the familiar old landscape of the American farm, this navigational trope is now standard fare within a genre where narrators increasingly admit to feeling disoriented, bewildered, and lost.[2]

At first glance, then, one might assume this phenomenon to be yet another sign of the unmappable and often unimaginable space of our globalized postmodern age. And yet this navigational or "cartographic" turn is far from new in the literature of American cultivation.[3] At least 130 years before the likes of Michael Pollan or Eric Schlosser, nineteenth-century writers responded similarly to the emergence of the first industrial farms. The strange operations they confronted, commonly known as "bonanza farms," often spanned tens of thousands of acres in the western territories. Not only did their immense size radically distinguish them from the more familiar family farms of the period; bonanza outfits were typically owned by large companies in distant cities, designed like factories, and run by professional managers. Like their twenty-first-century counterparts, then, the writers documenting this change in American farm life sought to reestablish spatial and cultural bearings in a national geography that had grown alarmingly unfamiliar. Scenes of mapping—both explicit and oblique—regularly appear in late nineteenth-century and Progressive-era agricultural journalism as well as the farm fiction of Frank Norris, Charles Chesnutt, Willa Cather, and others. With its intense interest in charts, cartography, and scale, this body of literature not only reflects the extraordinary mutations in space marking the period, but also reveals some key ways that turn-of-the-century Americans attempted to navigate a broader series of social upheavals and dislocations: the consolidation of corporate power in agricultural practice, the restructuring of farming's seasonal rhythms by capitalist technology, and most significantly, the unprecedented revolution in late nineteenth-century labor as the United States transitioned to an industrial economy, workers rapidly left farms for factories, and remaining farmers increasingly found themselves engaged in "manufacturing" without ever leaving their fields.

The restructuring of farming's spatial and social aspects, however, did not just shape late nineteenth-century agricultural writing; it also fueled the skyrocketing popularity—and transformed the very character—of domestic gardening literature itself. The period from 1885 to 1905 saw an explosion in circulation of gardening magazines, seed catalogs, books, newspaper articles, and advertisements, materials that increasingly played on the theme of gardening as an antidote to frayed nerves and the "encroachments of a ruthless civilization," as Progressive-era garden writer Elisabeth Morris put it (859). In creating a culture of nostalgia for "old-fashioned" or "grandmother's" gardens, these publications tapped into antimodern and anti-industrial sentiments already fueling the international Arts and Crafts movement. One contributor to *The Craftsman*, the Arts and Crafts' flagship publication, underscored this link between gardening, nostalgia, and therapeutic practice in her assertion that "[w]e are an overwrought people, too eager about everything except peace and contentment"; gardens, fortunately, offered "silence" and "peace" to "the restless spirit" of the age, even "heal[ing] the wounds of the busy world.... And so here in America of all things we need gardens" ("Pergolas" 33.)

However, in the pages to follow I do not mean simply to tell a story of nineteenth-century garden writing as yet another manifestation of antimodernist or Arts and Crafts disenchantment with industrial and bureaucratic life (much of which has already been examined against the backdrop of the period's rapidly modernizing cities).[4] Rather, our analysis here focuses on turn-of-the-century garden fantasy as a response to change on the *farm* itself. As we will see, gardens emerged as a foil to agriculture's increasingly commercial specialization, rigid divisions of labor, and exploded dimensions. With their enclosed structure and miniaturized scale, gardens offered a distinct sense of *place* over and against the vast and abstract expanses of *space* defining corporate agriculture of the period. Moreover, the artisanal labor commonly associated with gardening appealed to popular yearnings for simpler and more legible forms of manual work, a possibility that now seemed absent from agrarian lifeways and landscapes. Taken together, these features positioned the garden as a figure for navigating the scrambled zones of American farm life and the geography of production more broadly.

Not surprisingly, a good deal of nostalgia and romanticization run through these representations, many of which ignore the harsh facts of preindustrial farming and reproduce popular notions about traditional rural life as somehow "outside" our urban capitalist economy. Hamlin Garland, a Midwestern writer whose fiction explored the hardships of nineteenth-century agrarian life, powerfully captured this pastoralizing tendency in his 1891 *Main Travelled Roads*. When his protagonist, Howard McLane, now a successful easterner, returns to his family's desolate and impoverished Wisconsin farm, he prefers not to see the messy reality of these working landscapes, and so he surveys the garden "through half-shut eyes as the painters do" to soften and improve its effects (69).

Ultimately, however, I am less concerned with the accuracy of these fantasies than with what they tell us about the spatial disorientation and lost place-awareness arising from late nineteenth-century farm industrialization—and how the garden's appeal dramatizes a more pervasive desire to locate oneself in a legible and coherent scene at moments when, as literary theorist Fredric Jameson would put it, "the immediate and limited experience" of modern life can no longer "encompass and coincide with the true economic and social form that governs that experience" ("Cognitive" 349). Period garden fantasy, in short, lays bare a basic longing for the familiar, for knowing where you are.

In responding to this desire for restored legibility, Progressive-era writers recast the garden as a kind of "map" in its own right, loading their texts with spatial coordinates, diagrams, guided tours, and other cartographic dramatizations. And so, as our story returns to this earlier moment to reconstruct a prehistory to the defamiliarizing farm and food scenes of today, we rediscover the garden as a figure that people have repeatedly turned to in order to manage and map the personal upheavals produced by social and historical change.

Geographies of the American Farm: From Place to Space

> It is difficult to present the idea of the bigness of these farms to the person whose pre-conceived notion of a farm is a little checkerboard lying upon a hillside or in a valley. Seven thousand acres present the average bonanza farm . . . [and] distances across fields are so great that horseback communication is impracticable. Crews of workmen living at one end of the farm and operating it may not see the crews in other corners from season's end to season's end.
> —William White (1897)

In 1891 sociologist Walter Wyckoff embarked on an eighteen-month cross-country journey to document life as an itinerant worker in the United States, eventually publishing the account in *Scribner's* as "The Workers: An Experiment in Reality" (1897). The fourth installment of this ethnographic series profiles a modest farm in Pennsylvania where Wyckoff seeks work, opening with the author's initial impressions of the site. Wyckoff's description of his arrival has a faintly rehearsed quality; indeed, it seems almost to resemble the lines of a fairy tale that have been repeated again and again until one knows them by heart:

> The fences stood straight and stout, with an air of lasting security. On a rising ledge above the land was the farm-house, a small, unpainted wooden cottage.... Near it was a summer kitchen [garden], that seemed fairly to glow with the conscious pride in its cleanness, and the very footpath from the gate to the cottage door was swept like a threshing floor.

Before concluding this self-guided tour of the farmstead, Wyckoff interrupts his account to ask the family for work in their orchard. After his request is granted, the narrator resumes his portrait of the site; yet while the formulaic quality persists, the remaining lines register a subtle but important shift:

> The barn is on my right, a large, unpainted structure, stained by the weather to as dark a hue as the house, but there are no loose boards about it, nor any rifts among the shingles, and the doors hang true on their hinges, and meet in well-adjusted touch. The cow-yard and the pig-sty flank the lane, and the neatness of the yard and the tightness of the troughs makes clear that there is no waste of fodder there. Farther down on my left is the wagon house... (554)

Initially rendered as a static *map* in the first passage—a depiction itemizing a series of fixed objects in relation to each other ("above the land was," "near it was," a "footpath [connecting] the gate to the cottage")—Wyckoff's description gradually develops into something more like the *itinerary* of a subject who moves through this scene. Coordinates in the second passage are now rendered in relation to an individual immersed in a particular place ("The barn is on my right," "down on my left is the wagon house...").

From the immediate context of this passage, Wyckoff's drift from a panoptic, map-like description to a more physically immersed tour mode may seem puzzling. One plausible hint may be found in Michel de Certeau's analysis of the "spatial stories" people tell about familiar lived environments: as de Certeau argues, our impromptu descriptions of intimate places like homes overwhelmingly take the form of *itineraries* that narrate *movement* through space (i.e., "you enter, you go across, you turn...") rather than fixed tableaus (i.e., "X is to the left of Y") (119–20). Of course, in the opening moments of his visit, Wyckoff could not possibly develop the level of place-based familiarity that longtime residents have with their own homes. Yet perhaps the mere promise of work enhances his sense of embeddedness in the scene; after all, the offer of employment midway through this account directly coincides with Wyckoff's shift in spatial modifiers.[5]

Yet considered within the specific historical context of this late nineteenth-century moment, the impulse behind this rhetorical shift becomes clearer still. In moving away from panoptic formulations, Wyckoff's account follows a vector of desire toward the possibility of immersion in place, the possibility of dwelling in, moving through, and engaging with stable, familiar surroundings. Such a fantasy would have been immeasurably heightened by the broader trends transforming U.S. agriculture at the moment these lines were penned: as the industrialization and consolidation of American farms proceeded at ever-increasing rates in the final decades of the nineteenth century, the kinds of spaces where one might hope to enact such fantasies of stability, familiarity, or even spatial intelligibility were being steadily and systematically eliminated. In fact, by 1891 Wyckoff's account would have already seemed anachronistic, serving more as an exercise in folkloric documentation than any expression of a turn-of-the-century agrarian zeitgeist. That latter designation might instead apply to an account like "The Movement of Wheat" (1899), a profile of the new industrial bonanza farms written by journalist Ray Stannard Baker. Publishing his work in the muckraking magazine *McClure's*, Baker presented a sketch of agriculture from which not only specific preindustrial elements, but also the *farm itself*, seem to have vanished. The same holds true of the farmer. Where Wyckoff dwells on the pleasures of picking fruit alongside Mr. Hill, the avuncular and paradigmatic farmer profiled in "The Workers," a radically different farmer (or farm manager) presides over the new spatial order in Baker's account. As Baker writes of this figure,

> I saw him—in Chicago, Minneapolis, New York, Duluth, Buffalo, Detroit, and Toledo—he was always astonishing, he came so near to the realization of the cosmopolite. Every morning he knows the conditions of the weather in Chili [sic] and the progress of threshing in India. The United States Government hangs at his elbow a map showing the rising storm in Montana, which may reduce by two per cent the crops of northern Minnesota. His special newspapers inform him as to the prices in Mark Lane, London; in the Produce Exchange, New York; on the Board of Trade, Chicago.... The railroad companies quote him daily rates for shipments to Rio [de] Janeiro, Hamburg, and Hong Kong. (127)

Here, what remains of the "farm" has been stretched and warped across an international market space so vast and unwieldy that no single, identifiable site can represent it. Meanwhile, the figures populating this account occupy no place in particular and must consult official cartographies—maps supplied by "The United States Government"—in order to navigate the rapidly globalizing dimensions of their business. In short, Baker's piece can be seen as a product of historical trends reshaping the world according to modern paradigms of "*space*," a kind of "geometrical or topographical abstraction," as Lawrence Buell defines it (*Future* 63). Wyckoff's romantic farmstead portrait, on the other hand, has sought to recapture the fleeting possibility of "*place*," a meaning-rich and subjectively experienced social space (Tuan). Indeed, in that moment where Wyckoff shifts toward the language of the tour and itinerary, and literally flanks himself with barns and wagon houses, he restores an affectively charged mental and material geography precisely matching the idea of "place" as defined by philosopher Edward Casey: that which is "not so much the direct object of sight or thought or recollection as what we feel *with* and *around, under* and *above, before* and *behind* ourselves" (*Getting Back* 313; italics original).[6]

This distinction between abstract *space* and subjectively experienced *place* offers an essential framework for reading the difference between Wyckoff's and Baker's farm portraits, while it also situates the broader transformation of farm and garden representation explored in this chapter. Yet as central as the space/place gap is here, that split was hardly new to late nineteenth-century Western spatial representations. Long before American grain farmers began to rely on the government maps and "special newspapers" Baker cites in his profile, Enlightenment thinkers and scientists had already begun to reconceive space in abstract terms through the use of Euclidean geometry, perspectivism, and other technologies of representation that reduce *place*, at least in theory, to "position, or bare point" on "one of the XYZ axes that delineate the dimensionality of *space* as construed in Cartesian analytical geometry" (Casey, *Fate* 199). As geographer David Harvey argues, the modern era's translation of the elusive and diverse aspects of place—personal, symbolic, religious—into something more unified and objective was a vital strategy for consolidating imperial, class, and corporate power, since "the conquest and control of space . . . first requires that it be conceived of as something usable, malleable, and therefore capable of domination through human action" (*Condition* 254).[7]

This project arguably had its most far-reaching historical effect in the consolidation of land into private property—space parceled up as a commodity that could circulate on the market. And within the United States, perhaps the most enduring legacy of this process is found in the 1785 Land Ordinance, a congressional act that subdivided all areas in the public domain according to rectilinear survey lines that ran north–south and east–west "with complete disregard of the terrain" (Harvey 254). As Hildegard Johnson argues, this system "[made] it possible for the survey to be continuous not only in concept but in practice over thousands of square miles—the most extensive uninterrupted cadastral system in the world" (30). Notwithstanding the profound natural and topographical variety of the North American continent, surveyors partitioned space in a nearly uniform manner, presenting practical agriculture with some considerable difficulties but also, as Andro Linklater has noted, offering "great convenience [to a] financier tracking the rise and fall in land values." Indeed, the settlement grid, which Thomas Jefferson had originally envisioned as a mechanism for egalitarian property distribution (after, of course, Native inhabitants were evicted from those regions), turned out to be "ideal for buying, trading, and speculating" (Linklater 174).

Thus by the eve of the Civil War, this rectilinear and commodified organization of space would not have seemed novel to North Americans. Yet the sweeping changes to farm life in the final decades of the nineteenth century did transform rural landscapes into something that might have been unrecognizable to observers from just a generation earlier. From the earliest days of colonization up through the Civil War, farmers made up the majority of the nation's workforce; by 1890, however, that number had fallen to roughly 43 percent, and then dropped even further to 30 percent in the next two decades. Moreover, as historian Gilbert Fite points out, the value of agricultural output was eclipsed by industrial production at the end of the century, and even those who remained in farming increasingly saw the geography of rural life morph into something strikingly unfamiliar (8–9).

These quantitative figures only begin to suggest the deeper, qualitative transformations that attended them. The same dynamics that enabled such a downsizing of the agricultural labor force also made it difficult for small, independent growers to remain competitive. In transitioning from intensive modes of human and animal labor to mechanized production, larger operations gained a distinct advantage: unlike smaller family farms, big business could mobilize the immense capital required to both restructure farm operations around fleets of machinery and acquire the extensive tracts of land that made such a shift profitable.[8] By 1865, 80 percent of wheat in the United States was harvested by machine (even though these machines were still hitched to farm animals), and as agricultural historians have argued, farm machinery was soon "at the center of the U.S. industrial revolution" (Otter 221; Federico 100). As political economist Henry George prophesied in 1871, "[A]t last the steam plough and the steam wagon have appeared—to develop, perhaps, in agriculture the same tendencies to concentration which the power loom and the triphammer have developed in manufacturing" (95).

Accordingly, the late nineteenth-century's industrialization of agriculture, as William Conlogue argues, was "not simply synonymous with the use of machinery or scientific models"; in fact, preindustrial farmers had formerly integrated both into their practices to varying degrees. Rather, farming's meaning and practice were redefined according to business principles formerly associated with industrial manufacturing: in place of traditional notions of the farmer as "husbandman" (as exemplified by Mr. Hill in "The Workers"), the modernized approach looked to industry to create "the most efficient, most profitable business in a new industrial order" (Conlogue 16). Under this paradigm, which came to be known as the "New Agriculture,"[9] period landowners increasingly recruited managers with backgrounds in business who were trained to efficiently coordinate large labor forces on immense and highly specialized tracts of land (Drache 91–92). The *Farm Journal* noted this shift in 1890 when it announced that "we farmers are manufacturers, and when we adopt the successful manufacturer's emphatic methods we shall succeed as well as they" (qtd. in Conlogue 17).[10]

One of the most frequently cited casualties of this economic restructuring was farming's age-old subsistence and home production activities.[11] Such a sacrifice allowed the vocation to become more fully integrated into the market economy, a process Karl Marx identifies as a vital episode within the longer arc of capitalism's rise to hegemony. Agricultural productivity that exceeds the needs of its individual laborers, as Marx argues, constitutes "the basis of capitalist production, which disengages a constantly increasing portion of society from the production of basic foodstuffs and transforms them into 'free heads,' ... making them available for exploitation in other spheres" (*Capital III* 786). In tracing the consequences of this transition in Europe, Marx noted that those who remained in agriculture increasingly served as a home market for an ever-expanding capitalist system, while their means of subsistence and their labor itself became "material elements of capital":

> Formerly, the peasant family produced the means of subsistence and the raw materials, which they themselves, for the most part, consumed. These raw materials and means of subsistence have now become commodities; the large farmer sells them, he finds his market in manufactures. Yarn, linen, coarse woolen stuffs—things whose raw materials had been within the reach of every peasant family, had been spun and woven by it for its own use—were now transformed into articles of manufacture, to which the country districts at once served for markets.... Thus, hand in hand with the expropriation of the self-supporting peasants, with their separation from their means of production, goes the destruction of rural domestic industry, the process of separation between manufacture and agriculture. (*Capital I* 747)

As this process reached a demographic tipping point at the close of the century in the United States, champions of industry framed the transition in naturalistic rhetoric—the next inevitable phase in an "agricultural evolution." And by the early twentieth century, analysts like Eugene Davenport were chiding American commentators who responded to census data on the decline of farmers "as if it were [a] national calamity," reminding readers that "if 100 per cent of our population had always remained in the country, there would be no market for the produce of land, a money income from farming would be impossible, and agriculture would forever remain a family industry." "Fortunately," he concludes, by 1912 farming was "assuming the form of other capitalized industries," which would enable it to complete its "ris[e] from the self-sufficing stage to the money-making stage" (49, 45).

As Henri Lefebvre reminds us, such shifts to a new mode of production entail the production of a new space, and thus we see immense tracts of uniformly planted monocultures begin to blanket the late nineteenth-century American landscape. In particular, crop "factories" on western bonanza farms grew to unprecedented and eerily homogenous dimensions (tens of thousands of acres were not uncommon) to accommodate the structure of mechanized farming and the principles of specialization and economies of scale. Perhaps the most vivid portrait of these landscapes appears in Frank Norris's novel *The Octopus* (1901), a story based on the conflict between wheat farmers in the San Joaquin Valley and the Pacific and Southwestern railroad (P&SW). As Norris describes them, the croplands in this "new order of things" lacked "so much as a twig" by which to secure one's bearings, and they unfolded in such a homogenous expanse that "in one leap the [viewer's] eye reached the fine, delicate line where earth and sky met, miles away" (58). And where Wyckoff's portrait included visual emblems of a farm that supported its resident's diverse material needs—a patchwork landscape with livestock pens supplying meat and dairy; cornfields for commercial sale and animal feed; orchards and gardens for growing fruits and vegetables; sheds and barns for repair—only two years later the *Fargo Daily Argus* (1883) marveled at the implausible absence of these same elements, especially the kitchen garden. "The absence of familiar vegetables will strike most travelers," it reported of the Dakota bonanza farms, "for everybody rushed into wheat culture and pays high prices for food on the table. You would fancy that a man could at least spare an acre for potatoes, lettuce, parsnips, turnips, cabbage, and other garden truck, but no: except for a few corn patches, you see nothing but wheat" (qtd. in Drache 131).[12]

While the simple disappearance of features like subsistence gardens puzzled journalists charting the new contours of American agriculture, more global and "invisible" changes also heightened their sense of dislocation. Turn-of-the-century developments in transportation and communications technologies were revolutionizing subjective experiences of time and space, linking farms to remote events like the South American weather conditions and Hong Kong shipping rates cited in Baker's essay. Such processes plainly align with the broader condition of modernity during this period that geographer Nigel Thrift summarizes as "both a progressive shrinking of the world and its simultaneous enlargement" (8). Yet while Thrift maintains that the nineteenth-century's great time-space compression should be understood chiefly as a "metropolitan phenomenon" (17), the telegraph and commodity ticker—technologies that assimilated regional distinctions into the colossal machinery of global markets—irrevocably altered the rhythms and perception of lifeways on the farm as well. Indeed, many scholarly discussions of this "great acceleration" have overwhelmingly focused on the ways it was experienced in urban space (since, as these accounts presume, its effects were most acute there). But those transformations were just as pronounced on the farm.[13] In fact, a broad cross-section of agricultural literature shows these technologies directly eroding a sense of place among farming communities. William White's 1897 account of the bonanza farm for *Scribner's*, "The Business of a Wheat Farm," testifies that the ticker allows "a rainfall in India or a hot wind in South America [to be] felt upon the Dakota farm in a few hours" (547). Likewise, *The Octopus* depicts grain cultivation on a particular stretch of California soil as "connected by wire with San Francisco, and through that city with Minneapolis, Duluth, Chicago, New York, and . . . Liverpool," making this local acreage "merely a part of an enormous whole, a unit in the vast agglomeration of wheat land the whole world round" (54). Not only do such scenes indicate an explosion in existing spatial and temporal parameters; they also suggest how global markets and technologies hastened the standardization of agricultural practice, eclipsing each farm's cultural, ecological, and temporal idiosyncrasies, and refashioning quality, character, and condition into internationally translatable units, quantities, and categories.[14]

Like the telegraph and commodity ticker, rail transportation also transformed the experience and representation of space and place in Progressive-era farm literature. In fact, the railroad quickly became a force that wholly reshaped the social and economic meaning of farming. As historian William Cronon has noted of this period, "Everything that moved by railroad—and every place through which the railroad ran—became linked to the imperatives of corporate capital" (*Nature* 81). Rail systems helped nationalize agricultural markets and accelerate exchanges between metropolis and hinterland, not only transforming the time horizons for commodity production and distribution but also increasingly severing farm production from the particularities of different geographical regions. Much of the railroad's commercial success derived from its ability to operate independently of environmental and climactic factors: wet weather in late fall through spring no longer compelled a slowdown in agricultural exchange as it always had, and as Cronon points out, farmers could now travel to urban markets as the need arose. Certain events like the fall harvest continued to shape patterns of trade, but rail transportation greatly diminished other seasonal economic cycles driven by fluxes in temperature and precipitation (75–76). The imperatives of rail schedules and timetables further moved timekeeping itself toward the mechanical rhythm of the clock and away from daily and seasonal rhythms.

Small wonder, then, that the novel *My Ántonia* (1918), Willa Cather's elegy for the bygone era of pioneer farming in Nebraska, opens in the interior of a moving train years after the central action of the novel has taken place. From the insulation of this railcar, the narrator (who also happens to work as a lawyer for one of the great western railroads) reminisces about the fading agrarian lifeways as he and other passengers "flashed though never-ending miles of ripe wheat" (1). The great fields of prairie agriculture that are the novel's principal setting and subject now find themselves relegated to something the traveler merely "flashes through" en route to somewhere else.

And so despite Nigel Thrift's focus on this time-space revolution as an overwhelmingly "metropolitan phenomenon" in the Progressive era, we also see farm portraits exemplify this claim that period responses to modernization were generally expressed "via some kind of discourse on *speed*—or space divided by time" (17, 7). In fact, the momentum of Baker's "The Movement of Wheat" is so relentless that, although it examines grain production, the piece could easily stand alongside the most dizzying accounts of urban unrest. It is, after all, the *movement* of wheat, rather than its cultivation per se, that constitutes the essay's focal point. Baker marvels at agriculture's success in shattering its own former spatial barriers and "increasing marvelously the rapidity and efficiency of [the grain's] distribution," a feat made possible by technologies allowing farmers to communicate with city markets and "take advantage of any advance in price" at a mere "moment's notice" (130). This frenzied pace defines every aspect of his article, with the author depicting wheat production "advancing rapidly westward"; noting transactions at the grain elevator conducted "with a rapidity fairly dizzying to the outsider"; and remarking that unlike earlier quality-inspection practices (individualized assessments that were "full of time-consuming details"), the new, standardized grading system has been so streamlined that "no portion of the great business moves with more ease and efficiency" (130, 132). Finally, in keeping with these accelerated flows of commodities and information, the farmworkers themselves are redefined by the imperatives of speed and mobility. These itinerant figures begin the summer's work with the ripening of grain in Oklahoma and proceed from there to harvests in Nebraska and Kansas. By the time a laborer arrives in the Dakotas, Baker writers, "he is one of an army of more than 50,000 men," part of a labor force endlessly on the move, "drawn from St. Paul, Chicago, and even farther east" (129–30).

Thus, where the classic farm elements of Wyckoff's "The Workers" are wistfully presented with "an air of lasting security" (554), it is in fact images of fluidity—oceans, tides, streams, and rivers—that came to constitute the metaphors *du jour* in period representations of grain production, a domain where any stable sense of reality or place dissolved. What had once existed in the discrete form of the bushel now morphs into "vast tides of wheat" in Baker's article (125–26); moves in "flood[s]" and "torrent[s]" in Norris's novel (319, 321); and flows across space as "rivers of wheat" in Anthony Trollope's *North America* (1862), an account where even the grain elevators of the Midwest no longer serve as sturdy "storehouses" but rather as "a channel or a river course for the flooding freshets of corn" (164, 159). Swept up in such turbulent historical currents, American writers found themselves in need of a new set of maps and a new rhetorical strategy for representing farm and food production.

Imagining the Landscape

> [Annie Derrick] had been sitting, thoughtful, in her long chair . . . her glance losing itself in the immensity of Los Muertos [ranch]. . . . As far as the eye could reach, it was empty of all life, bare, mournful, absolutely still; and, as she looked, there seemed to her morbid imagination—diseased and disturbed with long brooding, sick with the monotony of repeated sensation—to be disengaged from all this immensity, a sense of a vast oppression, formless, disquieting. The terror of sheer bigness grew slowly in her mind; loneliness beyond words gradually enveloped her. She was lost in all these limitless reaches of space. Had she been abandoned in mid-ocean, in an open boat, her terror could hardly have been greater.
> —Frank Norris, *The Octopus* (1901)

In the years immediately following the Civil War, the general spatial reference for the family farm remained something on the order of the Homestead Act's 160-acre parcel—the amount of land a single family could typically cultivate on its own (Conlogue 29). Yet by 1890, as writers found themselves multiplying their existing concept of the farm by extraordinary factors, this older spatial reference quickly became obsolete. Indeed, scale emerged as a central problem within Progressive-era fiction and journalism; single units had to be increased by factors of a thousand, while whole days were reduced to single moments. Baker's "The Movement of Wheat" reported that grain traders now facilitated deals in such immense quantities "that thousands have become units to him: when he sells '10 wheat,' he means 10,000 bushels, not ten bushels" (127). Similarly, the *Bankers' Magazine* of London marveled at the scale of transactions across the Atlantic and offered the following calculus in its profile of American futures traders:

> Their dealings create a free market for grain such as exists nowhere else. Through them millions of bushels can be bought or sold any morning. Orders which might take days to execute at Liverpool or Mark Lane are the work of a moment in Chicago.... So on all the way through, in every branch of the wheat business, from growing it to making markets for it, the American is *facile princeps*. He handles millions of bushels where European dealers seldom get beyond thousands, and his methods are proportionately massive. (qtd. in Baker 136)

Illustrators for these bonanza features confronted a similar obstacle: the artist accompanying a *Harper's* journalist on assignment in the Northwest balked at the prospect of fitting its interminable farmscapes onto a canvas, noting that a person "might as well try to paint a dead calm in mid-ocean" (Van Dyke 806). Baker skirted this problem by simply leaving panoramic images out of his article (save one depicting fall harvest, presented as a medium long-shot to showcase the military-like arrangement of horses and machinery). Instead, his illustrator opted for a simple comparative sketch in which symbols representing different-sized wheat bushels bore the names of various countries and were arranged in a line of descending order to depict the different levels of agricultural productivity among those nations.[15] If writers were to help late nineteenth-century Americans accurately recalibrate their ideas of farming, invoking images of the barnyard and garden would hardly suffice now.

In response to these mutations in space, writers turned to mapping and navigational strategies to make sense of the New Agriculture. Some of the most notable developments in this cartographic turn emerged around 1880, when eastern journals began to deploy teams of correspondents to the Dakotas to document the peculiar new face of American farming. In an introductory remark bearing uncanny symmetries with Pollan's framing of *The Omnivore's Dilemma* 125 years later, journalist Henry Van Dyke reports that in preparing to write his piece for *Harper's*, he determined that "the only way to find out anything" about the Red River operations "was to go thither and behold with our own eyes."[16] He tells of his team packing their trunks

PLOUGHING.

COMPARATIVE WHEAT PRODUCTION OF THE DIFFERENT COUNTRIES.

FIGURES 5A AND 5B. *Above:* illustration from C. C. Coffin's "Dakota Wheat Fields" (1880). Courtesy of University of Washington Libraries, Special Collections, UW 38892. *Below:* illustration from Ray Stannard Baker's "The Movement of Wheat" (1899).

with sketchbooks and notebooks, "[buying] a supply of ammunition and a patent filter," and "set[ting] out to see for ourselves" (801-2)—a dramatic setup that became a stock convention of the genre, setting reader expectations more commonly associated with foreign travelogues and expedition tales than some profile of the very home turf of Americana.[17] Moreover, in their effort to provide readers with tools to calculate these new dimensions, writers often turned to urban images and figures—evidently the only spatial vocabulary adequate for conveying the scale of these massive croplands. William White oriented readers by asking them to imagine a train loaded with the wheat grown on a single Dakota farm, explaining that if such a rig came "charging down Fifth Avenue and Broadway in New York, the 'rear end' brakeman would be craning his neck from the caboose to catch sight of the Vanderbilt mansion while the engineer and fireman were enjoying themselves bumping the cable-car down by Union Square" (534). The *Atlantic Monthly* likewise drew on urban measurements to render the exploded proportions of American agriculture: "Most persons in reading of fields described by hundreds and thousands of acres can form but little idea of their actual or comparative extent," wrote journalist Poultney Bigelow. To "assist to a better understanding of the size of these fields and farms," he explains that Manhattan Island has an area of roughly 14,000 acres," while the Grandin farm featured in his article spans 40,000 acres, or "space enough for three cities like New York" (40).

Fiction writers of the period also adopted mapping strategies in depicting industrial farming. In a letter to his editor, Norris underscores the importance cartography would play in *The Octopus*, explaining that "[i]n the front matter I am going—maybe—to insert a list of dramatis personae and—This *surely*—a map of the locality" ("Letter" 6; italics in original). Indeed, as William Conlogue has noted, the novel is punctuated throughout with scenes featuring carefully charted maps of the colossal California wheat fields, schemes that reduce the operations to a more manageable scale. The first such diagram appears in the business office at Los Muertos ranch, where "every watercourse, depression, and elevation, together with the indications of the varying depths of the clays and loams in the soil" is "accurately plotted" in a bird's-eye format (Norris 53). The ranch's vast acreage has been subdivided into four principal operations—unsentimentally referred to as One, Two, Three, and Four—each of which falls under the management of a different superintendent who in turn reports to Magnus and Harran Derrick. No individual rancher himself could possibly hope to orchestrate and cultivate (or even see, for that matter) all the terrain involved here, a point Norris underscores when Harran places a telephone call to assess the progress on division Four, situated

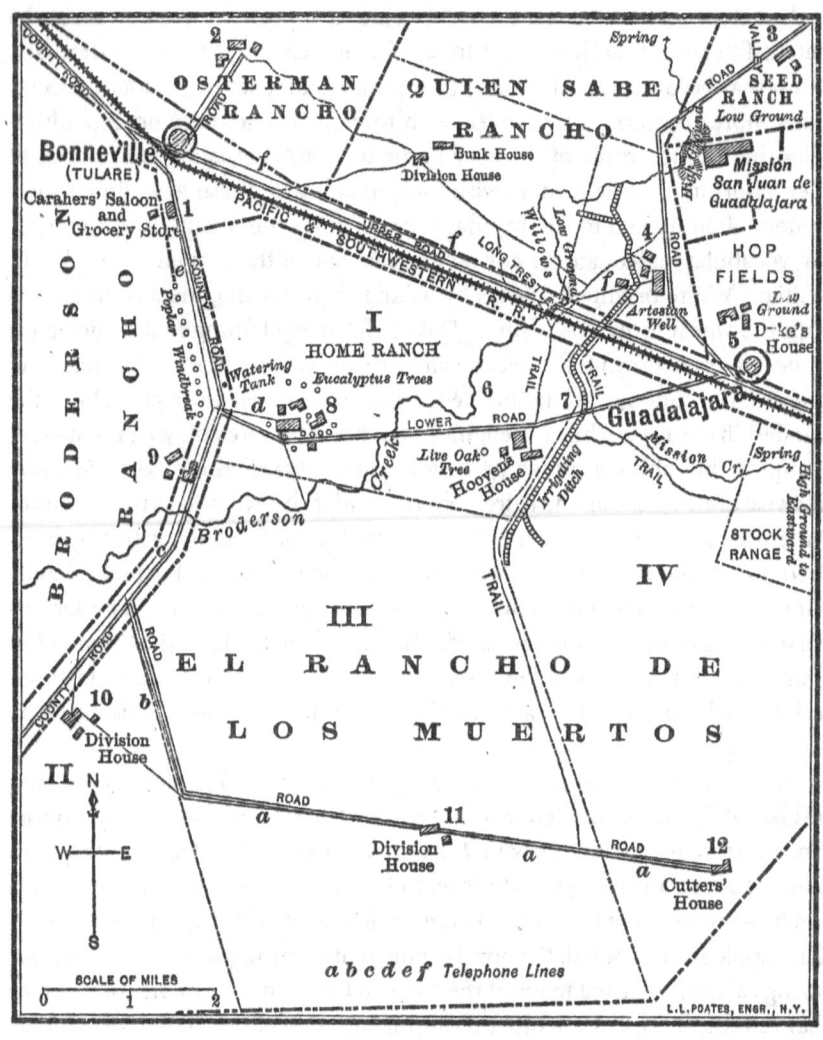

2. Osterman's Ranch House.
4. Annixter's Ranch House.
8. Derrick's Ranch House.
9. Broderson's Ranch House.

MAP OF THE COUNTRY DESCRIBED IN "THE OCTOPUS."

FIGURE 6. Map featured in Frank Norris's *The Octopus* depicting California's San Joaquin Valley (1901).

eleven miles away at the farm's "far southeastern extremity, where few people ever went, close to the line fence, a dot, a speck, lost in the immensity of open country" (54). By way of this dramatization we understand the map hanging next to the telephone as no mere convenience but rather a genuine imperative, something Magnus ceremonializes by centering it directly "between the windows" in his command center, establishing this panoptic technology as *the* central perspective or "window" through which the surrounding grainfields are viewed (53). Looking back from twenty-first-century farm fiction like Ruth Ozeki's *All Over Creation* (2003), where GPS software now puts potato growers in front of computers where they spend their days "trying to input data and generate readouts and maps" (127), Norris seems to prefigure this postmodern trend with striking fidelity.

Yet this very tool for orienting people to the geography of the American farm also suggests the *impossibility* of securing the kind of intimate experiential place knowledge that might otherwise come from direct engagement with one's environment. As de Certeau argues, maps and other panoramic technologies are essentially a "'theoretical' (that is, visual) simulacrum . . . whose condition of possibility is an oblivion and a misunderstanding of [our everyday] practices." Put another way, these abstract representations make us into voyeurs, disentangling us from the "murky intertwining daily behaviors" that otherwise immerse us in our material world and allow us to experience it as a dynamic process as opposed to a static, inanimate thing (93).[18] In fact, the very maps that might aid and orient Progressive-era readers (and fictional farmers) to these mutating landscapes and changing lifeways often serve as a tool for further conversion of rural space into fragmented and homogenized abstractions, into representations that reduce the rich diversity of our material landscape to mere units of identical value. As Harvey reminds us, the totalizing spatial representations of official cartography, "stripped of all elements of fantasy and religious belief, as well as any sign of the experiences involved in their production," offer "functional systems for the factual ordering of phenomena in space . . . [defining] property rights in land, territorial boundaries, domains of administration and social control, communication routes, etc." (*Condition* 249). A central scene from *The Octopus* juxtaposes the P&SW map (which invalidates all land claims falling outside this master document) with the claims of Annixter, a farmer who has invested his labor in one of the railroad's holdings under the presumption that he will someday purchase the land that has since become his home. In refusing Annixter's offer, the land agent has only to appeal to the map, which depicts present boundaries of ownership and "sections belonging to the Corporation *accurately plotted*," but gives no representation to Annixter's extensive improvements, the home he has made there, or his eight-year tenure working the soil (193; italics added). Subsequently, when a great bundle of maps is dropped off at the office of Lyman Derrick (a representative for California's wheat farmers), every spatial feature save those depicting the railroad holdings has been effaced from the illustrations. Wherever the rail lines do not run, the commissioner's map appears as a blank, white void, "and it seemed as if all the colour which should have gone to vivify the various counties, towns, and cities"—not to mention the farms and other spatial features, both built and natural—"had been absorbed by that huge, sprawling organism," a vast "network of red lines" that exclusively represent the P&SW's property claims (288).

Against these highly abstract and increasingly placeless figurations, a handful of Norris's characters "countermap" their surroundings in ways that seek to restore their experiential and qualitative dimensions. While Magnus Derrick uses cartographic tools to "accurately plo[t]" each feature of his wheat empire, his wife, Annie, opts for a kind of mental mapping of the scene, projecting her imagination onto a preindustrial, even quasi-animistic agricultural landscape (53). Faced with the sense of "losing [herself] in the immensity of Los Muertos" ranch, she summons up memories of the Ohio farm where she passed her childhood, a home remembered as "cosey, comfortable, home-like, where the farmers loved their land . . . nourishing it as though it were a thing almost conscious" (180, 59). Indeed, Annie carries out the very mental operations that Kevin Lynch and Fredric Jameson profile in their analysis of everyday strategies for countering alienation in modern space. Such a procedure, as Jameson describes it, involves "the practical reconquest of a sense of place and the construction or reconstruction of an articulated ensemble which can be retained in memory and which the individual subject can map and remap along the moments of mobile, alternative trajectories" (*Postmodernism* 51). Accordingly, Annie summons a mnemonic farm-space "neatly partitioned into the water lot, the cow pasture, the corn lot, the barley field, and wheat farm," and in rehearsing this old catechism of the agrarian scene, her inventory preserves each element in familiar, legible units (Norris 59). Moreover, the dimensions of Annie's old homestead are not only scaled to the capacity of an individual's imagination and experience but also to the capacities of the human body. No fleet of machines is necessary for cultivation on this scale, and Annie mourns the passing of a less disjointed arrangement in which "the seed was sown by hand and a single two-horse plough was sufficient for the entire farm" (59).

Notwithstanding the nostalgia in Annie's memory of preindustrial cultivation, her longing for immersive physical contact (a world where seed is "sown by hand") offers important insight into the way erosion of place was experienced at the level of the body itself. Since, as Edward Casey argues, "[b]odies and places are connatural terms," things that "interanimate each other," the new mechanized farm procedures often impaired the individual's sense of place by displacing human bodies in the realm of agriculture ("How to Get" 24).[19] Journalists profiling the New Agriculture continually remarked on the body's disappearance from (or altered place within) these scenes, describing the farmer who "plows and reaps and threshes with machinery without so much as touching his product with his hands" (Baker 130), threshers who are "merely assistants to a machine," and other farmhands whose work requires them to "only press buttons" (White 533).[20] Read in this light, Annie's nostalgia for manual work on the land is intimately linked with her antipathy toward the abstract, mechanized spaces causing her disorientation.

Yet in juxtaposing these scientific or technologically mediated constructions of space with phenomenological representations (like Annie's mental map), I do not mean simply to endorse one as a remedy to the other's alienating effects. After all, these two symbolic languages of space inevitably mingle, overlap, and complement each other, and as de Certeau has shown, discourses of the itinerary often incorporate planar projections as well ("There, there's a door, you take the next one"). In this way, he asserts, "an element of mapping is the presupposition of a certain itinerary."[21] What is ultimately at stake in the preceding juxtapositions, then, is not so much the formal difference between representational modes but rather their historical segregation. As Marxist geographers remind us, the rise of scientific discourse over the past five centuries coincided with a process in which the map "disengaged itself from the itineraries that were the condition of its possibility" (de Certeau 119–20). Premodern technologies for representing space and place were less "illustrations" or "iconic glosses on the text" than narrative figurations populated with characters who often participated in the story of that map's production: explorers, guides, mythical figures and creatures, and (perhaps most iconically) figures like the sailing ship, which "indicated the maritime expedition that made it possible to represent the coastlines." Yet fifteenth- and sixteenth-century European cartography increasingly came to represent maps as autonomous objects, and as de Certeau summarizes, "the map gradually wins out over these figures; it colonizes space; it eliminates little by little the pictural figurations of the practices that produce it" (120–21).

In late nineteenth-century North America, perhaps no group better understood the impact of this shift from subjective to more Cartesian or administrative representations of space than those whose sustenance depended on intimate knowledge of the land. The collected stories of Charles Chesnutt's *The Conjure Woman* (1899) vividly highlight the stakes of that contradiction by juxtaposing the character of Julius—a former slave for whom North Carolina's vineyards and plantations are an experiential and symbolically charged terrain, a homescape invested with stories, desires, religious beliefs, and idiosyncratic cultural practices—with a northern businessman who sees the land solely in terms of its property boundaries and commercial value. The latter figure, John, relocates to North Carolina to make his fortune in grape cultivation, expressing interest in this region on account of the fact that "labor was cheap, and land could be bought for a mere song" (118). Julius, on the other hand, relates to the land in ways that cannot be reduced to such calculations: born, raised, enslaved, and emancipated on the very plantation John intends to buy, Julius has been squatting and living off the land since it fell into economic "ruin" after the war. Indeed, the northern entrepreneur marvels at Julius's intimate knowledge of "the roads and watercourses," "the qualities of the various soils and what they would produce, and where the best hunting and fishing were to be had," as well as his "marvelous hand in the management of horses and dogs." Yet despite that appreciation, John equates Julius's experiential knowledge of the land with a primitive worldview, a mere effect of "the simplicity of a life that had kept him close to nature." And such an archaic relation to space, in John's view, proceeds from one cause above all: the failure to regard the land as an investment strategy. As he puts it, "Toward my tract of land and the things that were on it—the creeks, the swamps, the hills, the meadows, the stones, the trees—[Julius] maintained a peculiar personal attitude, that might be called predial rather than proprietary" (136–37). It is true that Julius's "predial" outlook (literally, an ethos "of the land" rather than "over the land") does not readily translate into an artful sense of its commercial potential or features. Yet as nature writer Barry Lopez points out, although mental maps and everyday orderings of place may "correspond poorly in spatial terms with maps of the same areas prepared with survey tools and cartographic instruments," they are nonetheless "proven, accurate guides of the landscape. They are living conceptions, idiosyncratically created, stripped of the superfluous, instantly adaptable. Their validity is not susceptible of contradiction" (295). For this reason, the new proprietor finds it necessary to hire Julius as a kind of spatial interlocutor, a guide who acquaints him with the dimensions, qualities, and capabilities of this property, a resident expert from whom he repeatedly solicits advice on which regions to plant, clear, and develop. Ultimately, then, it is John's so-called proprietary attitude toward the vineyard that proves crude and unsophisticated. And nothing highlights that one-dimensionality more conspicuously than his interpretation of the storytelling practices bound up with Julius's perspective on place.

While Julius may be seen as the classic trickster or Scheherazade figure in *The Conjure Woman*—one who spins tales to protect his material interests and the way of life by which he sustained himself prior to John's arrival—the purpose of his storytelling is not ultimately reducible to motives for pure personal gain or even self-preservation, as John is wont to conclude. It is true that Julius has an interest in protecting specific areas where he secretly distills alcohol or gathers grapes and honey, and he does indeed use his narrative arts to steer the new landowner away from those zones.[22] Yet to understand the oral histories and other colorful anecdotes Julius deploys as mere "scheming" is to read his relation to place through the same "proprietary" lens that reduces land to an inert resource for private use and commercial gain. For Julius, stripping this rural landscape of those oral histories and folktales would leave it without meaning and coherence. Indeed, as Kent Ryden reminds us, all geographies of human significance are filled with such "imaginative landmarks" and "unseen layers of usage, memory, and significance" (40). As the vineyard's former cultivator, Julius offers a perspective on place that is inseparable from the larger constellation of individual and collective histories, practices and beliefs suffusing this rural geography. Accordingly, his propensity for storytelling provides more than just a "local color" element to *The Conjure Woman* tales; it serves to highlight the poverty and limitations of purely Cartesian understandings of place.

Yet even as Chesnutt represents this North Carolina landscape through these two contradictory perspectives, the actual spatial referent itself remains the same, as-yet-unmodified preindustrial space. After all, within *The Conjure Woman*'s physical world, northern investors and developers are just arriving on the scene, leaving the greatest spatial transformations still "pending," as it were, over the horizon. Within less than a generation, however, these harbingers of change would be confronted as a fait accompli. For the protagonist of Willa Cather's *My Ántonia* (1918), returning to Nebraska after a twenty-year absence presents a childhood landscape now unequivocally and irreparably transformed by industrial development. Jim Burden discovers that the old road to his grandfather's farm has been plowed under when the new highways were surveyed, and a number of other bearings from his youth are now gone as well.[23] This mismatch between remembered and actual landscapes signals a key dramatic tension in *My Ántonia*, a novel that explores both the lasting impact of Nebraska's prairie landscapes on children who grew up there in the nineteenth century, and the way such memories can be undercut when the physical spaces of one's youth dissolve. Moreover, as Cather's narrative suggests, it is not just geographical place but all the myriad features of a material culture that preserve our personal and collective sense of self. This landscape of meaning-rich objects, as cultural anthropologist Nadia Seremetakis argues, secures memory and gives us access to the past by carrying "the sensorial offprint of its human use and triggered desires." When it is discarded, she notes, "an entire anthropology is thrown away with it" (10). Edward Casey makes a similar argument in his discussion of place as that which "gathers": places "keep such unbodylike entities as thoughts and memories" ("How to Get" 25).[24] Jim's disorienting homecoming toward the end of the novel thus underscores what is ultimately at stake in the rural upheavals of this era: as Cather presents it, they left Midwestern farming communities struggling not only to apprehend what the new farm *is*, but also to remember what it once *was*.

Such a predicament proves all the more acute for Jim Burden, since his position as an attorney for the expanding western railroads makes him complicit in the very upheavals causing this dislocation. This contradiction may go a long way in explaining Jim's reluctance to fully acknowledge the extent of these transformations (and their implications for those who still wish to count themselves among Crèvecoeur's celebrated "race of cultivators"). When the changed landmarks of his childhood fail to reconnect him with desired memories of Nebraska's preindustrial "golden age," Jim goes looking for them in a separate pilgrimage to Ántonia's farm. More than anything, it is a walking tour of Ántonia's grounds that helps reestablish the bearings Jim seeks, allowing him to finally declare that "everything was as it should be": no sooner have the old friends been reunited than Jim sets off on a ritualized walk from one landmark to the next, surveying the farmhouse and fruit cellar, the cattleyards, two ponds, a summer rye field, an ash grove, and the apple orchard. These images, "fixed there like the old woodcuts of one's first primer," trigger the appropriate and desired "succession of such pictures" (223, 218, 226). Additionally, this closing walking tour—where place is fixed and secure, and where Jim alone moves through the scene—provides an important counterbalance to the novel's opening scene, which features Jim as an enclosed railcar *passenger*, a spectator viewing the landscape outside his window hurl past him.

And yet for all the seeming stability and resolution here, there is something amiss in this final scene. Despite Jim's claim to immediately "recognize" the farm ensemble, this cannot possibly be so: he has never stepped foot on this particular site, as we learn that Ántonia herself settled here sometime after Jim left Nebraska as a young adult. Thus his "recognition" of this place must instead come from the act of matching these entirely new and previously unvisited grounds to a more general archetype carried in the mind. Indeed, during his initial approach to Ántonia's farm, Jim superimposes that imaginary landscape—an iconic ensemble nearly identical to the mental map carried by Annie Derrick—onto the one before him, reciting its standard details as if from memory: "I knew I must be nearing my destination. Set back on a swell of land at my right, I saw a wide farm house, with a red barn and an ash grove, and cattle-yards in front" (212). Much like Jim's propensity to embalm Ántonia, whom he now encounters less as an individual than a "universal" and "immemorial" peasant figure—an "image in the mind," as he puts it (226)—the iconic farm ensemble at the novel's end is no longer a viable, living thing in the present but rather a memorial to a doomed world. And so the western farm geography shares its fate with Jim's childhood friend—both person and place frozen in time so that a grown man may intermittently visit these preserved remnants of boyhood, all the while profiting from the very industrial process wiping out the lifeways and landscapes he eulogizes. Like Ántonia, the classic farmstead scene serves chiefly to provide instrumental practice with a sentimental alibi.[25]

The Garden as Map

> We cannot separate the function of the miniature from a nostalgia for preindustrial labor, a nostalgia for craft.... Whereas industrial labor is marked by the prevalence of repetition over skill and part over whole, the miniature object represents an antithetical mode of production: production by the hand, a production that is unique and authentic.
> —Susan Stewart (1984)

While the late nineteenth century might have been a bad time for nostalgic farm kids like Jim, it was something of a golden era for American garden writers. Readership of gardening literature exploded in these years: the first catalog-based seed business, which sent out a mere 750 catalogs in 1875, had increased that number to over one million by 1896, and consumption of other print materials—from magazines and books to advertisements and primers—rapidly followed suit (Mickey 118). New titles like *The Garden Magazine, Country Life in America, House Beautiful,* and *House and Garden* all appeared in the final decades of the century, and less-specialized magazines already in circulation—*Atlantic Monthly, Scribner's, The Independent, The Woman's Home Companion,* and *The Ladies' Home Journal*—increasingly featured pieces on domestic gardening as well.

Such developments were partly catalyzed by broader economic developments and advances in print technology: improved rail transportation and expanded mail service (with reduced rates for certain print materials) combined with lower printing costs and the advent of chromolithography to make mass-produced, color-illustrated catalogs and magazines newly affordable and accessible to American readers.[26] Meanwhile, the Arts and Crafts movement tapped into antimodernist sentiment and nostalgic yearnings for the "authentic" experience of folk and medieval craft production, an angst fueled by the stresses of urbanization and the instrumental rationality of an increasingly bureaucratic, corporate-consumer culture. Old-fashioned cottage gardens quickly became icons of the movement, evoking nostalgia for rustic lifeways, manual labor, and soil-based production practices.

Yet I argue that the unique character and powerful allure of garden fantasy in this period cannot be fully explained by developments in print culture, advertising, or antiurban angst. Agriculture's transformation also lies at the heart of this story, as long-entrenched meanings and perceptions linking American identity with a particular mode of production were wholly upended. For many of those who felt disoriented in the face of these upheavals, the garden represented something familiar, intelligible, and secure. Indeed, by the 1910s and 1920s, gardening had become a kind of shorthand for the act of reestablishing one's bearings—and once again, Willa Cather's work offers a useful angle of vision into the garden's meaning within these national fantasies and anxieties.

The most striking example, perhaps, is found in *Death Comes for the Archbishop* (1927), a novel in which Cather depicts the Catholic clergy's efforts to establish a diocese in New Mexico. In one of the opening scenes, readers follow a solitary horseman, Bishop Jean Latour, as he searches for bearings and navigational clues in the southwestern deserts:

> He had lost his way, and was trying to get back to the trail, with only his compass and his sense of direction for guides. The difficulty was that the country in which he found himself was so featureless—or rather, that it was crowded with features, all exactly alike. As far as he could see, on every side, the landscape was heaped up into monotonous red sand-hills, not much larger than haycocks, and very much the shape of haycocks. One could not have believed that in the number of square miles a man is able to sweep with the eye could be so many uniform red hills. (17)

In sketching this agonizing ordeal, Cather likens the episode to "wandering in some geometrical nightmare" (17). Eventually, however, Latour is relieved from his bewildering state by an agent of deliverance that takes its form as something both exceedingly old and uncannily new: he comes upon a garden oasis.

To be clear, I do not mean to hastily equate the Bishop's arrival at *Agua Secreta*—an Edenic village of "brilliant gardens," clover fields, and cottonwoods in the midst of this desert—with some simplistic resolution to the anxieties and perceived dislocations of Cather's period. This stretch of New Mexico desert is clearly no farm, and of course Cather's novel itself appears a full thirty years after turn-of-the-century writers began sounding the alarm on the effects of industrial agribusiness and its monocultural productions. And yet while this opening scene is no straightforward allegory of the New Agriculture's upheavals or the garden's promised relief, given Cather's lifelong focus on farm modernization in the West, it seems impossible to overlook the landscape type producing Latour's disorientation here. This is no tangled, overgrown wilderness where readers might typically expect a wanderer to lose his way; rather, Cather presents a landscape of hypermathematical *regularity* whose "uniform" and "monotonous" features cause a paralyzing sense of atopia (17). Indeed, its primary features—conical sand hills that so emphatically remind Latour of "haycocks" that the word is repeated twice in a single line—are all "exactly like one another" and are "repeated so many hundred times upon [Latour's] retina" that he begins to think "he would never see anything else" (17–18).

In short, Cather's endless mirage of mathematically spaced haycocks conjures the same hyperrational or "geometrical" regularity characterizing the monocultures of industrial agribusiness. And although *Death Comes* features farming merely as a peripheral concern, the social and environmental transformations of Cather's generation distinctly infuse this scene's patterns and meanings. Her inclusion of the garden in this opening moment does not merely reenact tired old religious allegories of the wasteland and paradise; rather, it draws on a more recent spatial ideal that had become a persistent leitmotif for a generation of writers seeking to navigate the strange dimensions of industrial agriculture.[27] Facing a national geography that had quickly grown unfamiliar, writers and growers increasingly turned to gardens to reestablish their bearings, invoking the figure as an explicit foil to industrial agriculture.

This thesis is borne out by three recurring elements characterizing the Progressive-era garden as a foil to the industrialized farm. First, the garden's distinct boundaries generated a coherent *place* over and against the more amorphous expanses of *space* coming to dominate commercial agriculture. Second, writers imagined gardens on a much smaller *scale* than their industrial counterparts, constructing "miniaturized" presentations that helped intensify their perceived intimacy and navigability. Finally, as farming became increasingly mechanized, specialized, and automated, gardening publications paid tribute to the pleasures of varied, *artisanal labor* in "old-fashioned" domestic plots.

The garden's first function here—establishing explicit boundaries—draws on one of the classic spatial features of gardens throughout history. The very etymology of the English term runs back to Old Norse *gard*, meaning "fence or enclosure." Michael Pollan explains that enclosure was especially pronounced in the iconic garden of the Middle Ages and early Renaissance—the *hortus conclusus*—which "offered a kind of refuge, a well-protected and scrupulously ordered place set apart from the dangerous and chaotic world that lay just over the wall" (*Second* 292–93). Conservative garden writers of the late nineteenth century like Alice Morse Earle increasingly called for a return to those older, clearly bounded designs, lamenting the "modern fashion in American towns of pulling down walls and fences, removing the boundaries of lawns," and leaving people's domestic lives exposed, "in full view of every passer-by" (66, 53). She devotes an entire chapter of *Old Time Gardens* (1901) exclusively to boundaries—hedges, fences, walls, and more—unequivocally asserting that "every garden must have boundaries, definite and high" (399). The profusion of photographs and descriptions she offers in this section explicitly seeks to halt the trend toward open-lawn styles that Andrew Jackson Downing and his successors has popularized.

Yet as gardening nonfiction debated the pros and cons of these aesthetic details, fictional accounts of the American farm more graphically dramatized the express role that boundaries played in restoring a *sense of place* amidst a disorienting, expanding, and increasingly homogenized landscape. This function is especially prominent in Cather's and Norris's novels. In *My Ántonia*, readers first encounter the vast landscapes of Nebraska through the eyes of Jim Burden, whose initial notion of the farm was established on a small, traditional family plot in Virginia. His move to the great cornfields of the Midwest—a territory blanketed with croplands "larger than any field [he] had ever seen" (12)—thus presents the protagonist with a radically novel spatial order.[28] During his first excursion to the vegetable garden, Jim nearly becomes lost in this featureless expanse, noting that without the guidance of his grandmother, "he should never have found the garden." As befits a curious child, Jim initially prefers the novelty of the unbounded cornfields to the familiar domesticity of a garden plot that carries "very little interest" for him, and instead indulges in fantasies that "the world ended here [in the prairie fields]: only the ground and sun and sky were left, and if one went a little farther there would be only sun and sky, and one would float off into them" (12–13). Yet after his grandmother leaves him alone, Jim does not, in fact, opt to set himself adrift on the endless prairies or massive cornfields that blanket them along the western skyline, but rather "grounds" himself by lying with his back against a warm pumpkin in his grandmother's garden, sheltered from the wind in its draw-bottom (14). Within this arrangement, the pumpkin (and by extension the garden itself) serves as a kind of buoy, moored by its vines to the prairie floor where Jim can fasten himself in place rather than "float off" in the interminable sea of Nebraska's wide-open fields.[29] The garden's role in securing place becomes even more pronounced when Jim visits Ántonia's farm at the novel's end. With the industrialization of prairie agriculture now an irrefutable fact, the garden-sanctuary is reinforced to an almost hyperbolic degree, with not one but three borders placed around it. As Jim describes the grape arbor where he reconnects with Ántonia, it is "surrounded by a triple enclosure; the wire fence, then the hedge of thorny locusts, then the mulberry hedge which kept out the hot winds of summer and held fast to the protecting snows of winter" (219).

As we have already seen, characters in Norris's *The Octopus* also experience a sense of atopia amid the bonanza farm's Euclidean croplands—spaces that unfold in a "flat monotony" and "expan[d] to infinity" (58). The only relief to this immense, rationalized arrangement comes from the San Joaquin mission garden, a plot that carves out "a tiny corner"—in short, a *place*—amid the sheer, unbounded space "stretch[ing] in all directions around it" (140). Indeed, if the "new order of things" in *The Octopus* is defined by industrial monocultures "bounded only by the horizon" (60), then the enclosed garden provides its ideal counterfigure.

Yet it is not just the perimeters of that mission garden that restore a sense of place to this vast and featureless landscape. Its contents are also vividly detailed and meticulously mapped out for readers, allowing us to visualize the coordinates of every landmark and accordingly find our way through a coherent ensemble. Spatial modifiers literally overflow descriptions of the mission garden: in a single paragraph, Norris exhaustively maps out walls that "*surrounded* the garden"; a "site *marked* . . . by a line of eight great pear trees"; an arched portal "in the *south* wall," "*in front* of the Mission," and "directly *opposite*" the pear trees; gravel walks "*bordered* with mignonette" weaving "*among* the flower beds" that lie "*underneath* the magnolia trees"; a fountain "in the *center*" and a sun dial "just *beyond, between* the fountain and the pear trees." Finally, the garden's most symbolically charged features—the gravestones— receive an even greater spatial dramatization. These sit "*on the other side* of the fountain, and *directly opposite* the door of the Mission, *ranged against* the wall," with Angéle Varian's resting place (the most important among these already-privileged place markers) even further plotted out: "the last one, the ninth, at the end of the line, nearest the pear trees, was marked by a little headstone" (139–40; italics added throughout). It hardly seems accidental that the mounting sequence of place-designators here culminates with such a figure: after all, gravestones remind us that the importance of *marking a place* becomes exponentially heightened when what that marker refers to is absence as such. Thus, the gravestone (memorializing the departed Angéle) and the cloister garden around it (memorializing sacred, preindustrial space—perhaps even the possibility of *place* itself) both signify something already perceived to have passed from the world. Indeed, the moment we step beyond the garden walls and into the bonanza wheat ranches surrounding them, we are once again "lost in [its] limitless reaches of space," set adrift in a virtual nowhere that makes Annie Derrick feel like she's been "abandoned in mid-ocean, in an open boat" (Norris 180).

Second, scale itself became a central feature in distinguishing turn-of-the-century garden representation from the upheavals of commercial agriculture. As Susan Stewart argues in her book *On Longing*, miniaturization has long been a way of emphasizing "a mental world of proportion, control, and balance," while the gigantic represents a "physical world of disorder and disproportion" (74). Not surprisingly, the miniature ideal became virtually synonymous with turn-of-the-century domestic gardens, while figures of the gigantic were affixed to the realm of industrial farming—from real-life croplands to narrative conventions of the agrarian "tall tale." Indeed, both spatial and narrative exaggerations were legion in early accounts of the bonanza farm, such as those compiled by Hiram Drache in *The Day of the Bonanza* (1964).[30] One particularly illustrative piece in this historical collection describes the Casselton bonanza of the 1870s, which, according to the son of a field hand, boasted "the biggest farm that ever lay out of doors." The speaker here tells of his father plowing a furrow alongside the head rancher, Dalrymple, and cutting a groove that extends

> over 40 miles long, and so straight you could snap a chalk line in it from one end to the other without touching either side. [The two men] headed in a northwesterly direction and plowed straight for two days. When they stopped at night Dalrymple asked my father if he thought they had gone far enough and he replied, "I hope you don't go any farther, or we may never get back." (70)

Some bonanza tales claimed even greater feats of labor: in one testimony from the early 1880s, a worker reports to have "seen a man on one of our big farms start out in the spring and plow a straight furrow until fall. Then he turned around and harvested back" (71).

It is important to note here that such tales do not merely express the amplification of farming's dimensions but also, more importantly, a *qualitative* mutation in the way farms were experienced by their laborers. From this view, scale and disproportion become ways of addressing class position and disempowerment—in particular, the inability to comprehend one's place in a larger social and economic order (how one's work fits into wider systems of production, who controls and profits from that system, who consumes the products of one's labor and where, etc.). William White, whose bonanza account is no tall tale but rather a journalistic report on actual labor conditions in the 1890s, notes that geographic distances had become too great for even horseback communication to remain feasible on the ranches: "Crews of workmen living at one end of the farm and operating it may not see the crews in other corners from season's end to season's end," he wrote (534). Geography thus appears as only one facet of the much larger problem of "distance" and estrangement, recalling us to Fredric Jameson's definition of alienation as a "gap between the local positioning of the individual subject and the totality of class structures in which he or she is situated, a gap between phenomenological perception and a reality that transcends all individual thinking or experience" (*Postmodernism* 415–16).

Little wonder, then, that conventions of the gigantic in the literature of New Agriculture express class struggle and exploitation not only through rhetorical amplification but also by way of more literal, "animate" giants. In *North America* (1862), Anthony Trollope depicts the grain elevators just then emerging across western farmscapes as "monsters," structures with enormous elephant-like trunks for siphoning grain, one of which "continues to devour" vast quantities of produce "till the corn within its reach has all been swallowed, masticated, and digested." Meanwhile, the laborers tending this giant are reduced to its diminutive feeders and caretakers, endlessly and furiously "shovel[ing] the corn up towards its maw, so that at every swallow [the elevator] should take in all that he can hold" (162–63). Ray Stannard Baker similarly characterizes this new feature in American agriculture, dubbing it the "Mammoth Elevator" (135), while Norris depicts the wheat fields of *The Octopus* as "Titans" and the steam harvester at the novel's end as a "hippopotamus," a "dinosaur," and a "prodigious monster, insatiable, with iron teeth, gnashing and threshing into the fields of standing wheat; devouring always, never glutted, never satiated, swallowing an entire harvest" (616). Across these caricatures, inequality and the exploitation of labor are communicated by means of disproportions in scale: on one hand, the workers infinitesimal as ants (and like insects of a swarm, dehumanized and interchangeable); and on the other hand, the colossal and fully animated figures of industrial agribusiness.

Against these various expressions of the gigantic, Progressive-era garden representation miniaturized cultivation, emphatically distinguishing itself from the industrial order by arresting the flow of time as such. As Stewart explains, the miniature presents "a world clearly limited in space but frozen"; and although its tiny, meticulously detailed ensembles "bring historical events 'to life,' to immediacy," they ultimately do so in order "to erase their history, to lose us within their presentness." As she argues, "the transcendence presented by the miniature is a spatial transcendence . . . which erases the productive possibilities of understanding through time" (48, 60). In *The Octopus*, paradoxically, the various emblems of time in the tiny and carefully preserved mission garden overwhelmingly suggest the *absence* of time's effects. The fountain at the courtyard's center—"flowing steadily, marking off the lapse of seconds, the progress of hours, the cycles of years, the inevitable march of centuries"—remains itself wholly unchanged. Images of hibernation suffuse the garden, and characters seeking solace here habitually visit at night when all the "multitudinous life of the daytime drowsed and dozed." Even the site's timepiece—a crumbling old sundial—proves useless for tracking time or change, since the numerals on its face are "worn away, illegible" (140). These various characterizations of timelessness dissociate the garden entirely from the linear trajectory of industrial wheat farming, which Norris depicts as an agent of historical progress and even a force behind "the march of empire rolling westward" (319–20). The "sudden and abrupt revolution" it generates is explicitly shut out by the garden walls: "outside" the mission garden, as Norris writes, "the great grim world went clashing through its grooves, but in here never an echo of the grinding of its wheels entered to jar upon the subdued modulation of the fountain's uninterrupted murmur" (140).

Miniaturization is also a common feature within nonfiction garden writing itself, with writers increasingly celebrating plots of "Lilliputian" and "postage-stamp" dimensions (Dyer 270–71); yet within this genre, "disproportion" is explicitly determined by the ability or inability of a gardener to cultivate a given space herself.[31] Growers cross the boundary line out of the miniature's world of balance and symmetry once they must hire a third party to do the work, a concession that became increasingly taboo in domestic gardening circles of the period. In fact, the refusal to outsource work eventually came to be something like an obligatory oath for induction into the cult of early twentieth-century gardening.[32] In 1912 Hanna Rion professed, "I should as soon think of asking a secretary to write my book, or the cook to assist in a water color painting, as to permit a gardener to plant or dig among my flowers" (35), while B. Y. Morrison, chief editor of the *American Horticultural Society's Magazine*, asserted that his essays were "not for the people who leave their gardens to the care of the hired man" (15). Yet any such do-it-yourself commitments would only be possible if plots remained small. Thus, when Frances Duncan insists that "[t]o hire a man to plant [one's garden] destroys the peculiar charm," she appeals directly to this inverse-relation between scale and pleasure in domestic gardening: "When one has settled the fine earth about the roots with his own fingers," she writes, one establishes "an intimacy and fellowship with a beloved object" that would only diminish were there whole "acres of it" (158). Indeed, when Richardson Wright, who served as editor of *House and Garden* for over thirty-five years, reflected back on this turn-of-the-century cult of smallness in an entry on "Little Gardens" (1929), he remembered chiefly that the ladies of his local garden club had always "yawned politely behind their hands at the big estates which had been laid out by professionals and maintained by an army of gardeners; but when they came to the little home-made and home-tended gardens, they went into ecstasies" (46).

Finally, the desire for less-disjointed and less-mechanized forms of work constituted a third recurring feature of turn-of-the-century garden representation. Such desires were closely linked with the miniaturized scale of domestic plots, which did not require the armies of hired (and increasingly itinerant) laborers found on larger commercial operations. As Susan Stewart notes, fantasies of unalienated, artisanal production are often linked to matters of scale, and her own examples of model ship- and model train-building practices closely resemble the case of home gardening as a foil to industrial farming: as Stewart explains, these hobby activities "completely transform the mode of production of the original as they miniaturize it: they produce a representation of a product of alienated labor, a representation which itself is constructed by artisanal labor" (58). Small wonder that these desires intensified during a historical moment marked by the transition from a producer culture (one that longed to imagine itself in small entrepreneurial or Jeffersonian agricultural terms) to the consumer economy of a more bureaucratic and industrialized state. Work regimens once dictated by natural rhythms were increasingly being regulated by clocks and managerial schedules, with Frederick Taylor developing his early principles for the scientific workplace in the 1880s and 1890s. Contemporary Arts and Crafts proponents like Irene Sargent noted that such trends toward de-skilling, mass production, and division of labor were fueling revolutionary agitation among workers, "the play of whose intelligence is confined to the endless repetition of a single mental process, and whose physical exercise is restricted to the working of certain unvarying muscles" (9).

Yet above all, it was the business and professional class that expressed the greatest anxiety over this sense that daily life had become not only "overcivilized" but also "insubstantial" and "curiously unreal," as historian Jackson Lears has argued (*No Place* xvi, 71). Compared with farm laborers, this group enjoyed significantly greater freedom from the brutalizing demands of manual labor; yet their insulated, bureaucratic work-lives fragmented their labor and led many to feel they were "isolated from the hard, substantial reality of things." Fantasies of recovering the "authentic" experience associated with manual labor (the "simple life" of subsistence farming or skilled craftsmanship) led many white-collar Americans to look wistfully toward premodern skilled artisans, whose activity they imagined as "necessary and demanding ... rooted in a genuine community ... a model of hardness and wholeness" (Lears 60).

Those middle-class fantasies found powerful expression in the American-style Arts and Crafts ideology just as the movement was popularizing the so-called "old-fashioned" garden designs inspired by cottages of the English peasantry.[33] Essays with titles like "Old Time Gardens," "The Gardens of Our Grandmothers," and "Our Old Timey Garden" proliferated in the period, while the work of Alice Morse Earle (1851–1911), a historian and Arts and Crafts champion, popularized all things colonial. Her comprehensive *Old Time Gardens* included over two hundred vintage photographs of gardens in New England and the Middle Atlantic states, quickly becoming one of the most popular garden books of the twentieth century (M. B. Hill 77–78).

The types of plants and flowers found in cottage gardens also lent to their special appeal, since these botanical elements were integral to modes of home production rapidly disappearing in this period. As historian Susan Lanman explains, "Tinned foods, patent medicines, industrial dyes and mass produced spirits were rapidly replacing foods, medicines, dyes, herbal wines and other domestically manufactured products dependent on abundant cottage gardens and plants gathered from the surrounding countryside" (209). In fact, some writers troubled by the social and environmental effects of industrial expansion went so far as to devise hierarchies of flower color according to their perceived association with factory production. Lanman notes that magenta flowers had the misfortune of resembling a newly popular aniline dye (recently discovered as a by-product of gas manufacturing and widely adopted for mass-produced fabrics), and as such they were derided by nostalgia-prone gardeners on both sides of the Atlantic. In 1918 popular garden writer Louise Beebe Wilder observed how widespread was this "custom to despise magenta":

> [I]n all my gardening experience I have met only one person who confessed admiration for this colour and I have come across but one garden writer who boldly put down in print his admiration for it. Indeed nearly every writer upon garden topics pauses in his praise of other flower colours to give the despised one a rap in passing. Mr. Bowles writes of "that awful form of floral original sin, magenta"; Miss Jekyll calls it "malignant magenta"; and Mrs. Earle, usually so sympathetic and tender toward all flowers, says that even the word magenta, seen often in the pages of her charming book, "makes the black and white look cheap." (94–95)

Yet, ironically, the turn to old-fashioned or cottage gardens as a remedy to industrial consumer culture was promoted by an industry whose own products had become increasingly mass-marketed. Gardening publications appealed to public anxieties and desires through mass-produced images of wholesome activity and happy, middle-class suburban life. And just as brands like Quaker Oats and Cracker Jack (first marketed in the late 1880s and 1890s) became familiar national brands associated with a specific icon, the grandmother's and English cottage garden became a standardized product through consistent repetition in garden publications. As garden historian Thomas Mickey points out, this domestic landscape typically included the same features and arrangement: "carefully sited trees, a group of shrubs, a lawn, and often carpet beds of annuals on the lawn [with] the kitchen garden . . . behind the house" (229–30). Indeed, demand for richly illustrated depictions of this ensemble in catalogs and advertisements led one seed company to wonder if it was now in the business of selling not seeds but rather images as such: as the editor of D. M. Ferry's catalog asked in 1882, "Is the trade so enormously profitable that they can afford to distribute gratuitously so beautiful and costly a book simply as an advertisement? That we, in company with every other seedsman in England and America, find it necessary to annually send out such a book indicates that there is something in the trade which demands it" (qtd. in Mickey 67–68). Growers were hardly oblivious to the commercial nature of this trend, with some complaining that gardening had become just another marketing gimmick—hardly a retreat from the increasing commodification of everyday life. Many mocked the very notion of "content in a garden," a phrase that had entered the popular vocabulary and became a kind of period trademark after Candace Wheeler, a prominent Arts and Crafts writer, published a series of essays under that banner. As Winifred Kirkland wrote in her essay "Discontent in the Garden," "[T]he gardening mania is but one more example of the modern unrest, so extensively advertised. True, there might be content in the garden if owners were ever satisfied with them as they are; but they are haunted by new combinations and new experiments" as promoted and sold in horticultural literature (853).

Yet for those dissatisfied with the tedium of the office or the drudgery of factory and domestic work, even the most standardized and mass-marketed gardens differed from other ready-made goods in important ways by inviting—and indeed demanding—hands-on participation and skilled, ongoing care. Growers may well have bought into a prepackaged template, but it was the experience and process of physical *production* that so appealed to paper-shuffling workers as well as to those simply struggling to navigate a world they found increasingly mechanized, fragmented, and remote from the "hard, substantial reality of things." In redirecting the effort of their bodies toward creative production that yielded food and blooms, domestic gardening allowed participants to intimately experience the cycles of soil, seeds, roots, and rain.

Indeed, the desire to highlight the effects of one's work gave rise to a convention of "touring" in period gardening literature, where readers or visitors were walked (either physically or narratively) from one feature to the next within the garden grounds. This tour custom directed explicit attention to the self-created nature of these landscapes, where each feature testified to time invested, skills honed, and decisions and selections reflecting idiosyncratic preferences, both aesthetic and gustatory (Cheney). Even without visitors, gardeners reported starting each day with "a brief but unhurried tour" of their grounds (Dyer 285). The custom thus played a double function in both showcasing the meticulous work process involved in maintaining this geography and reinforcing immersive modes of place-awareness—situating individuals in familiar and intelligible settings. Just as the garden's miniature scale promised to restore intimate forms of hand-tending that a commercial farm's dimensions and organization would never permit, these self-guided circuits promised to reestablish spatial bearings through direct engagement in place.

Thus, in a period when the farm's geographic and social dimensions had grown every day more unfamiliar and inconceivable, writers elevated basic properties of the domestic garden—its coherent boundaries, manageable scale, and promise of integrated production—as a standard bearer of legibility, a geography that could not only be traced and walked but whose circuits of consumption and production could also be mapped onto the daily lives of growers, readers, and visitors.

Such desires for more "mappable" spaces and modes of production continue to mobilize alternative food movements today, where a new genre of "locavore memoirs" and other "postindustrial pastorals" seeks to make sense of "an abstract and globalized food system via the interpersonal, the intimate, and the everyday" (Carruth 153). And given that commitment, it should come as no surprise that time and again, gardens crop up in twenty-first-century publications and movements much as they did in earlier generations, imagined by writers as antidotes to the social and ecological dislocations that motivate their inquiries.

Indeed, it is hardly an accident that Michael Pollan—the navigator who guides us through our postmodern food labyrinth in a blockbuster series of books, film appearances, and national speaking tours—originally gained prominence as one of North America's most well-known gardeners, a vocation that now seems something like a prerequisite for this navigational role. Granted, the connections linking all seeds and horticultural acts to intricate social, historical, and biological webs make it doubtful that any food chain could ever be characterized by the "brevity and simplicity" that Pollan seeks in his self-cultivated meals (an admission he explicitly makes himself) (409). And yet as an expression of the sheer desire to live and eat in "full consciousness" of the vast circuits and actors involved, the garden remains a powerful ideal today, much as it was a century and a half before. Indeed, even if our food webs remain confoundingly intricate, gardens have given generations of writers and growers reason to hope for more transparency in the myriad lines connecting these points.

CHAPTER 3

Resensualizing the Garden
From Surface to Substance in Midcentury Food Writing

> You can't get good ice cream anymore.... It tastes like gum and chalk.... Melons don't ripen, grapes are sour.... Butter tastes like the printed paper it's wrapped in. Whipped cream comes in aerosol bombs and isn't whipped and isn't cream. People serve it, people eat it. Two hundred and fifty million educated Americans will go to their graves and never know the difference.... That's what Paradise is—never knowing the difference.
> —Joseph Heller (1974)

It is no coincidence that one of the low points for kitchen gardens in the United States came during a high point in America's love affair with industrialized "convenience foods," a midcentury era famous for Jell-O mold salads and canned-food casseroles, the advent of TV dinners and fast food, the rise of the gleaming, ultramodern supermarket, and a dubious parade of imitation foods that have since become gastronomic punch lines: aerosol Cheez spray and Marshmallow Fluff, instant mashed potato buds and nondairy creamer, Kool-Aid, Pop-Tarts, sprayable cooking oil and a thousand other synthetic pseudofoods. The 1950s and 1960s were also a golden age of the suburban lawn, a landscape where modern, self-respecting Americans were more likely to be found grilling burgers or cranking up gas-powered mowers than puttering around in some old-fashioned turnip patch to grow rations for storage cellars they no longer had. Indeed, with an unprecedented number of Americans indulging in flashy new products and technological gadgetry—not to mention astronaut-endorsed, space-age novelties like Tang and Instant Breakfast—it seems surprising that anyone still bothered with old-fashioned, labor-intensive, home-grown garden fare at all.

Eventually, however, the 1960s and 1970s counterculture rebelled against a food industry it saw as homogenized, toxic, and synthetic. Public alarm over chemical pesticides spread in response to Rachel Carson's *Silent Spring* (1962) and a growing environmental movement, while plant-based diets became a form of social protest following publications like Frances Moore Lappé's *Diet for a Small Planet* (1971), which linked the Western food system to global hunger. Meanwhile, the counterculture vilified corporate agribusiness for driving family farms toward extinction; and hadn't all those new "convenience" meals originated from the military-industrial complex as spoil-proof, ready-to-eat rations for GIs in the field?

Rising health concerns were also memorably summarized in Doris Grant's somewhat hyperbolic claims about America's industrial diet in *Your Bread and Your Life* (1961): "Before our food reaches the table," she wrote, "it is poisoned in the soil, disinfected, bleached, softened, dyed, tinned, bottled, packaged, fortified, irradiated, thickened, frozen, flaked, sprayed, embalmed, flavored, extended, emulsified, gassed, deodorized, stabilized, hydrolized, polished, neutralized, or subjected to atomic fall-out" (15). This led a rising number of Americans to experiment with growing their own food on communes and other back-to-the-land movements that promoted subsistence gardening as an "alternative to supermarket America" (Edgington 282). Even those with no opportunity or interest in getting dirt on their hands helped diversify the midcentury food landscape by rejecting white flour, white sugar, and white bread, and gradually popularizing (or helping reintroduce) "brown foods," organic, vegetarian, small-is-beautiful, and many other practices that later crystallized as the familiar characters of today's "alternative" food movement (local and seasonal eating, Slow Food, school gardening programs, fair trade, farm-to-table restaurants—and, increasingly, restaurants with their own on-site food gardens).[1]

Additionally, interest in saving the dwindling number of family farms gave rise to the resurgence of market gardening programs in U.S. cities, where local growers could sell crops directly to urban residents.[2] One of the milestones in this movement was the creation of the New York City Greenmarket in 1975, a story John McPhee recounted in his now-classic essay "Giving Good Weight" after spending that opening season selling peppers alongside its local farmers. Such open-air street markets had all but disappeared in New York after the 1930s (indeed, they were systematically eliminated across the United States during the first half of the twentieth century), leaving consumers little choice beyond the supermarket's chemically preserved, "mummified" food. According to Barry Benepe, one of the Greenmarket founders, when local Jersey and Long Island peaches were at their luscious peak in summertime, "you'd go to a New York City supermarket and find hard, green nuggets for peaches, with no juice and no flavor. It was an insult" (qtd. in Kamp 278). Meanwhile, the New York metropolitan region had been hemorrhaging prime farmland since

World War II, as local growers found themselves both unable to compete with large-scale industrial agriculture out west and squeezed more locally by suburban development that was converting farmland into highways, shopping centers, and housing. Seeking a remedy, a group of activists led by Benepe invited a handful of local farmers and market gardeners to load their pickup trucks with fresh produce and set up an outdoor market in a lot along 59th Street. The summer of 1975's so-called Greenmarket was an instant sensation: beginning from that single site with seven growers from Long Island, New Jersey, and upstate New York, the number of participants doubled within a month and quickly spread to sites in Brooklyn, Harlem, Union Square, and other neighborhoods. The program was also hailed as a success in meeting its triple goal of keeping farmers solvent (many credited the Greenmarket for their survival), bringing high-quality fresh produce to urban residents at unusually low prices (consistently less than prices at supermarkets and corner grocers), and promoting community revitalization through European-style open-air markets at a moment when New York was staggering through its infamous 1970s financial crisis.[3]

Yet McPhee's story, along with many other accounts in food and gardening literature of this period, illuminates something more than just a revolt against the agricultural establishment. These texts also highlight a kind of revolt of the senses, an expression of longing for intimate bodily contact with the world of plant crops and soil-based life—indeed, a longing for restored emotional, narrative, and sensory intensity in the everyday objects we consume. Against a sterilized and mass-produced postwar food culture that commentators increasingly characterized as all surface with no content, the Greenmarket offered a carnival for the senses, a realm rich with embodied experience where fall pippin apples were "green as grass and curl your teeth," and slim peppers became a "small red grenade [that] explodes on [one's] tongue." Moreover, it was not just the intensity of taste that drew people into these market gardeners' midst: here, the full sensorium is activated by the "opiate aroma of peaches"; the "hammering sun" falling on growers' backs; visitors sweating and pressing against each other; onion tops "brittle and dry"; the rhythmic sound of vendors chanting jingles; the residue of "powdery soil"; bodies "soaked to the skin" as shoppers brave the rain for beautiful lettuce; the crowd's "thick heat"; a farmer's hands "rough, callused, cracked," "fingers like bananas"; the burning sensation of biting a hot pepper; the cool relief when a fistful of green beans is stuffed in the mouth to neutralize it (McPhee 6, 9, 20, 58, 64, 67, 25, 68).

Above all, McPhee's account is filled with the sheer, overwhelming desire to *touch*: New Yorkers long accustomed to the city's cellophane-wrapped, rock-hard fruit put their hands on everything in the Greenmarket, "press[ing] on the melons until their thumbs go through." Many handled the goods so passionately that growers complained: "[T]hey're brutal on the fruit," one reported, while another added, "[w]e have to leave them touch tomatoes, but when they do my guts go up and down. They paw them until if you stuck a pin in them they'd explode" (12). At times, the desires lurking in such gestures erupted into more frenzied acts. As one farmer recalled of his first day at 59th Street, he arrived before sunrise to find a growing crowd already waiting to buy his produce, and he ultimately panicked as those shoppers lunged at the bins of fresh Jersey corn he was pulling off his truck: "They went after the corn so fast I just dumped it on the ground. The people fell on it, stripped it, threw the husks around. They were fighting, grabbing, snatching at anything they could get their hands on.... We sold a full truck in five hours. It was as if there was a famine going on" (17).

Since we may safely assume that this "famine" had little to do with pure caloric need, it invites us to consider the less visible desires and deficiencies that did give rise to it, and how the objects prompting these acts took on such intense affective charge. By what process do common market-garden goods—its heaping towers of melons and plums, its brimming bins of berries and herbs—become intimately linked with a longing for embodied, sensual contact, the impulse to touch, taste, smell, and consume? How do these plant foods organize our fantasies and memories, and how do we, in turn, assign meaning and value to them? In what way do their meanings change across different scenes of encounter—the supermarket, the garden, the city, the farm stand? How do soil-based objects become repositories of the past, and what happens when the layers of memory invested in them—along with their vital sensory dimensions—are sapped, when they are reduced to a purely visual existence?

Food critics of the 1970s such as John and Karen Hess may well have been correct in diagnosing their fellow Americans as "starved for flavor"; indeed, they argued that such a condition explained the period fad for "incendiary chilies" and other spicy dishes "guaranteed to create a sensation on the palate": "When the actors have to set fire to the house to get a reaction from the audience," they wrote, "then the theater is in trouble" (54). Yet such single-sensory explanations omit an important part of the story. Perhaps progressive reformer and family-farm activist Jim Hightower got closer to the heart of the matter in suggesting that *nature itself* had somehow disappeared from midcentury food. After all, as he wrote in 1975, food "nourishes and pleases us in a way that automobiles and television sets cannot—it literally is part of us. To industrialize food, to make it conform to technologies and systems, is to industrialize ourselves and finally to surrender the quality of our lives to the mass-produced standard of big business" (229).

As I argue in the pages that follow, such garden- and food-related longings in McPhee's story and other midcentury accounts—from Eleanor Perenyi's alarmed writing about the dwindling variety in seed catalogs to Hightower's advocacy for small farms and John and Karen Hess's stinging food reviews—reveal more than what we may already know about the blandness of supermarket produce and luscious superiority of garden-fresh varieties. More significantly, these accounts offer insight into the way historical transformations are experienced at the level of the senses: how the industrialization of our diets, along with capitalism's tendency to reduce all values to market values, can reshape bodily encounters with the natural world and even undermine memories and identities that arise from those zones of contact. Indeed, if gardens are a realm where people seek experiences and pleasures denied to them in their daily lives, then the fantasies at work in midcentury farmers' markets throw light on an impoverished modern condition where scientific reductionism had disenchanted human relations to nature (including food) and even estranged individuals from their own bodies and biological processes.

Granted, McPhee's frenzied Greenmarket shoppers are not gardeners or farmers but simply people seeking contact with that which comes from the soil outside their city. Moreover, many of the midcentury accounts and spaces explored in this chapter are not conventional "gardens" or instances of "garden writing." Yet this idiosyncrasy may all the better confirm how the mere trace of the garden—even the simple presence of fruits and foliage in paved urban realms—can activate powerful fantasies and desires, and even reanimate the sensory dimensions of natural objects that seemed to have atrophied in other spheres of consumer culture.

As such, midcentury reflections on food and farmers' markets remind us that garden-based fantasy is infinitely more inclusive and vast than specialized approaches may suggest. After all, while the verb form of "garden" evokes an activity chiefly involving those directly engaged in cultivation tasks (gardening as an *act* of digging, planting, and harvest), zooming out to view "the garden" as a fundamental source of life reveals an infinite set of actors and participants involved in its process. In short, this broader view allows us to see the garden's story as the story of all who take pleasure in eating—growers and consumers alike.

A Famine of the Senses: Seeking the Garden in a Cellophane Age

> Let your condiments be in the condition of your senses.
> To appreciate the flavor of these wild apples requires vigorous and healthy senses, papillae firm and erect on the tongue and palate, not easily flattened and tamed.
> —Henry David Thoreau (1862)

> We lost our tail, though not our tailbone, eons ago. It appears to me that the next vestigial organ may be the taste bud.
> —Shana Alexander (1974)

On most days during his summer working as a Greenmarket vendor, John McPhee claims he ate "something like a dozen plums, four apples, seven pears, six peaches, ten nectarines, six tomatoes, and a green pepper" (20). If that daily fruit and vegetable intake sounds unusual by today's dietary standards, it was equally so in 1976, a moment when half of every U.S. food dollar was now spent on processed food, and McDonald's had overtaken the Army and Department of Agriculture's school lunch program as the biggest feeder in the nation (Hightower 78, 81). One could cite an endless list of figures to illustrate this unprecedented transformation in America's food culture during the latter half of the twentieth century: indeed, as *Fast Food Nation* author Eric Schlosser notes, what Western people eat changed more in the forty years following World War II than it had in the previous forty thousand years (7). Historically, humans have consumed over fifty thousand different plant species across the world, yet by the end of the twentieth century nearly 90 percent of our diet came from a mere fifteen crops, with the big four industrial plants—corn, soy, wheat, and rice—making up more than two-thirds of that caloric intake (FAO "Staple Foods" and "Agrobiodiversity").[4]

This profound consolidation of biodiversity in our diets is not the result of eating towering stacks of corn or tubs of fresh soybeans three times a day. Rather, these calories are primarily consumed as processed foods. After World War II, farmers stopped growing thousands of plant varietals formerly raised for the table, focusing instead on the shortlist of crops purchased by international distributors and processed-food manufacturers. Today's North American consumers, as Barbara Kingsolver notes, "now get to taste less than one percent of the vegetable varieties that were grown here a century ago." "Those old-timers now lurk only in backyard gardens and on farms that specialize in direct sales," although a growing number of those heirlooms have been lost entirely (*Animal* 49). Suffice it to say, these changes signal an extraordinary narrowing and simplification of the human diet.

Of course, from the perspective of someone strolling the endless lanes of the modern supermarket, where thousands of new products are introduced every year, it may be easy to conclude the very opposite—that we now consume a greater diversity than ever in our history. And yet those infinite proliferations in product diversity are merely skin-deep, with industrial processors using novel forms, stabilizers and texturizers, artificial flavoring, branding campaigns, and ever-changing packaging to mask what is essentially a monocultural farm system and an unprecedented homogenization of global food cultures (Pentecost; Pollan, *Omnivore*). As the special assistant for Consumer Affairs in the 1970s remarked, "The key to wider acceptance of pre-packaging by consumers is to offer a wide range of choice in packaging" (Hess 284). Just compare this industrial food system's four-ingredient version of diversity to the more than seven thousand varieties of *apples alone* listed by the U.S. Department of Agriculture at the end of the nineteenth century—a fruit whose dizzying variety goes well beyond botanical categories to also include cultural, geographic, sensory, historical, and narrative aspects that Thoreau once cataloged (and further enhanced with whimsically invented Latin names) in his essay on New England's wild fruits:

> There is, first of all, the Wood-Apple (*Malus sylvatica*); the Blue-Jay Apple; the Apple which grows in Dells in the Woods, (*sylvestrivallis*) also in Hollows in Pastures (*campestrivallis*); the Apple that grows in an old Cellar-Hole (*Malus cellaris*); the Meadow-Apple; the Partridge-Apple; the Truant's Apple, (*Cessatoris,*) which no boy will ever go by without knocking off some, however late it may be; the Saunterer's Apple,—you must lose yourself before you can find the way to that; the Beauty of the Air (*Decus Aëris*); December-Eating; the Frozen-Thawed, (*gelato-soluta,*) good only in that state; . . . Wine of New England; the Chickaree Apple ; the Green Apple (*Malus viridis*);—this has many synonyms; in an imperfect state, it is the *Cholera morbifera aut dysenterifera, puerulis dilectissima;*— the Apple which Atalanta stopped to pick up; the Hedge Apple (*Malus Sepium*); the Slug-Apple (*limacea*); the Railroad-Apple, which perhaps came from a core thrown out of the cars; the Apple whose Fruit we tasted in our Youth; our Particular Apple, not to be found in any catalogue,—*Pedestrium Solatium*; also the Apple where hangs the Forgotten Scythe; Iduna's Apples, and the Apples which Loki found in the Wood; and a great many more I have on my list, too numerous to mention,—all of them good. As Bodaeus exclaims, referring to the cultivated kinds, and adapting Virgil to his case, so I, adapting Bodaeus,—
>
> Not if I had a hundred tongues, a hundred mouths,
> An iron voice, could I describe all the forms
> And reckon up all the names of these *wild apples*. ("Wild" 523–24)

FIGURE 7. Tom Wesselmann (1931–2004). *Still Life #30* (1963). Oil enamel and synthetic polymer paint on composition board. Gift of Philip Johnson. Digital Image © The Museum of Modern Art / Licensed by SCALA / Art Resource, N.Y. Art © Estate of Tom Wesselmann / Licensed by VAGA, New York, N.Y.

Yet as food writers John and Karen Hess complained in 1972, "the only apple most Americans eat today is the Delicious"—either the Red or the Golden, a color-coded designation that turned out to be quite handy since their identical taste made it otherwise impossible to tell them apart (44).

Naturally, these transformations in the consumer realm have been shaped by historical developments in the realm of food production across the twentieth century as the shift to mechanization, monocultures, and economies of scale pumped out unprecedented quantities of standardized crops (eventually genetically engineered to express identical traits) for industrial processors.[5] As Michael Pollan points out, in its transition from whole to processed foods the industry adopted an economic model based on "adding value" to cheap raw materials, ingeniously "figur[ing] out how to break these two big seeds [corn and soy] down into their chemical building blocks and then reassemble them in myriad packaged food products" (*Defense* 117). Thus, crops formerly grown as food for people and livestock now became what Barbara Kingsolver calls a "standardized raw material for a new extractive industry," one whose principles might seem more appropriate to mining than food production. Particularly in the years following World War II, the food industry's mills and factories were retooled for a "multibranched production line" every bit as complex as those that "turn iron and aluminum ores into the likes of automobiles, paper clips, and antiperspirants" (Kingsolver, *Animal* 13). Here, primary materials like wheat, corn, and soy are broken down to their basic molecular structure and then converted into hydrogenated oil, high-fructose corn syrup, and thousands of other food-like products and chemicals bearing little or no resemblance to the field crops from which they originate.[6] And notwithstanding the disparaging responses of writers like Joseph Heller, Doris Grant, or Shana Alexander, who claimed that "grocery stores selling fresh produce have all but disappeared, and supermarket shelves offer miles and miles of frozen, dehydrated, processed, dyed, adulterated glop" (Alexander 34), millions of consumers in the 1950s and 1960s were unabashedly enthused by the increasingly processed nature of American food. Indeed, not only was it quick, convenient, and relatively cheap to whip up a recipe from Poppy Cannon's *The Can Opener Cookbook* (1951), but it was also considered *chic* to serve a "modern" dinner of Hamburger Helper, instant mashed potatoes, Pillsbury crescent rolls, Hawaiian Punch, and Jell-O topped with Reddi-wip for dessert (Wyman 8–10).

Yet there is more than just technology and economics at work beneath the twentieth-century shrinking of biological (as well as cultural) diversity in the North American diet. These developments also reflect a reductive, Cartesian worldview in Western science and thought, a mode that has historically sought mastery over nature and promoted quantitative, mechanistic understandings of the world through mathematical analysis and abstract, objective expression. Within the nutritional sciences, that legacy is readily apparent in the focus on breaking foods down into isolated variables and chemical components, a trend that was supercharged when chemists discovered vitamins in the 1920s. Now, plant foods in their living wholeness—an infinitely complex amalgamation of skins, seeds, juices, membranes, worm-bites, soil symbionts, and such—were disassembled into tidy sets of isolated components, parts that could then be reassembled into superior (value-added) forms. Eventually, even Nobel Prize winners like John Boyd-Orr, chief of the United Nations Food and Agriculture Organization, predicted that if continued population growth made it unfeasible to feed the world through conventional farming, we could always "call in the chemists, who can synthesize nearly all the constituents of food except mineral elements" (qtd. in Otter 235). And why not? In regarding the dark and complex world beneath our feet as a mere composite of neutral material, scientists had already isolated many key soil components and begun replicating them in the form of synthetic fertilizers and other chemical inputs. What if the same logic were now applied to food crops themselves? After all, as industry experts put it in Pohl and Kornbluth's satirical 1953 science fiction classic, *The Space Merchants*, "If 'Nature' had intended us to eat fresh vegetables, it wouldn't have given us niacin or ascorbic acid" (14).

By the 1960s and 1970s, this outlook had gone beyond the realm of speculation to reshape foods themselves. The proliferation of these "nonagricultural" ingredients was parodied in a 1971 National Education Television skit where Marshall Efron dons a chef's hat and uses ingredients on a Morton's lemon-cream pie box to guide viewers through the process of making this dessert at home, mixing together monosodium phosphate, ammonium bicarbonate, sodium caseinate, sugar, emulsifiers, polysorbate #60, imitation flavor, and artificial coloring. Holding up the final product—a "modern" and "factory fresh" creation—he presents the quintessential postmodern dessert: "No lemons, no eggs, no cream. Just pie" (National Education Television). Executives at Morton were unapologetic: "Eventually, we'll have to depend on artificial foods to feed the world's population," argued the president of Morton's Frozen Foods Division. "By using artificial ingredients now, we're helping in their development" (Feldberg, A-19). Indeed, as historian Chris Otter points out, chemists had already been developing synthetic foods and flavoring for some time: saccharin, derived from coal tar, was first developed in 1876, but only later in the twentieth century did it (along with other fossil-fuel-derived and nonagricultural "foods") become widespread in everyday foods (235).

Yet like the myth of mastery underlying Francis Bacon's dream of a modernized paradise in *New Atlantis* (1627)—a future where humanity achieves total control over nature by engineering synthetic fruits and even extending the growing season itself—twentieth-century food science betrays a profound hubris as well as a kind of biophobia, a disdain for the messy variability of fleshy, wild nature with its gooey secretions, teeming microbes, smelly waste, and random ways. Indeed, as Warren Belasco argues in *Meals to Come*, his meticulously researched analysis of twentieth-century speculation around the future of food, one of the persistent themes of these nutritional endeavors has always been a desire "to solve dirt farming's perennial inefficiencies by doing away with conventional agriculture entirely" (37). That ethos is handily summarized by chemist Jacob Rosin in his 1953 *The Road to Abundance* (just one of hundreds of similar scientific and government publications Belasco cites), which calls on us "to recognize that our dependence ... upon the dilatory and inefficient plant is a cruel bondage. We have given the plant almost the entire 'floor space' of the planet, and devoted to it by far the largest part of our energies. And in return we have not gotten enough food to go round" (9, 57).

This Cartesian outlook—particularly the representation of technology rather than biology as the source of modern abundance—went well beyond midcentury laboratories, extending into realms like advertising, World's Fair exhibitions, and American literature. As Jackson Lears has shown, around 1900 advertising adopted a mode of representation he describes as a "disembodiment of abundance"—an aesthetic and ideological practice that found its most pronounced expression in agricultural ads. Here, "with startling abruptness, machine replaced *mater*; mythic emblems of fecundity yielded to unadorned photographs of male-operated threshers and harvesters," and the popular slogan "every farm a factory" underscored a "disenchantment of familiar agrarian imagery" (*Fables* 120–21). As modern science became increasingly "reified and venerated as an autonomous force," traditional emblems of abundance—fleshy, nature-based, and otherwise carnivalesque motifs—gave way to images of mass-produced abundance. Advertising depicted a material world largely disengaged from the soil, where food seemed to originate from factories and patent medicines from "well-lighted laboratories rather than dark forests" (Lears 120).

Belasco also traces this ideology across the disparate representations of agriculture at the 1890s versus 1930s World's Fairs (*Meals* 154, 186). While guidebooks for the 1893 Chicago Exhibition had described a palace of agriculture adorned with motifs of "abundance" and "fertility," including "Edenic vine-olive-fig designs" and a statue of Diana under the central dome, the 1933 and 1939 fairs focused on technological innovation, showcasing breakthroughs in irrigation, pesticides, mechanization, and hybridization (White and Ingleheart 168). In fact, separate halls dedicated to agriculture and horticulture (the largest buildings in 1893) were now absent from the twentieth-century fairs. Agriculture had been "demoted to a sub-field of The Chemist's research," as Belasco puts it, and the food chain once associated with farms now led back to the laboratory: as the New York Fair's science director confidently projected in 1939, meals in the World of Tomorrow would be fabricated in chemical plants, thereby "liberating" us from soil-based agriculture. Eventually, he concluded, foods would simply "abandon all pretense of imitating nature" (Wendt 214).

Yet perhaps the most memorable and vivid examples of this representational shift toward the synthetic future of food come from the examples in American literature and film that Belasco examines.[7] Decades before highly processed convenience foods proliferated in postwar kitchens and supermarkets, their imaginative seeds had already begun to sprout in science fiction, particularly between 1910 and 1940, as an increasing number of writers depicted future generations turning from soil-based organic foods to synthetic "food analogs." As Belasco shows, these futurists typically split between two camps, either imagining that revolution as a desperate response to overpopulation and the degradation of biological food chains (the prediction of Malthusian camps) or as a triumph of science and engineering that would liberate humans from biological constraints by devising more efficient alternatives to the old-fashioned act of chewing and digesting gross organic matter (the dream of technological utopians). Yet whether dystopian or celebratory in tone, their accounts largely imagined food within the framework of a Fordist economy that favored processes of simplification, fragmentation, automation, purity, and standardization in defiance of season, culture, geography, time, craftsmanship, and diversity (Belasco, *Meals* 166).

Patrons of Hugo Gernsback's "Scientific Restaurant" in 2660 swapped traditional dining utensils for buttons and tubes that delivered a liquefied slurry of food-flavored nutrients straight into their mouths (84–87). Feminist science fiction texts of the 1920s, as Jane Donawerth shows, featured a simplified and sanitary fare in the form of synthetic "liquid food," "foamy concoctions," and "chemical nourishments" (138–39). Meanwhile, citizens of Huxley's *Brave New World* consumed "cup[s] of caffeine solution," vitamin A pâté, and "vitaminized beef-surrogate" (118, 167, 152); people of the thirty-first century featured in one *Amazing Stories* piece lived on the "essences" of vegetables and meat to "avoid taking waste matter into [their] stomachs" (qtd. in Donawerth 138–39); and countless other sci-fi populations dined on the ever-popular "meal-in-a-pill," what Belasco calls the "reductio ad absurdum of all simplification schemes" (*Meals* 115).

It would seem, then, that midcentury Americans unwilling to drink the Kool-Aid served up by these biophobic industrial ideologies should either "grow their own" or stick with food from the old-fashioned wing of American supermarkets: the produce section. Yet even here, things weren't quite what they used to be. Whole-food cultivars—the everyday fruits and vegetables found in backyard gardens—increasingly joined their industrialized cousins (crops destined to become jelly beans and Cool Whip) in the march toward rationalized standardization. This shift went well beyond the practice of shrink-wrapping fresh produce, which had increasingly become an industry standard in the early 1970s; the contents within this packaging also changed. As John and Karen Hess lamented in *The Taste of America* (1972), "The taste of the seasons is gone; it has been replaced by 'carrying quality'"—the ability of produce to withstand machine harvesting and long-distance transportation. As they continued, "Tomatoes are picked hard green and gassed with ethylene . . . whereupon they turn a sort of neon red. Of course, they taste like nothing at all, but the taste of real tomatoes has so far faded from memory that, even for local market, farmers now pick tomatoes that are just turning pink" (39–40). While the Hesses' elite foodie credentials may tempt some to dismiss their criticism as overblown, the practices they highlight had indeed become standard in commercial farming. Corporate growers increasingly engineered fruits and vegetables to require less hand cultivation; to grow to identical heights and "ripen" all at once for mechanical harvesting; to tolerate the stresses of transportation; to respond to forced chemical-ripening off the vine; and to have lengthy shelf lives and uniform appearance (Barndt 38). Home gardening followed similar trends, with writers like Katharine White, Eleanor Perenyi, and Ruth Stout noting that old-fashioned, heirloom food plants and flowers were being pushed out of the seed catalogs and nurseries to make room for flashy new hybrids with bigger fruit or blooms—even if this meant sacrificing flavor and aroma. Gardeners in search of heirloom seeds were increasingly forced to turn to informal economies and personal networks like rural market bulletins—lists of classified advertisements for herbs and ornamental perennials. Indeed, this commitment to preserving regional gardening knowledge, culture, and networks of exchange constituted a decades-long correspondence (posthumously published as *Gardening for Love*) of celebrated garden writer Elizabeth Lawrence, who scoured the market bulletins for relics of a disappearing world, for "names not to be found in catalogs: the white coronation rose, the lady-of-the-lake, and the old fashion Betsy rose that blooms all summer" (38).

It is certainly fair to ask why industrial agriculture couldn't simultaneously improve carrying quality *and* sensual aspects like flavor, smell, texture, and juiciness. As it turns out, in many cases those two sets of priorities are indeed at odds with each other. Russ Parsons notes that industrial producers do consider taste, but to maximize profit they must also factor in whether a given crop will be a heavy bearer; whether it will appear at times that fetch the highest prices (early and late in the season); whether it will "appear consistently, rather than in fits and starts, so [farms] can keep a steady crew employed"; whether it will hold up during harvesting and shipping; and—of crucial importance—whether it will look good, since many supermarket shoppers "buy with their eyes." Of course, it must also "taste good enough, that goes without saying. But if the rest of the criteria aren't met, all the flavor in the world won't mean a thing," he notes (21). And on top of these criteria comes an added level of rationalization: regardless of product type, a single grower's goods frequently arrive at the supermarket mixed with produce from other sources, reducing incentive to take the extra risks involved in growing better-tasting fruit (which typically requires leaving items on the branch or vine where they are exposed to chance events as they ripen, all the while becoming softer and more delicate). In light of these competing considerations, then, a typical rule of thumb for large commercial growers is to harvest fruit "as soon as it reaches the minimum quality standard" (Parsons 118–19). With farm operations increasingly adopting this practice after World War II, the Hesses wondered aloud that anyone was still consuming supermarket produce at all. As they wistfully reflect on the old Washington Market they used to frequent, "in tomato time, one could find fruit, tart, sweet, and bursting with juice. . . . Now, there is not a ripe-picked tomato to be found *even in tomato time*. . . . So we can have tomatoes year-round but now we cannot buy tomatoes worth eating at any time of year. Nor strawberries. In fact, we can no longer tell the difference between tomatoes and strawberries" (40).

Bland tomatoes are, or course, a far cry from the complete "disembodiment" of food represented in science fiction, where scientists in Jules Verne's stories create meals of "nutritious air [that would] enable us to take our nourishment . . . only by breathing" (111). Or are they? From the perspective of those concerned with the desensualization of eating, food plants were becoming little more than visual reminders of their former selves—pure surface, pure sign—hardly different from the lemonless and creamless "lemon cream pie." Indeed, this distress over the triumph of the image became a persistent theme in garden and food writing of the 1970s.[8] In *Eat Your Heart Out*, Jim Hightower complained that new strains of "picture-book red" tomatoes dazzled the eye but failed to engage other bodily senses with the textures and flavors of summer that people used to wait for all year (95). Journalist Alden Whitman likewise admitted that the strawberries of 1973 "may well be bigger and redder" than those grown in his grandmother's garden, but to him they tasted like "so much sawdust or asbestos flaking" (15). Meanwhile, John and Karen Hess conceded that the deep color and gleaming shine of the Red Delicious gave it the flawless appearance of "an apple in a child's coloring book" but found it so devoid of taste that "[o]ne might as well follow the direction on a carton of Ritz Crackers and make a 'Mock Apple Pie: no apples needed!' It is indeed a short step from Delicious to no apples at all" (44). These intimations that basic plant foods had somehow become disembodied replicas of their preindustrial selves are even more explicit in Peter Lamborn Wilson's *Avant Gardening* (1999): although this manifesto appears some twenty-five years later, Wilson tracks his grievance back to this very period in the 1970s, a moment when apples began to "taste pretty much like raw potatoes and look like Jungian archetypes." Once available in thousands of distinct varieties and manifestations that Thoreau celebrated, the apple in Wilson's account becomes "part of the body of the Image, the global *imaginaire*, the universal unchanging mystical vortex of control, of hegemony, of separation. The Apple transcends the mere accidental bodies of random russets, winesaps, pippins, this windfall or that sour green one, good for pie, or this bruised one, good for cider." "The wizards of genetics triumph," he concludes, "and soon there is only one pure Apple" (21). In this way, the eating of soil-based foods—an act conventionally regarded as one of our most intimate and unassailable connections to the flesh and substance of the natural world, "one of the few real things left in our lives" (229), as Hightower dramatically declared in 1975—now seemed to dissolve with the rest of consumer culture into the insubstantial realm of the postmodern simulacrum.

Such concerns provide a key insight into the more curious scenes from John McPhee's account of the Greenmarket's opening season—scenes where New Yorkers maul the fruit, rush the fresh Jersey corn, and nearly break into fights like "there was a famine going on" (17). If we read these gestures as symptoms of depleted sensory experience in midcentury food culture, they raise important questions about how our sensorium is both embedded in material culture and essential to our relation with the past. In "The Memory of the Senses," cultural anthropologist Nadia Seremetakis elaborates on such questions by examining everyday objects as agents that "sustain our relationship to the historical as a sensory dimension." Reflecting on her childhood in Greece, Seremetakis recalls a favorite regional peach, the *rodhakino*, that was "phased out" by globalizing market forces—taking with it a "mosaic of enmeshed memories, tastes, [and] aromas"—and replaced by a watery, tasteless "surrogate" (2). Looking back from 1994 at the long restructuring project of the European Economic Community, national trade agreements, World Bank loan requirements, and more, Seremetakis is perhaps better positioned than midcentury observers to identify this eradication of specific tastes and local material cultures of production as a largely invisible and undocumented casualty of neoliberalism—a process resulting not only in economic change but also "a massive resocialization of existing consumer cultures and sensibilities, as well as a reorganization of public memory." Yet her perception of this commercialized, "surrogate" food culture—a realm "emptied of specific cultural content" and experienced as a "surface with no past"—is certainly nascent within the writings of the 1970s as well (3, 2). And perhaps no trope captured its sensory impact more vividly than the "hollow" fruits of garden writing.

As industrial standardization and consolidation seemed to gut the content of basic foodstuffs, figures of "hollowness," "surface," "density," and "weight" proliferated in garden and food literature, supplying a common vocabulary through which to articulate the difference between a material culture perceived as layered with personal, historical, and regional associations, on one hand, and a fragmented landscape of meaningless objects without history or depth on the other. "Hollowness," in particular, became code for objects devoid of shared emotion and experience, objects that no longer supplied the kind of meaning-rich sensory encounters that Nadia Seremetakis identifies with "commensal depth."[9]

Garden writer Eleanor Perenyi renders what is arguably the period's image *par excellence* of this evisceration of farm and garden products. As the pages of her 1970s gardening catalogs are transformed by the commercial priorities that Hightower, Hess, and others denounce, Perenyi comes across advertisements for "improved" tomato varieties with "fewer seed cavities"; some even offer "a 'hollow' tomato," what Perenyi describes as "all wall with no flesh or seeds, a prefabricated receptacle for tuna-fish salad" (218). In creating this tidy new model, breeders had effectively gutted the fruit's messy innards (even though the juicy seed pockets are the very key to a good tomato's flavor), leaving gardeners to subsist on a mere shell of the tomato's former self. As we shall see in the following section, this trope of "hollowness" also migrates between particular objects and the broader context of our capitalist economy, which translates the infinite variety of qualitative difference into a single common denominator and "irreparably . . . hollows out the core of things, their individuality, their specific value, and their incomparability," as philosopher Georg Simmel puts it in his classic critique of modern capitalism (330).

And so although the meal-in-a-pill did not materialize as predicted by early twentieth-century science fiction, garden and gastronomic writing seemed to suggest that the transition to a diet of "images" or "essences" had come to pass all the same. Little wonder, then, that McPhee's portrait of the New York Greenmarket puts such extraordinary emphasis on the simple desire to touch and weigh the dense biomass of these trucked-in fruits. Indeed, the opening lines of "Giving Good Weight" zero in on shoppers probing items with their fingers and hands, squeezing, palming, and pushing their thumbs into the fleshy bellies and cores of summer fruit. As McPhee writes,

> You people come into the market—the Greenmarket, in the open air under the downpouring sun—and you slit the tomatoes with your fingernails. With your

thumbs, you excavate the cheese. You choose your string beans one at a time. You pulp the nectarines and rape the sweet corn. You are something wonderful, you are—people of the city—and we, who are almost without exception strangers here, are as absorbed with you as you seem to be with the numbers on our hanging scales. (3)

While the near-violent gestures framing this opening moment—the gashing of skins, the pulping and stripping of summer fruit and corn—might initially seem out of place amid the market's quaint umbrellas and cheerful milieu, within the context of this moment they emerge as genuine acts of celebration and multisensory indulgence, a reembodiment and resensualization of organic matter. Indeed, against proliferating anxieties that fresh produce had dissolved into the mere *idea* of produce, with hollow tomatoes and apple-archetypes overtaking both garden writing and actual dinner plates, the opening gestures in "Giving Good Weight" assume extraordinary significance by simply reorienting the reader's perception of fruit as inescapably *embodied*—as something composed of skin, flesh, innards, even husk-like garments that get stripped from the farmer's corncob figurines.

McPhee's restoration of the fleshy density and substance of these Greenmarket items is further expressed through a near-compulsive focus on their weight. As he writes in the passage above, visitors are utterly "absorbed" with the numbers on the farmers' hanging scales, a fixation that quickly becomes a central motif of the story—a kind of refrain to the soundtrack McPhee creates in sampling the market's densely textured sounds and rhythms. The cacophony he relates is layered with shoppers' voices as they probe every dimension of the garden bounty: when something was planted or picked; how crisp, sweet, juicy, or tart it is; where it was grown; why it is fuzzy; whether the skin can be eaten; how one selects, prepares, cooks, combines, preserves, and more. Yet as those individuals hand over their selections, these endlessly diverse exchanges almost always conclude with a single line: "Will you weigh these?" Vendors further underscore the mnemonic quality of this refrain, chanting out their activity of weighing goods on the scale with a mantra-like cadence: "Two and a quarter pounds at three pounds for a dollar comes to, let's see. Seventy-five cents. Five and a half pounds at three for a dollar twenty-five, call it two and a quarter. That's three dollars.' 'Even?' 'Even'" (31). Of course given the Greenmarket's prolific botanical variety and shoppers' desire for proximity to something they perceive as "tangible" and "real," this particular refrain may seem directly at odds with the prevailing spirit of the story (a point we will explore at greater length in the next section). After all, in its "all-day conversion of weight to cash," as McPhee puts it, the scale's express

FIGURE 8. The first Greenmarket was held in a parking lot across from the 59th Street Bridge, New York City (1976). Photo courtesy of GrowNYC.

purpose is to change discrete, fleshy things into abstract numeric value, an operation that may be seen as complicit in the very economic system Georg Simmel faults for "fill[ing] the daily life ... of so many people with weighing, calculating, enumerating and the reduction of qualitative values to quantitative terms" (328). Yet in light of proliferating expressions of hollowed-out objects and our atrophied experience of everyday material culture, McPhee's persistent reference to this metrological instrument is hardly an off-message slip. Indeed, as transactions between grower and buyer repeatedly highlight the precise weight of plums, onions, eggplants, and grapes, the device seems to call us back to the density and fullness of living matter under which the scale gives way.

McPhee emphasizes that association by staging weight as a distinctly liminal property, an attribute poised at a kind of sensory and conceptual threshold: like money, it expresses a quantified value, and yet that quantification cannot be uncoupled from the irreducible density and embodied heft of a given object. This dual property is embodied by vendors and growers who exhibit an intimate kinesthetic knowledge of the objects they handle. The most experienced even seem to have fine-tuned scales built into their hands and muscles, allowing them to accurately calculate the weights of bulging sacks of beans before confirming them on the scale—a trick that draws crowds of fascinated onlookers ("Did you see that? He knew exactly how much it weighed!") (5). In thus foregrounding the embodied aspects of weight, as opposed to its more abstract, quantitative expression, McPhee's scale dramatizes a basic sensual property that had suddenly come to matter in extraordinary new ways.

This fascination with nature's raw weight is hardly exclusive to shoppers browsing the Greenmarket; indeed, it has long been ubiquitous within garden writing, where growers endlessly reflect on the near-mystical process by which light is changed to biomass. Michael Pollan admits that every fall he is newly astonished by the garden's increase, the way it generates "[s]o much sheer, indubitable *mass*, none of which existed just a few months ago except in the prospect of a handful of seeds." When he hauls this immense load to storage, Pollan reflects how "beyond the impressive bulk, there's the unexpected weight of it all—almost as if we're shouldering not just baskets of produce but fall's gravity itself, the same ripe force that bows the sunflower heads and bends low the boughs of apple trees" (*Second* 170; italics original).[10] That harvest increase strikes Thoreau with a similar sense of weighted meaning in "Wild Apples," where he describes trees in autumn so loaded with fruit that every limb is pulled back toward the earth, and the groaning lower branches must be supported by poles so that they "looked like pictures of banian-trees." Indeed, as he concludes, "Pliny says that apples are the heaviest of all things, and that the oxen begin to sweat at the mere sight of a load of them" (515–16). Contemporary garden writer William Alexander likewise punctuates his narrative with repeated reflections on nature's staggering output, breathlessly voicing his wonder at the miracle of tiny kernels mutating into "bushels of tomatoes [and] thirty-pound watermelons" (259). Like Pliny's oxen he develops a kinesthetic sense of nature's fecundity, using his own muscle power to heave hundreds of pounds of apples uphill for winter storage (230–31).[11]

Yet the organic matter of home gardens, truck farms, and traditional food cultures is also imbued with properties that cannot be measured or weighed: cultural, regional, and historical meanings that give these objects additional layers of density and depth. In *A Sense of Things*, Bill Brown reminds us of the mysterious substratum we perceive in the things making up our material culture—congealed fantasies, anxieties, values, and affections, even the power to "keep the past proximate, to incorporate the past into our daily lives" (12). As an object is invested with surplus meanings, it can even become what Seremetakis calls "a separate and distinct (monadic) memory-form in-itself... carr[ying] within it the sensorial off-print of its human use and triggered desires" (10). Thus, Greenmarket visitors are often transported immediately from present physical forms to linked places and memories—associations that seem to have atrophied in routine encounters with mass-produced food. A *New York Times* feature on the electrified response of shoppers during the market's first summer quotes Manhattan resident Julia Pfannschmidt, who praises the luscious peaches and claims she had "never tasted good [ones] from a supermarket," but then in the next breath drifts to her home country and memories of its fruit, adding, "I'm from Germany, so I know about peaches. We used to make Rhine wine, peach wine" ("E. 59th"). Such responses seem to reverse the blocked pathways in writing on industrial food consumption, where, for example, Alden Whitman's "sawdust"-flavored strawberries warp existing associations with specific people, places, and contexts: as he writes, "Every time I bite into a modern strawberry . . . I get a reverse *déjà-goût* of those luscious, tasteful strawberries that my grandmother tended in her backyard" (15).

Like the senses themselves, which act as a repository and recordkeeper of spontaneous material experience, gardening and food literature also serve as a site of "alternative memory and temporality" (Seremetakis 20), particularly during this midcentury period when their pages became ever-expanding inventories of departed tastes and lost smells. Thus, while it may be tempting to dismiss these elegies as the nostalgic indulgence of writers projecting back to idealized childhood gardens or farms, the genre tells a powerful story about the "extinction of experience"[12] accompanying transformations in agriculture and regional foodways, along with the radical simplification of biodiversity in our food system—the kinds of transitions our sensorium may suspect before statistics officialize them.

These hidden zones of countermemory become especially important when we note that official histories of global agriculture are overwhelmingly narrated as high-profile, sensational events (international trade agreements, large-scale health and environmental impacts, the development of new biotechnologies, legal battles over the genetic modification of crops) rather than as individually experienced changes (the subtle loss of flavor of an apple). Yet as Seremetakis argues, that privileging of official histories—and indeed, the very split "between public and private memory, the narrated and unnarrated"—reveals the extent to which private, everyday experience is marginalized and "organized around the reproduction of inattention, and therefore the extent to which a good deal of historical experience is relegated to forgetfulness" (20). Ultimately, the "cultural construction of the 'public' and the sayable," as Seremetakis argues, "in turn creates zones of privatized, inadmissible memory and experience that operate as spaces of social amnesia and anesthesia," even though what is experienced as a mere "background of organic, continuous time" is itself a political-cultural creation (19).

Furthermore, the sensory changes resulting from these economic and political transformations tend to "occur microscopically through everyday accretion; so, that which shifts the material culture of perception is itself imperceptible and only reappears after the fact in fairy tales, myths, and memories that hover at the margins of speech" (Seremetakis 3). To illuminate her point, Seremetakis zeroes in again on the fact that the *rodhakino* peach disappeared almost without notice: only at length does she consciously grasp that it is no longer carried in markets (and that the trees themselves have vanished from Greece's orchards). When she casually mentions this in conversations, her friends and relatives "responded as if the peach is always out there although they did not happen to eat it lately." "People only alluded to the disappearance of the older peach by remarking on the tastelessness of new varieties," she writes, "a comment that was often extended to all food, 'nothing tastes as good as the past'" (1). This dynamic is especially prominent in the fairy-tale quality of gardening and food literature, along with its capacity to reactivate buried memories or give rise to recognitions that somewhere along the way, some part of our material culture unceremoniously vanished. Although he grew up in a part of New Jersey that produced "world-famous truck-farm delicacies in season" well into the 1950s, Wilson's full awareness of the gulf between the old Jersey tomato and today's version (which tastes to him like "red dye #3") does not fully crystallize until decades later when browsing a seed catalog. The catalyst comes from a wistful entry in the catalog, "Remember the way tomatoes *used* to taste?" Reading this passage, Wilson is overwhelmed by an awareness suddenly awakened from hibernation—a recognition of the mass attrition of beloved objects linked to local production and consumption experiences from decades past ("Avant Gardening" 28–29).

Yet while the potency of such a response may be preserved (or even intensified) over time on the individual level, it is markedly diminished for individuals lacking personal memories of the objects triggering such responses—a lapse reminding us that sensory memory comes with a kind of intergenerational shelf life. In Perenyi's writing on floral scents lost in creating today's flashier hybrid blooms, the complex structure of loss (like the one Seremetakis depicts) is replaced by the mere flash of surprise for younger generations when they first encounter the heady smell of surviving heirloom roses and sweet peas (accustomed as they are to the "dusty little madeleines" with "no power to summon the memory of things past" now sold by commercial florists) (198, 214–16). This same concern informs Perenyi's expectation that future generations will not even know to miss the sublime flavor and messy lakes of seeds in preindustrialized tomatoes (218–19). Such forecasts may have been easier to dismiss if voiced only by aging gardeners and snooty food critics who joked about midcentury kids growing up to pine for "Kool-Aid like my mother used to make" (Hess xi). But they were also confirmed by 1970s food industry researchers and flavor scientists, generating headlines in the *Wall Street Journal* that summarized this new normal: "Fresh Foods Taste Peculiar If You Grew Up Eating Instant, Frozen or Canned" (1974). Citing research on this growing phenomenon, food industry executives maintained that after years of producing artificial flavors, some of the pressure was now off to replicate the qualities of fresh whole food, freeing up their flavor technicians to pursue "imitations of imitations" as they developed new products. The director of flavor creation for International Flavors and Fragrances, Inc., even cited an industry term for this growing preference for artificial: flavor scientists called it the "Pineapple-Juice Bias" after a study showing that most Americans were now used to canned pineapple juice, which has a slight metallic flavor from the container, and therefore overwhelmingly rejected fresh juice as tasting unfamiliar and even not "real" (Bralove 1).

And so, despite valid criticisms of the social privilege often underlying food and garden writing's preoccupation with tasteless, processed foods,[13] we must also keep in mind that at stake here is nothing less than the retraining of the body as a sensory field and what Seremetakis would call a massive "reorganization of public memory." After all, she argues,

> The capacity to replicate a sensorial culture resides in a dynamic interaction between perception, memory and a landscape of artifacts, organic and inorganic. This capacity can atrophy when that landscape, as a repository and horizon of historical experience, emotions, embedded sensibilities and hence social identities, dissolves into disconnected pieces. (3, 8)

Indeed, within this pervasive context of dissolution and disintegration, we often forget even to look for those alternative structures of feeling and hidden spheres of sensory experience. Few of the Greenmarket patrons seem aware of these simple pleasures as something they may be seeking, voicing surprise at the potency of their involuntary responses to plant foods. Farmers, vendors, and city organizers also seem caught off guard by the sheer ordinariness giving rise to this profusion of elated responses, filling their accounts with gleeful exclamations overheard in the Greenmarket: "I'd forgotten what tomatoes taste like"; "In nine years in the city, I've never seen food like this"; "I'm finally discovering what real vegetables smell like"; "My bean hasn't snapped in years"; "Everybody's smiling"; "It smells like the country!"; "I feel like I'm in another time!" (McPhee 10, 64; Benepe 20). One New Yorker who parts the tassels on an ear of corn exclaims to nearby shoppers, "Oh, look at the lovely worm!" while a young basketball player shouts to his friend as they shoulder through the crowd, "This is where it is, man. This is where it is!" (Hess, Preface 2; McPhee 29).

This elation is further heightened by the Greenmarket's urban context—a landscape not commonly celebrated for biological variation. McPhee borders on the manic in listing the names of all the produce filling these lots, both common and exotic forms that proliferate wildly and overspill the pages of "Giving Good Weight." Like an ethnobotanist surveying this market landscape, the narrator looks out from the post where he sells peppers to document a stunning biodiversity:

> Gold Star cantaloupes. Patty Pan squash. Burpless cucumbers. Cranberry beans. Silver Queen corn. Sweet Sue bicolor corn, with its concise tight kernels, its well-filled tips and butts. Boston salad lettuce. Parris Island romaine lettuce. Ithaca iceberg crunchy pale lettuce. Orange tomatoes. Cherry Bell tomatoes. Moreton Hybrid, Jet Star, Setmore, Supersonic, Roma, Saladette tomatoes. Campbell 38s. Campbell 1327s. Big Boy, Big Girl, Redpak, Ramapo, Rutgers London-broil thick-slice tomatoes. Clean-shouldered, super-globed Fantastic tomatoes . . . (6)

Other shoppers wistfully remark on the presence of farmers themselves, talking as if these figures had stepped right out of a fairytale. One visitor holding a bundle of chicory lettuce tells a *Times* reporter, "I get goose bumps just looking at these farmers coming from where there are real trees and plants. . . . Everyone's so happy to have them here" ("E. 59th").

The childlike wonder in this allusion to a land of "real trees and plants" seems as good a summary as any for the Greenmarket's appeal. Like the market fruits themselves, loaded with memory, meaning, and complex sensory structures, these truck farmers become bearers of a vast landscape of pastoral fantasy—so much so that, with their arrival in New York City, they seem to "spill into its center the colors of the country. Greengage plums. Ruby Red onions. Yellow crookneck squash. Sweet white Spanish onions. Starking Delicious plums"—a garden bounty that utterly transforms the concrete and commotion of 1970s Harlem and Brooklyn into spaces blooming with biodiversity, lost flavors, smells, memories, and associations (6). Indeed, what ultimately emerges from this urban scene very much resembles a garden, a space where people come to smell, touch, sample, and select the fruits of the earth "in the open air under the downpouring sun" (3).

Little wonder, then, that New Yorkers are so hungry for the Greenmarket goods, so overcome with desires to physically immerse themselves in this space (in one moment, shoppers actually "plunge" like "splashing bears" into the peppers [9]). It might even be that the images with which McPhee opens his story—people sinking their fingers into the core of all the goods encountered here, literally pushing their thumbs into the bellies of summer fruits and "excavat[ing] the cheese"—are likewise informed by this fantasy of the garden, a fantasy evoked by gestures that seem to transform consumers themselves into gardeners, individuals who ritualistically plunge, probe, plow, and dig, who come to the market to sink their hands into the soil-based substance of life.

"Under the Downpouring Sun": Street Markets, Gardens, and the Reenchantment of Urban Space

> To appreciate the wild and sharp flavors of these October fruits, it is necessary that you be breathing the sharp October or November air. . . . They must be eaten in the fields, when your system is all aglow with exercise, when the frosty weather nips your fingers, the wind rattles the bare boughs or rustles the few remaining leaves, and the jay is heard screaming around. What is sour in the house a bracing walk makes sweet. Some of these apples might be labelled, "To be eaten in the wind."
> —Henry David Thoreau (1862)

In his essay "Wild Apples," Thoreau expresses a notion that has since become an article of faith for twenty-first-century locavores and Slow Food advocates: when it comes to the pleasures of food, place matters. Celebrating the wild apples of New England, Thoreau calls attention to the unique experience of eating fruits that "have hung in the wind and frost and rain till they have absorbed the qualities of the weather or season, and thus are highly *seasoned*, and they *pierce* and *sting* and *permeate* us with their spirit." Indeed, he argues that fruits deracinated from their earthy context lose something of that essence: the same wild apple that is "spirited and racy" when eaten in the fields or woods takes on "a harsh and crabbed taste" if consumed indoors. "The palate rejects it [indoors], as it does haws and acorns, and demands a tamed one; for there you miss the November air, which is the sauce it is to be eaten with." And so in singing the praises of these apples' remarkable flavor, Thoreau paints a vivid, sensory-rich portrait of the autumn *landscapes* in which they are found, along with the body's experience of such environments.

One cannot help but note the same dynamic at work in the Greenmarket portrayed by McPhee, where the pleasure of its items is heightened by the gardenlike feel of this space—an association engendered not only by the profusion of ripe, aromatic garden goods but also the thicket of hanging plants and flowers swaying from the stands—"baskets of zebra plants, ferns, coleus, and begonias" that "add to the lushness of the scene" (Benepe 7).

Of course, the paved neighborhoods of Harlem and Union Square—spaces filled with traffic and rimmed by the Manhattan skyline—are a far cry from the rustic countryside Thoreau preferred. Yet as McPhee demonstrates, encounters with nature's rich colors, flavors, and other sensory associations can occur even in the most urban places. Like the welcome "volunteers" that episodically shoot up in every garden patch, the Greenmarket's carnival of botanic variety seems to spontaneously burst into being on alternating summer days across various New York neighborhoods. And just as Thoreau's bitter indoor apples taste delightful in the crisp open air, the Greenmarket goods—along with visitors themselves—seem dramatically transformed by the venue in which they are situated. Indeed, this quirky heterotopia opens a space within which alternative meanings and values attach to natural objects, and a certain playfulness and generosity emerge in the act of exchange—shifting perceptions in ways that disrupt established conventions of market exchange and, by extension, the naturalized relation between objects and commodity value as such.

This elusive transformational quality is not just characteristic of the Greenmarket space McPhee profiled in 1976; contemporary farmers' markets are commonly recognized as sites of affective intensity where the experience of time and social exchange markedly differ from that of other retail spaces.[14] While product quality and desire to support local, sustainable agriculture are a significant part of the appeal for market-goers, scholars Wendy Parkins and Geoffrey Craig observe that people who patronize these "slow spaces" commonly emphasize their unique atmosphere, quoting visitor responses that highlight experiential qualities ranging from their "community feel" to a sense of the market as "another (and more pleasant) world." They also note subtle behavioral shifts within these spaces: in contrast to other shopping experiences, Parkins and Craig show that people at outdoor farmers' markets are more likely to chat with each other and note "it is rare to see someone in a hurry" (92).[15] In its report on the New York Greenmarket's first year in operation, the Center on the Environment noted a similar phenomenon: "The country like atmosphere and the easy-going manner of the farmers seems to encourage a relaxed attitude on the part of many shoppers. Strangers would find themselves in conversation about the food, the farmers, or any manner of subjects, and friends arranged to rendezvous and shop together. The farmers, delighted to find a generally warm and appreciative crowd of people, returned the good feelings in kind by answering questions, giving cooking advice, and telling anecdotes while weighing purchases" (Benepe 20). As Parkins and Craig reflect, the somewhat "makeshift nature" of these outdoor venues "subtly marks [them] as a different kind of space to inhabit and move around in, where different kinds of social practices from those routinely associated with food shopping are possible." Within this context, they argue, visitor statements like "'There's just a feel about it' can be seen not so much as an imprecise or tentative attempt to capture an affective experience in words as [a reminder] of the depth of sensory contact which people associate with the markets" (92–93).

These experiential dimensions have undoubtedly contributed to the skyrocketing popularity of farmers' markets in the early twenty-first century, as their numbers rose from 1,755 in 1994, to 3,706 in 2004, and then to 8,669 in 2016 according to the USDA's Agricultural Marketing Service (USDA).[16] Yet direct-to-consumer food models are hardly new today—nor were they in 1976 when the Greenmarket program launched in New York City. Before the advent of refrigerated railcars and trucks in the late nineteenth century—and later, the postwar spread of home refrigerator ownership—towns and cities were fed by the surrounding countryside, with goods following the season. This arrangement actually yielded surprising variety in most regions of the United States, with goods picked in the cool morning or evening hours often arriving on local consumers' tables "within a half a day" (Freidberg, *Fresh*; Hess 39). Even the densest urban centers benefitted from these arrangements: New York, of course, sits just across the border from America's fabled "Garden State" of New Jersey. Through the late 1930s, an informal assemblage of pushcart vendors in New York sold produce directly to the public in open-air markets. The system was especially popular in lower-income districts where vendors (the overwhelming majority of whom were recent immigrants) could sell goods on the streets unencumbered by the overhead of rent, utilities, and taxes. Meanwhile, shoppers enjoyed lower prices than those at more established stores: according to Florence Brobeck, a journalist covering the push to eliminate this system beginning in 1936, one could buy sweet peppers and cucumbers for a penny, heads of lettuce for two cents—"all kinds of garden stuff at prices much less than the greengrocers charge." This led Thomas Dwyer, commissioner of the Department of Public Markets, to identify the pushcart markets as "the poor man's market" in 1928 (Bluestone 292). Brobeck also observed that participants in these open-air gatherings were "accustomed to ... a more casual way of buying and selling and the freedom of bargaining," while the decentralized nature of this arrangement gave rise to a colorful mosaic of ethnic and regional items reflecting the diversity of New York residents. Brobeck's profile listed just a small sample of ethnic produce one might encounter strolling through these informal "food bazaars" in 1936: Armenian, Syrian, Turkish, Persian, Swedish, Czech, Chinese, Jewish, and Italian.

Yet those very ethnic and class connotations, coupled with the pushcart system's unregulated, open-air setting, led city authorities to deem them (and, by extension, the "social undesirables" they hosted) as "unsanitary, unhealthy and unsafe" ("War on Pushcarts" 1940). Nor were these changes exclusive to New York: indeed, since the beginning of the twentieth century, outdoor markets had been aggressively dismantled across the United States as partisans of the City Beautiful Movement looked to "sanitize" and efficiently regulate public life. In place of these informal arrangements, New York erected new retail centers that city officials in 1936 characterized as "ultra-modern, efficient, hygienic and convenient" (Brobeck). Daniel Bluestone points out that proposals for eliminating New York pushcarts also redefined the vision and purpose of the street itself as the "exclusive province of smoothly circulating 'traffic'"—a modern ideal that eclipsed earlier social uses of those streets for "political activity, gregarious socializing, and popular amusements" (287). As noted in a 1940 *New York Times* article (ominously titled "War on Pushcarts Pressed by Mayor"), the few remaining produce vendors were now required to get permits and then corralled indoors into large, modern facilities like the Essex Street market. Like lab technicians, these sellers donned white coats, and in a moment that seemed to perfectly stage the decline of face-to-face encounters formerly characterizing the informal outdoor gatherings, Mayor La Guardia's disembodied voice addressed crowds via loudspeaker at the grand opening of this new indoor complex.

But above all, the modernization of food distribution in midcentury America was epitomized by the rise of the supermarket—the odorless, air-conditioned, hypersanitized complex of efficient consumption. These gleaming food centers were some of the heaviest early users of the "streamline moderne" aesthetic—a futuristic, aerodynamic style featuring curved corners, stainless steel, neon lighting, and Art Deco letters (Belasco 175). As Belasco explains, early supermarkets adopted a Taylorized scheme that admitted shoppers through one-way turnstiles where they then wandered through a maze of consumer items to maximize purchases. The trade journal *Progressive Grocer* even referred to the new markets as "scientific food stores" and a "machine" for efficient distribution, specifically laid out to "engineer sales" (*Meals* 174).

The rise of big supermarket chains also went hand-in-hand with the continued growth in corporate agriculture, industrial food processing, and national advertising; indeed, the scale of midcentury supermarkets was key to the very workings of this industrial model, luring shoppers with an unprecedented number of goods and a "one-stop" convenience. The number of supermarkets quadrupled between 1936 and 1946—and that was only the beginning (Freidberg, *Fresh* 185).

Changes on the consumer end of the economy also increased this shift away from direct sales by small local growers. As automobile and refrigerator ownership expanded, more shoppers were able to haul big purchases home and preserve them over longer periods of time, making daily purchases of fresh goods unnecessary. Civic promoters in New Orleans justified the eviction of farmers and distributors from the old French Markets on these very grounds, noting that the traditional practice of buying fresh produce and meat on a daily basis "was no longer viable in an age of automobiles, supermarkets and home freezers" (*New Orleans Statesman*; qtd. in Hess 37). Even the fabled Pike Place Market of Seattle, which dates back to 1907 and emerged as a cause célèbre of small farmers and local food long before the advent of Carlo Petrini and Michael Pollan, went into steep decline in the 1950s and 1960s as Seattleites moved into the suburbs and turned to supermarkets selling long-haul goods from California and Florida (Kamp 277).

Yet perhaps less visible than this overhaul in the consumer economy and urban infrastructure was the changed nature of daily social encounters. Russ Parsons reminds us that prior to the introduction of self-serve grocery stores, shoppers had directly interacted with store clerks who fetched items from behind a counter. Now those customers independently wandered the aisles selecting their own goods—a system that seemed so revolutionary in 1916 that Clarence Saunders's Piggly Wiggly stores received a patent for the system (9). Jim Hightower found this aspect of the modern supermarket just as troubling as its tasteless iceberg lettuce and indestructible ethylene-gassed tomatoes; and after learning the industry's plans in 1975 to begin installing automated scanners and self-checkout systems, he forecast the final death of interactions with grocery clerks that constituted "about the only human touch that remains in today's cavernous supermarkets" (231). Indeed, such developments would seem to make supermarkets virtually indistinguishable from a vending machine, having now eliminated both their spatial *and* social context.

The desire to resocialize and respatialize food, as many scholars have pointed out, thus became a significant factor in the late twentieth-century resurgence of direct-to-consumer markets, with "face-to-face" encounters commonly hailed as a key source of their pleasure—if not *the* "emblematic image"—of the farmers' market (Holloway and Kneafsey 270). Indeed, just a year after Hightower lamented the erosion of spontaneous social encounter in these corporate retail venues, McPhee profiled a dramatically different development in the streets of New York—a growers' market that seemed somehow enchanted by a medley of Fourier-style collisions and comminglings, by a sense of "mesmerism" produced through the "all-day touching of hands" (5). Given postwar trends toward the erosion of public space in the United States—trends that have only accelerated in the decades since—such exchanges offered powerful fuel for unmet desires.

The Greenmarket's social dimensions are arguably the lifeblood of "Giving Good Weight," where a riotous cultural variety vividly contrasts with the standardization and order of midcentury supermarkets. Within the Brooklyn market alone, McPhee identifies what he claims is the most varied human assemblage "anyone is likely to see in one place west of Suez": in a single glance visitors will note "Greeks. Italians. Russians. Finns. Haitians. Puerto Ricans. Nubians. Muslim women in veils of shocking pink. Sunnis in total black. Women in hiking shorts with babies in their backpacks." Across town, the Harlem Greenmarket is animated by activists wearing sandwich boards, someone trying to sell a case of "hot" (stolen) mangoes, a cyclist in yellow racing gloves who pays with food stamps, "men in cool Haspel cords and regimental ties, men in lipstick, men with blue eyelids. Corporate-echelon pinstripe men. Their silvered hair is in perfect coif; it appears to have been audited" (6–7).

This carnival-like scene, admittedly, does not make the Greenmarket a utopia. Pickpockets endlessly prey on shoppers, while shoppers palm extra produce from growers: "crime on such levels is part of the background here," McPhee writes, "something in the urban air, so many parts per million. The condition is accepted with a resignation that approaches nonchalance" (51). Even law-abiding New Yorkers fight viciously over heads of lettuce, and farmers paint honest competitors as frauds and phonies while the real opportunists occasionally cheat the system (and violate the Greenmarket's very mission) by purchasing trucked-in Florida produce from corporate giants to undersell the local growers. Yet on the whole, these episodes only seem to heighten the market's carnivalesque milieu, and the unsavory aspects are ultimately eclipsed by a sense of goodwill and openness between rural growers and urban buyers. Growers take up a cash collection for a customer who is robbed of her entire month's pay while shopping and even throw in a bonus of free fruits and vegetables. One vendor McPhee profiles, Derryck Brooks-Smith (a teacher who spends his summer months working in the Greenmarket), explains his special affection for customers in the Harlem Greenmarket, where fellow black New Yorkers tell him stories about the southern lives they left behind. Here, as Brooks-Smith puts it, he is "among my own people": "They talk about Georgia, about South Carolina. They have a feeling for the farm a lot of people in the city don't have." In turn, McPhee writes, Brooks-Smith shares his knowledge of nutrition and gives minilectures on architecture "in a manner that makes them conclude correctly that he is talking about them":

> He quotes Rimbaud to his customers. He fills up the sky for them with "permanganate sunsets" of Henry Miller.... They bring him things. Books, mainly. Cards of salutation and farewell, anticipating his return to school. "Peace, brother, may you always get back the true kindness you give." The message is handwritten.... He has always given them a little more than good weight. (29)

As that final line suggests, such exchanges represent more than just the goodwill between Greenmarket participants; this urban heterotopia also seems to extend the possibility of transforming perceptions of routine commercial activity itself—a possibility advanced, in part, by the practice of "giving good weight," which becomes a central metaphor for the account. McPhee borrows this phrase from the lexicon of fruit and vegetable vendors, where it literally means to be generous in the sale and dispensation of produce: as one grower remarks, "I give them two pounds always for a pound and a half" (62). Another farmer, Rich Hodson, notes that "[t]hree pounds, as we weigh them out, are anywhere from forty-eight to fifty-two ounces," and tells his vendors not to charge for an extra quarter pound (5). McPhee is hardly the only observer to have highlighted this aspect of the Greenmarket. Soon after its opening, acclaimed food writer Patricia Wells wrote an amused feature for the *New York Times*' "Best Buys" column on a farmer offering "however many shallots one could hold in the palm of the hand" for 75 cents.

This variability—an openness to wander from standardizing metrics in the act of exchange—arises in part from the informality of the Greenmarket. Bargaining, bartering, and gift-giving practices flourish in this space; vendors estimate weights and prices in a playfully offhand manner; the narrator is careless with money and repeatedly errs when making change; and time and again, activities with no clear commercial purpose overshadow the business of buying and selling. In one rather unremarkable moment McPhee becomes so absorbed watching a Harlem pickup game across the street that customers must recall him to his sales task—an exchange that typifies the capricious and elastic nature of this market's conventions:

> "Mister, will you weigh these peppers? Do you want to sell them to me or not?"
> "Sorry. Three and a half pounds. Take them for a dollar." Who wants to make change? (38)

As such, the Greenmarket presents something like a do-it-yourself economy, a space where participants can improvise in the act of exchange—endlessly tinkering with, bending, and reinventing the social and economic conventions comprising their activity. And as those individuals step outside the official "rules" of consumer practice, the very context in which meaning is ascribed to objects also transforms, allowing readers and participants to imagine alternative modes through which natural objects and other everyday items might accrue value and mediate social relations. One grower in McPhee's story enumerates and exalts layers and layers of noncommodity value in his tomatoes, decentering their exchange value as the goods move through his hands and into those of customers. One variety, he explains, comes from a remote corner of Afghanistan and will "send you into ecstasy," while "[t]he smaller ones are from Hunza, a little country in the Himalayas. The people of Hunza attribute their longevity to these tomatoes. Yes, three pounds for a dollar. They also attribute their longevity to yogurt and a friendly family" (28). Within this brief exchange, the grower begins to unpack a vast network of associations carried by the fruit: properties that are sensual, geographic, historic, cultural, and anecdotal; that pertain to health and ritual and regional belief. The commodity aspect, on the other hand, is mentioned primarily as an aside—an interruption, even—and certainly as one of the least interesting attributes of the tomato.

The gardeners' bazaars of the 1970s and today are hardly unique in their capacity to scramble everyday customs of commercial activity, no matter how novel they may seem in contemporary North American cities.[17] As Jackson Lears argues in *Fables of Abundance*, since the rise of Europe's great commercial fairs in the early modern period, market exchange has retained associations with a carnival atmosphere and its activities, "with fantastic and sensuous experience . . . even with the possibility of an almost magical self-transformation through the purchase of exotic artifacts in a fluid, anonymous social setting" (9). Lears reminds us that carnival itself was typically held in the marketplace and that its festivities "commingled with market fairs. References to fairs and Carnivals in the early modern period . . . were often virtually coextensive" (24). Even apart from the presence of carnival activities as such, the marketplace was commonly linked to animistic realms throughout the early modern period, presenting "a mix of the miraculous and the carnivalesque. The events that took place there and the commodities that were sold there . . . provide[d] magical connections between material and spiritual realms" (25). McPhee clearly taps into this tradition across his story, depicting even sober business calculations as games where growers amuse customers like carnival performers at fool-the-guesser booths ("Fantastic! You see that?

You see that? He knew exactly how much it weighed") (5). Meanwhile, the Greenmarket magnetizes additional subcultures of sellers and craftspeople—not the city-licensed vendors who peddle hot dogs from carts but "itinerant merchants of the most mercurial kind," including one man who pulls his old Chevrolet sedan to the curb in Brooklyn to sell Finnish porgies out of his trunk. In cleaning his catch on the street, the man transforms this space into a near-magical scene where the rather unappealing scales scraped from the fish drift through the Greenmarket like stardust or coruscating snowflakes: "Cleaning them, he spilled their innards into a bucket and their scales fell like snow on the street" (36).

Yet the transformative potential of this commingling of commerce and carnival is perhaps best expressed in bargaining and bartering activities themselves, which repeatedly disrupt the self-evident structure of exchange value within the Greenmarket. As Bill Brown points out, bargaining has been progressively eliminated from everyday retail experience in the United States since the nineteenth century, when early department stores standardized the use of fixed prices and thus sidestepped much of the traditional interaction between buyer and seller, narrowing the act of consumerism "to a relation between the consumer and the merchandise" (31). That institutionalized one-price rule also reinforces a sense of inevitability in regard to an object's commodity value in modern retail venues; in fact, it has become so entrenched in modern capitalist culture that everyday attempts to bargain are often viewed as near-deviant acts (participants in a 1970s study of American economic views and behaviors overwhelmingly reported feeling shame and awkwardness when sent into conventional retail settings to bargain; reciprocally, sales associates responded to these norm violations with "anxiety and anger" [Garfinkel 68–70]). Yet as these practices (re)surface in McPhee's bazaar, they help expose the arbitrariness and constructedness of commodity versions of value. While many wonder aloud at how superior the Greenmarket products are and vow never to return to the "unspeakable" produce of supermarkets (11), others complain of being defrauded, challenging sellers in a way that would seem scandalous in conventional retail spaces: "Wow! What a rip-off," or "Three pounds for a dollar is too much for tomatoes. You know that, don't you? I don't care how good they are" (9–10). With the market organized so that value must be reestablished in the context of every new transaction, the naturalized relation between the object and its commodity value becomes increasingly destabilized.[18] Eggs—cheap and utterly identical elsewhere—are meticulously examined here, one at a time, as if each were a distinct, peerless creation: as one Greenmarket farmer complains of these time-consuming inspections, "You'd think they were buying diamonds" (13). And as those objects engage the attention of market-goers on their own incommensurable terms, unhinging themselves from standardized prices and classifications, they more readily form new (and often unexpected) associations. Things that were distant suddenly seem close: homely eggs assume the importance of precious gems, common corn takes on the allure of winning lottery tickets (17). Meanwhile, items conventionally treated as equivalents—so many dollars for so many pounds of produce—become noninterchangeable. In one scene, a man who buys fresh squash refuses a bag filled with inedible coins in its place. After selecting his vegetables at a particularly crowded stand, he is accidentally handed another bag filled with fifty dollars in rolled coins yet amazes the vendor by returning later that day when he discovers the mix-up. Without a trace of self-righteousness—indeed, in a tone conveying his belief that he'd genuinely gotten the bad end of the deal—he returns the money and demands his vegetables: "Hey, this isn't squash! I didn't ask for money. I asked for squash" (55). In the process of unpairing these false equivalences (the very equivalences that overwhelmingly organize relations between people and objects in capitalist society), such exchanges not only scramble established hierarchies of value but also challenge the ascendancy of money itself. Encountered within this vibrant garden space, the Greenmarket objects break from their ontological status as mere inanimate things, activating the fantasies of consumers not sated by surface alone.

As one of the world's iconic capitals of commerce—a global mecca of bankers, Wall Street tycoons, and international trade deals—Manhattan may seem a rather unlikely place to situate this tribute to the soil, let alone reimagine the nature of a money economy that every day reduces a wondrous, multidimensional world of natural forms, use values, human desires, and subjective meanings to a common objective denominator. Indeed, McPhee never quite lets us forget the ubiquitous, nearly gravitational pull of that system, filling his account with icons like "iceberg lettuce crisp as new money," suspicious shoppers who glare at vendors with eyes "narrower than the sides of dimes," customers who dive for sinking coins through towering displays of produce, buyers and sellers, price haggling and petty theft—all of which move to a rhythm set by the constant "pulsations of the needle" on the produce scale (9, 57, 31).

And yet perhaps there is no better place to underscore the garden world's unique power to transform, to remind us that sun, rain, plants, and people who work the soil are our real source of value—not the towering institutions of Wall Street and the empty signifiers in which they trade. Bursting into being across the city on select summer afternoons, these transitory garden markets open a space not only for encountering colorful fruits and foliage, but also for altering the way visitors experience time, social exchange, and the miraculous layering of narrative, memory, and sensory value in everyday natural objects.

There are even moments when the dominant conversion process of capitalism itself seems to be reversed in the Greenmarket—a transmutation that McPhee stages in a single and remarkable moment of selling cabbage. Here, readers are subtly invited to imagine dollars changed back into crisp green leaves—a reverse conversion of money to garden produce, substitute to substance. As patrons buy up his produce, McPhee is plunged into a nonstop flurry of stripping the outermost leaves from cabbage heads (straight from the field, they are too big to fit in customers' baskets), and after a long morning of tendering dollars and coins and hastily stuffing the extra leaves wherever he can, he finds himself digging in his apron for some bills to change a twenty: but "all [he] come[s] up with is cabbage" (27).

Such fleeting impressions may have seemed reason enough for McPhee to tell the Greenmarket story, to invite us to imagine a realm where nature is more than a product for sale and value is more than a numeral. And the moment his growers box up their melons and berries and leafy green goods, the streets return to business as usual, leaving readers to reflect on the powerful role of these soil-based foods and spaces in triggering such visions in the first place. Indeed, it is hard to imagine another site that could produce quite the same effect, reminding us, once again, of the profound ways in which garden fantasy is implicated and intertwined with desires to experience the natural world—and one another—as a source of value that no scale or currency can accurately represent, desires that, as McPhee himself put it, simply "go right off the scale" (5).

CHAPTER 4

Against the Grain

Reinventing the Garden in Contemporary Utopia

> The more people have of new plants, and the more they delight in them, the happier and the better they will be; we will let them into Kew Gardens unwatched, and yet not a leaf is rifled; . . . and we make for them parks and gardens, where they may walk unrestrained and roll upon the grass even, and bask in the sunshine, and revel in pure air. And what is the consequence of this? We must condense the reply into one sentence—We have had no Revolution.
> —Anonymous (1854)

> After several months of tending, your garden will be ready for harvest. Why not invite friends and neighbors to share your first home-grown meal? You can turn it into an event, share your stories of guerrilla gardening exploits, show them before and after photographs, and eventually turn the conversation to abolishing capitalism.
> —*We Are Everywhere: The Irresistible Rise of Global Anti-Capitalism* (2003)

Most readers who pick up works of science fiction hardly do so looking for gardening wisdom. This is the genre, after all, that launches us out of the old world and into new ones, a literary niche filled with futuristic adventure, exciting space travel episodes, and of course lots of flashy high-tech gadgetry. Yet while these more conventional elements may indeed be standards of science fiction writing, one can also find a rich landscape of garden representation here, one that reveals some surprising developments in contemporary fantasies about social and political change, the right to the city, environmental activism, and daily life as a site of revolt.

One of the most striking examples of gardening's unexpected presence in science fiction appears in Kim Stanley Robinson's award-winning *Mars* trilogy (1993–96), a series whose meticulous focus on the creation of a more egalitarian society has made it a landmark in contemporary utopian literature. Robinson's narrative spans nearly two centuries to chronicle the settlement and terraforming of Mars through the viewpoints of a wide variety of characters. The story opens with a voyage to the sister planet, and it is during this long interplanetary commute that we are first introduced to the colonists as they debate the shape and nature of the sociopolitical order they hope to create. And yet during these critical moments—when key alliances are formed and ideological battles are waged over everything from property relations to the rights of nature to social implications in architectural design—chief botanist Hiroko Ai and her horticultural crew are, conspicuously, absent. Completely absorbed in their gardening, off "in a realm that had nothing to do with the rest of the ship" and its endless social debates, the gardeners have seemingly left the details of humanity's future to their more politically minded crewmates (*Red* 65). It comes as a bit of a surprise, then, when the botany team suddenly disappears from the base on Mars (and from the narrative itself) just a few months into the colonization process; and even more startling is the moment of their resurfacing at the end of the first novel, when we learn that these supposedly "apolitical" gardeners have secretly constructed an underground insurgent movement and have, in fact, plotted from the very outset to break away from fellow colonists and forge an even more radical social alternative.

The surprise element, of course, plays off of our lingering associations of gardening with the apolitical, escapist, and compensatory. Even seasoned garden writer Michael Pollan admits that he originally came to gardening—the very apotheosis of "the hobby"—"in the naïve belief it offered a fairly benign way to kill an afternoon" ("Introduction" vii). This association can be found everywhere. The very humor of Jerzy Kosinski's novel *Being There* (along with its 1979 filmic adaptation starring Peter Sellers) proceeds from the absurdity of a *gardener* inadvertently finding himself at the hub of American politics and ultimately becoming a presidential adviser. Two decades later in *The Constant Gardener* (2001), John le Carré used gardening as a device to signal the absence of political impulses: the hero of his political thriller, a fiery social-justice activist more concerned with helping people than tending her neglected and underwatered houseplants, uncovers a global pharmaceutical conspiracy, while her unwitting doormat of a husband (described in the book's marketing literature as a "complacent raiser of freesias") tinkers away in his garden plot, oblivious to the political corruption intensifying poverty and exploitation in Nairobi ("Amazon"). Humanities scholars also play off of this association, whether examining how gardens in historical novels "articulate [the] desire for withdrawal from civil strife" (Boccardi 6) or arguing, as historian Keith Thomas does, that the "preoccupation with gardening" may help "explain the relative lack of radical and political impulses among the

British proletariat" (240). Even—or perhaps especially—when tackling the most pressing social issues of our age, gardens are used as a political foil. In forecasting the devastating effects of climate change and global capitalism, Naomi Klein paints a terrifying picture of megadroughts and fires, floods, famine, climate refugees, and whole coastal communities swallowed by the sea, noting that such a future is inevitable if we persist in our present inaction, complacently "counting on a techno-fix or tending to our gardens" (4).

Yet despite the prevalence of these escapist and apolitical associations, such traditional formulations sharply contradict representations of gardening that have emerged within science fiction and utopian literature since the 1990s. From that opening reversal in the *Mars* trilogy to gardener-led insurgencies in Margaret Atwood's *Year of the Flood* and Marge Piercy's *He, She, and It*; from the postapocalyptic gardens established by the rebel Earthseed community in Octavia Butler's *Parable of the Sower* series to real-life urban coalitions like New York's "Green Guerrillas"; and from street growers in South Central Los Angeles playing up their "gangster" credentials to manifestos linking community gardening to "the rebel Zapatista movement" (Weinberg 45), depictions of gardening have taken a decidedly rebellious and anarchic turn. Of course, many of the literary works already explored in this book have also challenged conventional assumptions about gardens from their own time—whether imagining the garden as a figure of resistance to nineteenth-century divisions of labor, or to the abstractions of American agribusiness, or to capitalism's commodity logic. Yet contemporary writers, growers, and activists take up the question of politics and social change much more explicitly, extinguishing all lingering notions about the garden as a sanctuary from historical change or engaged political action. One need only consider Peter Lamborn Wilson's manifesto "Avant Gardening" (1999) to appreciate the force of this figurative reversal:

> Voltaire's cynical advice in *Candide*—"Cultivate your own garden"—can no longer be considered simply an amoral *bon mot*. The world has changed considerably since the Enlightenment. Meanings have shifted. "Cultivate your own garden" sounds more today like hot radical rhetoric. Growing a garden has become—at least potentially—an act of resistance. But it's not simply a gesture of refusal. It's a positive act. It's praxis. (9–10)

How is it, then, that something as innocuous as the garden—the supposed retreat of middle-aged suburbanites fussing over color schemes in petunia borders—has become a symbol for radical political resistance?

This chapter explores that question by looking at broad historical developments in utopian literary production, environmental thinking, and urban social-justice movements. We begin by tracking the evolution of garden representation in classical utopias, where these spaces served to suspend time in an unchanging, frozen state. As these literary formulations gradually moved from an emphasis on utopia as a final product toward the *process* and *unfolding* of utopia itself, they increasingly reframed the garden as a dynamic social practice as well, one that actively engages us in the perpetual remaking of our world. Garden representation also shifted alongside utopian literature's pedagogical function, which progressively came to serve less as an instructive blueprint for social change and more as an agent for activating *desires* that expose present structural failures and injustices.

The adoption of gardening as a symbol of political opposition also sheds light on broader trends that have reclaimed utopian representation from some distant time or place (the remote future or an isolated realm in the mythical past) toward more immediate forms of action. Among other things, the imminence of our current environmental crisis has heightened the urgency for change in the here and now. Consequently, while its broader impact may remain vastly inadequate to the scale of the problem, gardening's relative immediacy and ease of access give it a distinct appeal within the purview of everyday life; no scientific or policy expertise is needed here—only access to a few tools, seeds, and a small patch of dirt (authorized or no). Finally, the more radical profile of gardening practice becomes especially manifest in contemporary cities. While urban and pastoral modes historically were seen to be fundamentally at odds, today that antagonism has been remapped onto contradictions between dominant and differential space—between spaces that invite users to participate in shaping their social environments, and those that foreclose such open-ended, democratic interventions. Rather than fleeing to the countryside, then, community and guerilla gardeners directly engage the city's spatial regime, seizing those small gaps and fissures in the dominant order to experiment, appropriate, and selectively reject or reshape existing structures.

And so the classical garden utopia—timeless, immutable, at rest—is shattered by new modes that emphasize the process of fabrication and becoming over that of any fixed or finished object. For those clinging to the older literary and mythical associations, this may render the very notion of "paradise" unrecognizable; and yet, paradoxically, we might also argue that this shake-up signals the most quintessentially utopian phase of all for garden fantasy, making it available to the very process of transformation, reinvention, and reorganization at the heart of the utopian enterprise as such.

Gardening in Utopia: From Product to Process

> And the LORD God planted a garden eastward in Eden; and there he put the man whom he had formed. And out of the ground made the LORD God to grow every tree that is pleasant to the sight, and good for food.
> —Genesis 2:8–9

> [It's] a holy greening power we call viriditas, the driving force of the cosmos.... Because we are alive, the universe must be said to be alive. We are its consciousness as well as our own. We rise out of the cosmos and we see its mesh patterns and it strikes us as beautiful.... Our task in this world is to do everything we can to foster it. And one way to do that is to spread life everywhere. To aid it into existence where it was not before, as here on Mars.
> —Hiroko Ai, head botanist in Kim Stanley Robinson's *Green Mars* (1994)

The connections between gardens, utopian dreaming, and mythical expressions of fantasy are ancient and deeply intertwined. Long before Thomas More inaugurated the modern genre of utopian literature in 1516, gardens were inseparable from the idea of paradise. In both Judeo-Christian mythology and the beliefs of Islam, the Garden of Eden was the realm of earthly perfection, and similar versions of idealized gardens can be found across world cultures and historical periods, from the sacred gardens of various ancient Near Eastern civilizations to Greco-Roman beliefs in a lost Golden Age and Classical accounts of the Elysian Fields and the Isles of the Blessed. Historian Richard Heinberg cites evidence of the garden paradise as origin or destination in religions, cosmologies, and myths spanning ancient Mesopotamia, Iran, India, Egypt, China, Australia, North America, and Africa (49–54). Indeed, the English word "paradise" itself derives from the Persian term *pairidaeza*, a walled enclosure (from *pairi-*, "around," and *diz*, "to create, make").[1] Classical Persian gardens were arranged within those walls to evoke the four parts of the world, and many depictions of the Garden of Eden (originally named in the Septuagint with the Greek word *paradeisos*) share this basic arrangement as well.

In Western literature, even when fantasies of the ideal realm shifted from religion and myth to more humanist accounts (in short, when the otherworldly "paradise" became the human and political construct "utopia"), gardens lost little of their revered status. In his original *Utopia* (1516), Thomas More imagined a garden in the home of every townsperson, including

> both vines, fruits, herbs and flowers in [it]; and all is so well ordered and so finely kept, that [one] never saw gardens anywhere that were both so fruitful and so beautiful as theirs.... [T]here is, indeed, nothing belonging to the whole town that is both more useful and more pleasant. (32)

FIGURE 9. Map of Utopia by Ambrosius Holbein, printed in Thomas More's 1518 edition of *Utopia*. Courtesy of Princeton University Library, Rare Books and Special Collections.

In fact, our narrator and tour guide in *Utopia*, Raphael Hythloday, takes great pains to ensure that we recognize this place as mild, fertile, domesticated—in short, as gardenlike—by first conducting us through a brief tour of the desolate country surrounding it. Before arriving at the fabled island of Utopia, readers are made to traverse desert lands "parched by the perpetual heat of the sun" where "the soil was withered, all things looked dismally, and all places were either quite uninhabited, or abounded with wild beasts and serpents." Yet as Hythloday draws nearer to Utopia, the geography shifts entirely: "a new scene opened, all things grew milder, the air less burning, the soil more verdant, and even the beasts were less wild" (3).

Yet this lushly cultivated gardenland is more than just a defining feature of Utopia's geography; more importantly, "cultivation" is closely linked to the society's notion of citizenship and civilization as such. While Utopian citizens "cultivate their gardens with great care," receiving agricultural instruction from childhood on (each member spends at least two years farming in the countryside), the fierce and uncivilized Zapolet people inhabiting surrounding regions know nothing of cultivation, living "either by hunting or upon rapine" (32–33, 67). Through this juxtaposition, the non-Utopian—hunter, nomad, savage, slayer of animals—supplies the qualities against which Utopian citizenship and identity are defined: cultivator, settled, civilized, humane.[2] Indeed, the very meaning of cultivation emerges as inseparable from notions of civilization, with "culture" in its earliest use denoting the activity of caring for crops (Williams, *Keywords* 77). Beginning in the early sixteenth century, the tending of plant life extended metaphorically to a process of human (mental or spiritual) improvement and growth. More's *Utopia* is among the earliest-cited texts to use culture as a figure for human development: in one passage Hythloday explains that the citizens of Utopia are allowed as much time as necessary for "the culture and profit of their minds" (Williams 77).[3] This foundational text in the utopian genre thus helped solidify the very link between cultivation (gardening) and what came to represent the higher expression of human potential (capital-C "Culture"). Indeed, this island's own creation story uses cultivation (both personal and soil-based) to explicitly underscore the vast distance between the civilized and the savage: Utopia's ancestral race, More writes, was originally made up of "rude and uncivilized inhabitants" (much like their present Zapolet neighbors). Only gradually are they made "civil" by the founder, Utopus. Surely, then, it is no coincidence that one of the few details Hythloday provides about this enigmatic forefather is that "he who founded the town seems to have taken care of nothing more than of their gardens" (28, 32). To be Utopian (and thus to count as civilized) is necessarily to be a gardener or farmer, a settled cultivator of the soil rather than a nomad following beasts of the hunt.

However, the timeless, restful and unchanging gardens of Utopia—as well as those of traditional world religions and mythologies—are a far cry from the radicalized garden depictions in recent utopian literature and science fiction. And that disparity directly reflects the relatively frozen social orders and isolated geographies of those early traditional accounts. As geographer David Harvey has argued, the perfect society in More's *Utopia* is established through the act of creating an island—an isolated and self-contained geography that "strictly regulates a stabilized and unchanging social process." This foundational gesture immobilizes the dynamic nature of politics and history within an ideal and fixed social order, where "time's arrow ... is excluded in favor of perpetuating a happy stationary state" (*Spaces* 160). The archetypal garden paradise thus offered an ideal template for utopian society, with its *enclosed space* freezing time within the endlessly recurring cycles of nature.

Yet as utopian representation developed into its modern form, this temporal feature underwent a crucial shift: beginning in the late nineteenth century, utopian narratives began to include accounts of the historical process that had brought about their respective societies. Raymond Williams, E. P. Thompson, and Miguel Abensour all identify William Morris's *News from Nowhere* (1890) as a landmark in this generic shift, a distinction the novel earns through its "crucial insertion of the *transition* to utopia, which is not discovered, come across, or projected ... but fought for" (Williams, *Problems* 204). In this way, the traditional "blueprint" utopias—detailed and totalizing schemes depicting an alternative organizational model—gave way to "heuristic utopias": narratives that focused more directly on the pedagogy of desire and the process of social transition itself (Thompson, "Romanticism" 96).

Initially, that shift from blueprint to process continued to frame the physical world in the traditional way: the primary purpose of space and place was to furnish the "stage" or backdrop against which more primary actions unfolded. Of course, within Western literature more generally, this hierarchy has long been reflected in the prioritization of character and plot development over "setting."[4] Even while utopian narratives like *News from Nowhere* or Charlotte Perkins Gilman's *Herland* (1915) relate the historical events that bring their physical worlds into being, the reader only learns of these spatial transformations indirectly, through the recollection of characters who participated in a revolution or preserved its history for posterity. The *space* of utopia we encounter here already exists in a state of relative completion.

Since the 1990s, however, utopia has undergone a second major transformation, with the genre increasingly approaching space itself as a complex and dynamic social construction. And in this turn from "things in space" to the actual *production* of space, the idea of garden as noun has likewise been succeeded by garden as verb in much literary representation. Indeed, the inherently dynamic nature of gardening makes it a useful figure in highlighting the constructed nature of space, in imagining its role as a medium or force rather than just a thing, and in comprehending how space both shapes possibilities of human action and is, in turn, shaped by them. Moreover, the relative ease of access to gardening (as opposed to, say, utopian productions involving large-scale urban and architectural planning) also makes this a favored site for exploring how everyday practice creates patterns and meanings in lived social space.

This "spatial turn" in utopian representation and praxis, I argue, largely emerges from broader trends in twentieth-century critical theory and philosophy, most prominently formulated in Henri Lefebvre's Marxist analysis of everyday life, *The Production of Space* (1974). As Lefebvre asserts, "(social) space is a (social) product," and thus the space we produce and inhabit "also serves as a tool of thought and of action; in addition to being a means of production it is also a means of control, and hence of domination, of power" (26). Whether we are dealing with the permeation of technology in our daily lives, the distribution of wealth, environmental crisis, inequality, political and social oppression, or geopolitical conflict, we can no longer escape awareness of their "embracing spatialities," which political geographers like Edward Soja have mapped across contemporary lifeworlds at all scales, from the intimate spaces of our own bodies to vast global networks. Indeed, Soja reminds us that our social reality does not just coincidentally take place "in" space: "it is presuppositionally and ontologically spatial. *There is no unspatialized social reality*" (1, 46). Yet the influence of space in everyday life is hardly self-evident: indeed, Lefebvre's pioneering work remained largely overlooked until the 1990s, and he himself acknowledged the extent to which the premise of his inquiry seemed counterintuitive, noting that "[t]o speak of 'producing space' sounds bizarre, so great is the sway still held by the idea that empty space is prior to whatever ends up filling it" (15). Philosopher Michel Foucault also recognized this conceptual blind spot, pointing out that for much of the nineteenth and early twentieth centuries, not the spatial but the social and historical had been the primary objects of critical and philosophical inquiry: as he put it, "The great obsession of the nineteenth century was, as we know, history: with its themes of development and of suspension, of crisis and cycle, themes of the ever accumulating past, with its great preponderance of dead men and the menacing glaciation of the world" (22). Meanwhile, geography remained frozen into the background as the theater or container of action.

Yet as Lefebvre asserts, "space is neither a mere 'frame' . . . nor a form or container of a virtually neutral kind, designed simply to receive whatever is poured into it. Space is social morphology: it is to lived experience what form itself is to the living organism, and just as intimately bound up with function and structure" (93–94).

Within U.S. utopian fiction, this critical reorientation is especially visible between 1970 and 1990; indeed, we even see the shift when comparing novels from a single author bridging those two periods. In *Woman on the Edge of Time* (1976), for example, Marge Piercy explores the relationship between the present and a number of contending futures by way of a psychic time-traveler, Connie Ramos. Although Piercy constructs an intricate relation between the present and what is yet to come—a future that is always in flux and moving in many directions rather than along a simple linear track—the novel's various historical moments nonetheless occupy the same geographical region. The factor that makes all the narrative difference, as the title suggests, is time. Yet fifteen years later, her novel *He, She, and It* (1991) uses a landscape of fractal microgeographies to juxtapose a number of simultaneously existing worlds (utopias, dystopias, heterotopias) that are sharply differentiated (wealthy and insulated corporate enclaves, impoverished global slums, gang turfs, potentially revolutionary pockets within the megalopolis, free towns on the margins, and an underground feminist coalition waiting to emerge from a network of caves in the Middle East). Like Piercy's earlier novel, this latter work also alternates between two historical moments (near-future North America and seventeenth-century Prague); yet in *He, She, and It*, those twin narratives are now wholly analogous and could easily be uncoupled into two independent and self-contained stories. They are repetitions, recurrences, detachable parts endlessly reproduced by the same dynamic of uneven geographical development, without being necessarily intertwined at the linear level of the novel's plot.

In addition to being organized around these differential geographies, late twentieth- and early twenty-first-century utopias also pay meticulous attention to their production, maintenance, reproduction, and transformation. In *Archaeologies of the Future* (2005), literary theorist Frederic Jameson identifies contemporary utopian literature as "no longer the exhibit of an achieved Utopian construct, but rather the story of its production and the very process of construction as such" (217). Some of the most vivid examples of this shift can be seen in representations of "terraforming" in science fiction. Terraforming practices—the large-scale, coordinated transformation of planetary geographies, including aquatic and climactic features—figure prominently in both Ursula Le Guin's 1974 novel *The Dispossessed* and in Robinson's *Mars* trilogy (1993–96). Yet at the opening of Le Guin's work, this process has, for the most part, already occurred: we come to Le Guin's fictional planet of Anarres to find forests already planted, town and road construction completed, irrigation systems in place, and agricultural valleys fully developed. Whatever ongoing spatial transformations do continue in the present moment occur more or less at the periphery. That relatively completed stage thus provides a ready-made arena within which another set of "actions" can occur—an arrangement highly fitting for a story whose key protagonist is working within the field of temporal physics.[5] Yet when we skip forward to Robinson's novels twenty years later, the *process* of world building now comprises the centerpiece of narrative action. Indeed, the *Mars* narrative begins at a much earlier moment in the process of creating utopia, and from that point forward the material world remains endlessly under construction. From the initial phase of colonization, through the revolutions and intervening years, and up to the final scenes of the trilogy some two thousand pages later, Robinson meticulously details a material world being constructed, redesigned, and rebuilt: atmospheric domes are raised and beneath them whole cities are erected, only later to be submerged by oceans engineered by humans; meanwhile, the entire Martian surface is geothermally altered, split open, mined, liquefied, filled in, and shored up.

What makes Robinson's work especially relevant to our present discussion is his use of gardening itself as a shorthand for that terraforming process, a concrete metaphor for (utopian) world building as such. This horticultural analogy emerges in a rather epiphanic moment in the second novel (*Blue Mars*), where a major character—the scientist Sax Russell—tours a seeming "wilderness of rock" on the colossal massif outside the Martian city of Sabishii. Sax reflexively assumes this to be an abiological world, characterized solely by a "museum of rockscapes," "regolith," "ejecta," "rimless craters," "etched mesas," and other nonliving features. Yet as the scientist gradually adjusts his vision, the scene fundamentally transforms: "the closer he looked, the more he saw; and then, in one high basin, it seemed there were plants tucked everywhere." Upon learning that in fact the whole basin has been meticulously cultivated by hand, the soil engineered and imported, and the plant life expertly tailored to its environment, Sax wonders aloud: "These are gardens, then" (86–89).

Here, given the tremendous upheavals and transformations of the Martian environment, to invoke the figure of the garden is to dislocate it entirely from those deeply entrenched historical associations of permanence and invariability; in their place, Robinson's gardens appear as something radically processual and historical. The significance of recoding the garden's meaning in this scene is further emphasized by way of a familiar formal device. We know that Sax's epiphany here is quite deliberately meant to be read as a quintessential "utopian" moment since it is embedded in one of the genre's most distinctive conventions: the guided tour. Typically, the tourist would be a visitor from elsewhere, allowing them to relate observations back to readers from an outsider's perspective. Sax, however, is no visitor to Mars. In fact, as an original colonist, his tenure on the planet far exceeds that of his guides in this scene. Yet in this manner, the *Mars* narrative more fully avails itself of the utopian genre's unique ability to educate through estrangement, to make a recognizable subject seem unfamiliar.[6] As literary scholars often point out, one of the primary pedagogical roles of science fiction/utopia is to help readers rethink the spaces they *already* inhabit (Wegner 17): from the "no-place" of utopia, as Paul Ricoeur puts it, "an exterior glance [can be] cast on our reality, which suddenly looks strange, nothing more being taken for granted" (16). Sax's garden tour, then, is staged as an utterly self-reflexive moment that invites readers to reimagine our conventional associations between gardens and utopia. Indeed, this passage is packed with images of refocusing, reclassifying, and reidentification as Sax begins to note the evidence of cultivated plant life all around him: "one had to look for it"; "once attuned to the pale living colors ... they began to jump out," and so forth (87). Sax even finds himself reading up on the etymology of the word *garden:* "French, Teutonic, Old Norse, *gard*, enclosure. Seemed to share origins with *guard*, or keeping" (90). Yet not only does this staging explicitly call attention to the act of reevaluating old meanings; Robinson also seems intent on prompting those who subscribe to dualistic Western notions of the nature/culture split to think carefully about the figure of the garden. Relaying this conceptual shift through the character of Sax is no accident: when readers first encounter him in the opening debates of *Red Mars*, Sax serves as the group's hardline defender of an absolute division between nature and culture (the very intersection where gardens reside, of course), adamant in insisting that their only legitimate business on Mars is to conduct objective research on physical phenomena. As he reminds his fellow colonists, "We're a *scientific* station," and so the mission "doesn't have much politics to it" (60). In taking such a position, Sax establishes himself as the novel's most devoted adherent to the "Modern Constitution"—a distinctly Western worldview that philosopher Bruno Latour describes as rigidly dividing political spokespersons, who "represent the quarrelsome and calculating multitude of citizens," from scientific spokespersons, who represent nature, "the mute and material multitude of objects" (29). Because Sax subscribes to this exclusive division in knowledge, he struggles to make sense of the gardened landscapes outside Sabishii, explaining to his guide that he's "used to thinking of Mars as a kind of wilderness" (*Blue Mars* 89). This category distinction is pivotal, since regarding Mars as a wilderness (as the radically *nonhuman,* in the original sense of this term) designates it as a place unmarked by labor, history, social relations, and material exchange between human and nonhuman nature.[7] The wilderness label, in short, identifies this world with everything the garden is *not*. Discovering Mars as a garden thus frustrates Sax's habit of bracketing off nature from culture, or science from politics. And yet owing to its messy, mixed-up character—its integration of science, politics, art, nature, technology, and more—the garden ultimately supplies a kind of bridge by which Sax can finally think his way across two seemingly irreconcilable domains: the natural world of facts and the social world of subjects. This epiphany also allows him to recognize the limitations of his dualistic, Cartesian worldview as he observes how gardeners engaging the same natural-social terrain around Sabishii experience it not as an object for dispassionate, rational analysis but rather as "an aesthetic journey, filled with allusion and subtle variants of tradition that were invisible to him" (89).

Ultimately, these shifts in perspective open a space in which more utopian modes of production, world building, and environmental practice can be imagined in the *Mars* trilogy. Granted, terraforming does not automatically constitute a utopian practice in and of itself. Indeed, the process has already been underway long before colonists (including Sax) liberate themselves from the grip of corporate exploitation and its militarized enforcement. Yet insofar as Mars colonists increasingly come to associate their terraforming practice with gardening, their world-building project evolves into an entirely new form, gradually emerging as a kind of "third term" that would replace the two dominant modes of production preceding it in the narrative: on one hand, the noninterventionist philosophy of the "Reds" (Mars' counterpart to something like deep ecology back on Earth) and, on the other hand, the ruthless capitalist practices of the metanationals, which regard both land and labor in instrumental terms and devastate both in their endless drive for accumulation. So even while Sax finally recognizes that this new world is not "a wilderness," his guide also reminds him that its production and cultivation is not "powered by heavy industrial global methods" either, but rather "by the slow, steady, and intensely local process of working on individual patches of land" (89). Thus, pairing the book's prototypical "utopian moment" with a series of garden tropes is hardly accidental; indeed, the analogy provides a way of thinking about production that avoids both the exclusive and alienating idea of the wilderness as well as the equally alienating reality of treating Mars as a mere collection of social and material resources to be plundered for profit. As Robinson's gardeners perform their work, they remain mindful of the singularity of this living geography and "follow the inclination of the land," drawing on both the legacy of great cultivators and "develop[ing] visions of their own" (88–89). Ultimately, so transformed is this new model of production that Robinson's colonists coin an entirely new expression for their work: no longer terraformation but "areoformation" (from the Greek name for Mars, Ares), a democratic, self-managed, and ecologically reciprocal process, "a human-Mars interface that does justice to both" (*Blue* 89). As Robinson puts it in *Green Mars*,

> Life is tough and adaptable; it is the green force viriditas, pushing into the universe.... [O]ut on the cold surface new plants spread over the flanks of the glaciers, and down into the warm low basins, a slow inexorable surge. Of course all the genetic templates for our new biota are Terran; the minds designing them are Terran; but the Terrain is Martian. And terrain is a powerful genetic engineer, determining what flourishes and what doesn't, pushing along progressive differentiation, and thus the evolution of new species. And as the generations pass, all the members of a biosphere evolve together, adapting to their terrain in a complex communal response, a creative self-designing ability.... And eventually the designers' minds, along with everything else, have been forever changed.
> This is the process of areoformation. (2–3)

As an open-ended *epoch of production*, this garden world could hardly be farther from earlier utopian visions like William Morris's, where the narrator of *News from Nowhere* (1890) sleeps through the entire transformation of society, only to wake 150 years later to a ready-made, gardenlike England that has settled into "An Epoch of Rest" (the alternative title Morris used for the original edition of his book). Indeed, the older and newer generations in Robinson's narrative struggle to find a common point of reference in comprehending the massive transformative role settlers now play in cocreating their world, helping transform lifeless glaciers into ocean habitats and rockscapes into gardens and forests. Marveling at this process, the Earth-born cosmonaut Maya tries in vain to impress the new generations with the magnitude of their efforts and effects, insisting there had "never been any project anything like this on Earth." Her Martian counterparts, however, are hardly awed by the scale of their labor or the contribution each of them makes to that collective vision of the good life: "It was their work, their life—to them it *was* human scale, there was nothing unnatural about it." Within the emerging utopia on Mars, simply enough, "human work consisted of pharaonic projects like this" (*Green* 475).

Gardens in the Critical Dystopia

> Oh sing we now the Holy Weeds
> That flourish in the ditch,
> For they are for the meek in needs,
> They are not for the rich.
>
> You cannot buy them at the mall,
> Nor at the superstore,
> They are despised because they all
> Grow freely for the poor.
> —"The God's Gardeners Oral Hymnbook," in Atwood,
> *The Year of the Flood* (2009)
>
> Enjoy Park Greenery, City Says, but Not as Salad
> —*New York Times* headline (2011)

For every such garden blooming in utopia, a shadowy counterpart can also be found pushing through the rubble of dystopia, where dark visions of the future point back to present environmental issues and the urgency of social and ecological renewal. Unlike traditional religious and secular narratives that imagine paradise as either origin or destination, this strain of garden fantasy calls on us to reclaim a better world in the here and now, while playing on desires to move from a destructive role to one where humanity might act as earth's caretakers and restorationists. In addition, much of the nature fantasy in contemporary dystopian literature calls into question historically preferred garden modes like the picturesque, the "landscape garden," and other aesthetic traditions that have evoked paradise by concealing the labor (and very existence) of workers who create and maintain those spaces. Many dystopian writers seek to restore this visibility while also acknowledging nature's agency and collaboration in all acts of natural production. Finally, within dystopia's bleak and repressive context, gardens open a space for alternative structures of feeling, activating transgressive desires that can ultimately trigger acts of rebellion against the dominant order.

Gardens play an especially prominent role in the "critical dystopia," a reformulated genre that emerged in response to the conservative resurgence of the 1980s and 1990s. As utopian scholars Tom Moylan and Raffaella Baccolini point out, classic twentieth-century dystopias tended to imagine societies controlled by an all-powerful state (*Brave New World, 1984, Fahrenheit 451*, and the like), generally directing their critique at technology or government as such. In contrast, the more recent critical dystopias focus on the devastations of global capitalism. Moreover, where traditional dystopias are often defined by a near-paralyzing pessimism, the new generation tends to preserve a utopian core, "a locus of hope that contributes to deconstructing tradition and reconstructing alternatives" (Baccolini 13). As such, Moylan argues that the critical dystopia marks "a significant retrieval and refunctioning of the most progressive possibilities inherent in dystopian narrative" (188).

At first glance, readers of these works seem to find themselves in the familiar landscapes of dystopian hopelessness: Octavia Butler's *Parable of the Sower* (1993) opens in torched neighborhoods with "rugged, unwalled houses ... broken asphalt and rag and stick shacks of squatters and street poor" (110), while the "glop" of Marge Piercy's *He, She, and It* (1993) is "a crowded violent festering warren of the half-starved" where the unfortunate masses huddle at night in "filthy decaying passages" amidst "running sewage" and "muffled screams" (6, 31–32). Yet these same scenes are also dotted with subversive pocket geographies, reminding us of the vital ways that even small acts of resistance prevent the total saturation of state, military, or corporate oppression—not to mention paralyzing despair. Geography thus remains central to the critical dystopia's more (cautiously) hopeful orientation, with this patchwork of alternative holdouts and enclaves preserving some possibility of resistance. Garden fantasy thus finds good soil where it may flourish in these interstitial spaces. In Kim Stanley Robinson's *Three Californias Trilogy* (1984–90), survivors of nuclear war are partly sustained by gardening while rebuilding what becomes a utopian society in the final installment (*Pacific Edge*); in *He, She, and It*, the courtyard garden of a central character—the freedom fighter Malka—stands as the spatial and symbolic nerve center of the novel's beleaguered utopian holdout; and gardens offer a vital figure for survival, resistance, and redemption in Butler's *Parable* series. In opening *Parable of the Sower*, Butler introduces a multiracial enclave featuring gardens and orchards that enable the neighborhood to produce most of its own food (a vital survival activity rather than a quaint pastime here, since movement beyond the community walls is tantamount to suicide). Here in the gardens, future revolutionary leader Laura Olamina develops her "Earthseed" philosophy, and as she prepares for the inevitable raid that will wipe out her increasingly embattled neighborhood, she packs a survival kit including "a lot of plantable raw seed." In Butler's second volume, *Parable of the Talents*, this seed material enables a small group of survivors to start over by rebuilding a small sustainable community on the rubble of their devastated world. Indeed, the ultimate goal of Laura's Earthseed philosophy is to transform humanity into a species of intergalactic gardeners who will "scatter the Earth's living essence—human, plant, and animal—to extrasolar worlds" (*Talents* 46).

Yet arguably gardening takes its most prominent role in Margaret Atwood's critical dystopia, *The Year of the Flood* (2009), which puts a contemporary spin on humanity's fall from Eden by expanding signature trends of the Anthropocene—climate change, pervasive environmental pollution, and mass extinction—into a terrifying near-future context. In addition to visions of environmental devastation, Atwood depicts the utter collapse of public life, which allows a private security corporation (CorpSeCorps) to replace all semblance of democratic government. Like Butler, Piercy, and other dystopian contemporaries, Atwood presents a future that merely magnifies present social conditions, with the wealthy and well-connected living in guarded compounds while the rest of humanity fights for survival in the polluted "pleeblands" beyond. Yet amidst this toxic decay, an underground band known as "God's Gardeners" works to preserve and restore small pockets of the green world—along with cooperative social life itself—in vacant buildings, rooftops, and abandoned lots. Far from existing in some pregiven state of paradise, these garden utopias must be hacked out of a ruined landscape at great effort, a scenario that resituates the agency for producing apocalypse—and restoring paradise—squarely within human hands.

The Year of the Flood takes place in the aftermath of a viral pandemic released by a lone bioengineer to "cleanse" the world of its human scourge, relating prepandemic events through the flashbacks of a tiny handful of survivors. One of these perspectives is provided by Toby, a woman who flees her wage-slave job in the years before the plague to join the Gardeners. Like the patchwork gardens they cultivate to provide food and green spaces for life to flourish, the Gardeners' philosophy also has a mosaic quality, combining evolutionary and ecological principles with permaculture practice, tropes from Genesis and Apocalypse, and elements from various religious myths of the Great Flood. Upon first arriving in their midst, Toby invokes familiar tropes of Eden and paradise to describe the rooftop sanctuary they've established:

> Toby . . . gazed around it in wonder: it was so beautiful, with plants and flowers of many kinds she'd never seen before. There were vivid butterflies; from nearby came the vibration of bees. Each petal and leaf was fully alive, shining with awareness of her. Even the air of the Garden was different. She found herself crying with relief and gratitude. It was as if a large, benevolent hand had reached down and picked her up, and was holding her safe. (43)

Yet despite the rhetoric of deliverance by divine intervention here, this pocket utopia is not the divinely created paradise of biblical or other religious mythologies but rather a hard-won artifact of collective human effort. Alternately, apocalypse itself, which is predicted within the Gardeners' mythology through the figure of a "Waterless Flood," is neither supernatural nor inevitable but the outcome of human action. Indeed, the final collapse results from a collective failure to acknowledge and protect the ecological utopia we *already* inhabited prior to the Anthropocene (the Holocene)—the very geological age of peak biological diversity that enabled humans to flourish and evolve into their present form in the first place.[8] According to verses from *The God's Gardeners Oral Hymnbook*, no serpent, heavenly father, or tree of knowledge expels us from paradise; rather, the human "Spoilers" are actively suppressing it in the here and now, right beneath our feet:

Who is it tends the Garden,
The Garden oh so green?

'Twas once the finest Garden
That ever has been seen.

And in it God's dear Creatures
Did swim and fly and play;

But then came greedy Spoilers,
And killed them all away.

And all the Trees that flourished
And gave us wholesome fruit,

By waves of sand are buried,
Both leaf and branch and root.

And all the shining Water
Is turned to slime and mire,

And all the feathered Birds so bright
Have ceased their joyful choir.

Oh Garden, oh my Garden,
I'll mourn forevermore

Until the Gardeners arise,
And you to Life restore. (Atwood xi)

In expanding the traditionally enclosed garden concept (*hortus conclusus*) onto a planetary scale, the environmental vision put forth by this hymn is hardly new. Indeed, the mythology of God's Gardeners draws on a much longer lineage that might include Rousseau, the naturalist turn in eighteenth-century European garden design (with its extension of domestic gardens into surrounding landscapes), contemporary environmental movements, outdoor industries, and more. Collectively, such movements and environmental notions overturned inherited Western assumptions that the ideal natural landscape was one that humans improved by art, and as environmental writer

Rebecca Solnit puts it, "the world ever since has been regarded as once only gardens were" (*Storming* 257).

In addition to reimagining the entire natural world as a garden, Atwood also takes aim at conventional notions of the gardener as politically disengaged by depicting the private security corporation in her novel as indifferent to these small acts of subversive greening. In part, God's Gardeners are able to escape persecution from CorpSeCorps because *as gardeners*, they are reflexively presumed to be innocuous and/or indisposed to social resistance. As the group's leader, Adam One, explains, "[the authorities] view us as twisted fanatics who combine food extremism with bad fashion sense and a puritanical attitude towards shopping. But we own nothing they want, so we don't qualify as terrorists" (48). Yet while it is true that members like Adam One adhere to a rather pacifist—even fatalistic—philosophy, there also exists a more radical strain within the Gardeners. Under the leadership of Zeb, a militant subgroup refuses simply to bear witness to the ongoing social and environmental destruction of the Anthropocene, pushing for "bio-resistance" and an insurgency against corporate governance. In fact, the final novel of Atwood's *MaddAddam* trilogy reveals Zeb as a longtime member of broader resistance efforts to bring down CorpSeCorps.

Yet despite these progressive associations, not all green space in the critical dystopia carries a utopian promise. Alongside their hopeful and anarchic guerilla gardens, many of the same texts landscape the most oppressive zones with luxurious parks and leisure grounds. Such spaces serve as a kind of spatial counterpart to the dominant order, not only signifying regimes of wealth, empire, and exclusion but also rendering invisible the labor—and indeed the very existence of the working class—that creates and maintains them. Unlike the pocket gardens grown to provide food and sanctuary or promote biodiversity and community in utopian enclaves, the parks and leisure grounds of dystopia are expressly designed to appear free from artifice. In Piercy's *He, She, and It*, the green spaces of the corporate multinational dystopia (Yakamura-Stichen, or "Y-S") consist entirely of parks: here, amid an otherwise ecologically devastated world, "the top levels" disport themselves in Paradise Park, an exclusive country club where "[t]he president lives on a lake full of real water" (326). Such picturesque scenes evoke the ideal eighteenth- and nineteenth-century English landscape described by Raymond Williams in *The Country and the City*, one "emptied of rural labor and of laborers; a sylvan and watery prospect . . . from which the facts of production [have] been banished" (125). In Y-S, park users themselves do not participate in the cultivation of these green enclaves; the whole point of their "natural" design, in fact, is to suggest that *no one* does. For precisely this reason, Piercy's protagonists disguise themselves as gardeners when breaking into this protected corporate fortress, since that station allows them to pass anywhere virtually unseen; as the protagonist Shira explains, although landscape maintenance crews "were always about clipping, weeding, feeding . . . they were essentially invisible. No one spoke to them or knew them. It was a service like the water that flowed from the tap" (331). In Piercy's vision of dystopia, then, the gardener (like all day laborers and keepers of public and domestic tidiness) is someone whose very existence would only be noticed in her absence.

Ironically, this very aesthetic of the traditional English landscape gardens was originally envisioned as a kind of democratic rebellion against the "despotic" geometric gardens of the French aristocracy. Even those who know little about European landscape history are often at least familiar with the rivalry between the formal French gardens of the seventeenth century and the naturalistic English landscapes of the eighteenth—a kind of Montague-Capulet feud of the garden world, as it were. The rational geometry of the French formal mode was perhaps most famously expressed in the gardens of Versailles, a vast symmetrical landscape of radial paths, spear-like topiary in military formation, and avenues extending to the horizon (what Solnit calls a "Euclidean-Cartesian apogee" [*Storming* 255]) symbolizing King Louis XIV's absolute power over a unified France. In rejecting the aristocratic aura and obsessive control of nature inherent in such a mode, eighteenth-century English garden designers favored the "amiable Simplicity of unadorned Nature," as Alexander Pope famously put it ("Essay" 205). Yet as countless landscape historians have noted, those English gardens aspired to a very particular version of the natural, one more readily found in the paintings of Claude Lorrain and Nicolas Poussin than in everyday "natural" landscapes. This gardening mode—which aptly came to be known as the "picturesque"—reimagined the landscape in its entirety as a garden, typically featuring a lake or pond, gently rolling hills, and lawns punctuated by groves of trees, serpentine paths, "swept" views, and sometimes picturesque architectural structures (classical or gothic ruins, bridges or weathered sculpture) to evoke pastoral associations. Thus, as Solnit points out, "one of the great contradictions is that the English garden is imitating art in its attempt to imitate nature, and the nature it is willing to imitate is once again a very specific idealized thing" (*Storming* 257).

This "gardenless" form of gardening—subsequently imitated throughout the Western world and still ubiquitous today in public parks, golf courses, and other landscaped grounds—has become so familiar that we often fail to recognize it as a particular "design" at all. Yet such landscapes are hardly free from artifice; rather, they are expressly engineered to conceal it. Lancelot

"Capability" Brown, the celebrated eighteenth-century landscape architect who perfected this mode, moved entire hills for the right visual effect, created lakes with "organic" borders using dams and canals, and imported grazing herds to keep the grasses tidily clipped. Most famously, he popularized the "ha-ha," a recessed landscape feature that creates a vertical barrier to prevent access to a property owner's grounds without obstructing its sweeping views (the name "ha-ha" derives from the surprise experienced when one gets close enough for the buried wall to be seen). Pope thus summarized the whole philosophy behind this aesthetic mode with his quip that in gardening, "half the skill is decently to hide" ("Epistle IV" line 54).

Given these tendencies, eighteenth-century English landscape connoisseurs showed a disdain not only for the symmetrical patterns of formal gardens but also for their counterparts in productive agricultural land, deeming squared-off garden patches, vegetable rows, and beanstalks on stakes as violations of conventional beauty standards. Yet as Raymond Williams reminds us, the rectilinear grids of both formal gardens and agricultural land were in fact contemporaneous with rolling, organic lines and picturesque compositions; the two are, ultimately,

> related parts of the same process—superficially opposed in taste but only because in the one case the land is being organized for production, where tenants and laborers will work, while in the other case it is being organized for consumption—the view, the ordered proprietary repose, the prospect. (*Country* 124)

As we have already explored in discussions of American garden writing before Charles Dudley Warner, such divided landscape arrangements gave a spatial expression to ideological boundaries between the beautiful and the good, on one hand, and the necessary and useful on the other. As Herbert Marcuse reminds us, Classical philosophy long ago deemed "all activity relating to the material provision of life [as] in its essence untrue, bad, and ugly" (93). Contemporary utopian thinkers thus have good reason to be wary of class-coded landscapes aspiring to this particular aesthetic ideal. Indeed, the very survival activities so commonly depicted and celebrated in the critical dystopias have historically been prohibited or criminalized in many park spaces. Central Park, an iconic example of the English landscape mode in the heart of New York City, was itself created on a site where poor residents and squatters, predominantly poor immigrants and free African Americans, were already using the rugged, swampy central Manhattan landscape for subsistence activities: growing produce, raising animals, gathering garbage to feed livestock, and collecting animal bones for sale (Rosenzweig and Blackmar; Rossi). During the eviction of some 1,600 residents in 1857, Central

FIGURE 10. Central Park cartoon by Frank Leslie. From *Frank Leslie's Illustrated Newspaper* (June 19, 1869).

Park's engineer-in-chief justified sweeping away these untidy garden patches through a racialized rhetoric of primitivism and criminality, shuddering as he recalled how the original squatters, "principally of foreign birth," were "dwelling in rude huts of their own construction, and living off the refuse of the city" (Viele 556–57). All such rogue gardening practices were criminalized in the park thereafter, and the newly organized Central Park police mobilized patrols to stamp out subsistence activities: individuals could now be arrested for gathering plants, collecting and selling stones, harvesting tree branches for firewood—even digging in the soil.[9]

Yet since the nineteenth-century American public was largely unaccustomed to thinking about such natural environments as pure "scenery" (that is, as spaces one walked through like a museum rather than physically engaged like a garden or farm), authorities had to actively educate visitors about proper park conduct. Chief architects Frederick Law Olmsted and Calvert Vaux argued that the public should immediately be taught that a "wide distinction exists between [Central Park] and the general suburban country, in which it is the prevalent impression of a certain class that all trees, shrubs, fruit and flowers, are common property" (*Forty* 58–59).[10] Indeed, not only were visitors prohibited from gathering, cultivating, or eating the vegetation found here; in many cases they were forbidden from playing sports or even walking on lawns beyond designated pathways. Olmsted and Vaux deliberately arranged Central Park in a manner that forced people to stroll those paths, one of the few forms of "vigorous" activity aligned with their belief that tranquilizing recreation was best pursued through "the act of immersing oneself in the scenery rather than [through acts of] production or boisterous forms of play and sports" (Taylor 460). True to this ethos, an 1860s report codifying Central Park's use policy "acknowledged the 'pleasure found in walking on a lawn'" but nonetheless banned the practice since "such pleasure would interfere with the lawn's more important 'power to gratify by sight'" (qtd. in Rosenzweig and Blackmar 251).[11] In privileging the visual over the multisensory or productive, such regulations reinforced the doctrine of this period's ornamental gardening and landscape literature as well. Garden design books like Frank J. Scott's, as discussed in chapter 1, had urged homeowners to exercise restraint in planting food-bearing plants among their lawns, which threatened to "mak[e] the beauty of their grounds subordinate to the pleasures of the palate" (24). And while such tensions between the productive and picturesque garden may seem historically remote, they have indeed carried well into the twenty-first century. This became especially pronounced during the Great Recession, when Central Park patrol officers stepped up efforts to suppress a resurgent trend in foraging and issued public announcements that "New York's public lands are not a communal pantry" (Foderaro).

It is precisely these practices and prohibitions that have prompted other gardeners and garden writers today to attach a dystopian stigma to the lawn itself rather than to parks more generally. Urban gardening campaigns like "Food not Lawns" depict our suburban yards as "reek[ing] of gross waste and mindless affluence" (Flores 10), while garden writer Michael Pollan has effectively made a side career of denouncing lawns ("nature under totalitarian rule") for their suppression of biodiversity. Although these grassy spaces appear natural, they are chemically saturated and mechanically maintained subjugations of nature "as utter and complete as a parking lot," where "[e]very species [is] forcibly excluded from the landscape but one, and this is forbidden to grow longer than the owner's little finger" (*Second* 48). Lawns are also equated with social conformity in countless American landscape histories and radical gardening publications, where suburbia's closely shaven green expanse gives a uniform appearance to communities intolerant of untidy or iconoclastic neighbors. And predating all these critiques, in 1899 sociologist Thorstein Veblen noted how the lawn's appeal derived precisely from its uselessness. Maintained by grazing animals that kept grasses tidy and armies of landscapers performing other tasks, ornamental lawns signaled a "superior expensiveness or futility," thus explaining their near-universal popularity among the "well-to-do classes" of the West (81–82). Within American fiction, perhaps no novel has better captured this cult of conspicuous consumption than *The Great Gatsby*. Here, our narrator's first encounter with Tom and Daisy Buchanan's extraordinary affluence takes place not within their palatial estate but rather out on the lawn: as Nick Carraway looks across these splendid grounds, he describes a sprawling green carpet that "started at the beach and ran toward the front door for a quarter of a mile, jumping over sun-dials and brick walks and burning gardens—finally when it reached the house drifting up the side in bright vines as though from the momentum of its run" (11). Someone looking for an image of invasion or imperial conquest overrunning the landscape would hardly have to change a word if they wished to adapt such a line. More recently, Héctor Tobar's *The Barbarian Nurseries* (2011) used lawn maintenance to highlight the vast gulf between California's affluent white families and the domestic workers—largely Latinx immigrants—trapped in near-indentured servitude while maintaining those homes and landscapes. In the novel's opening scene, an incompetent white homeowner struggles to start his lawnmower after having just fired his head gardener, Pepe. Ironically, as the Latina housekeeper notes, the homeowner's children actually prefer to play in the lush secluded garden out back; the front lawn is only kept as a status symbol, signifying money a family can blow on something serving no other purpose whatsoever. And it is precisely this *inutility*—the lawn's failure to offer a productive interface with the rich life of our soil and plant communities—that scandalizes so many contemporary garden writers, prompting Pollan to characterize the New England lawn as a kind of *antifarm* or "lid" that has been clamped down on the region's agricultural past, where "the distance [property] owners have traveled from farming to middle-class respectability [can be measured] in the acres of unproductive lawn" (*Second* 277).

Such depictions surely provide insight for understanding why contemporary utopias and critical dystopias take such pains to render *visible* both the people and processes that create, maintain, and utilize their food gardens, allotments, "survival plots," and guerilla gardens. The plant hybrids sown across Mars in the final novel of Robinson's trilogy bear tiny insignias identifying the garden teams that cultivate them. Even as early as 1915, Charlotte Perkins Gilman reformulated utopia as a place of visibly staged, egalitarian production when she transformed the park concept into a garden: her feminist utopia *Herland* depicts "a land in a state of perfect cultivation," where even the forest trees are cared for "like so many cabbages." This entire country, Gilman writes, "looked like an enormous *park*, only that it was even more evidently an enormous *garden*"—the difference here being that gardens showcase the activity and maintenance they involve and serve as fully functional environments produced, inhabited, and consumed by their caretakers (10, 12; italics added). In *Second Nature*, Pollan even goes so far as to entertain fantasies of "seced[ing] from the national lawn" by replacing his entire yard with functional food gardens. As he complains, even households that *do* maintain vegetable gardens in the United States must "invariably relegate [them] to the backyard, leaving the front free to play its part in the picturesque park that the combined lawns of the neighborhood aspire to recall" (77, 282–83). Pollan thus rebels by situating his "productive" plots in clear view, even giving the steaming compost pile a respectable central placement. "What I like about such land," he explains, "is precisely what offended the classical garden designers: it betrays the human effort that went into its making" and "seems to tell the story" of its own production (298, 238, 283).

Yet notwithstanding these utopian reappropriations of the garden as a more transparent "arena for self-expression" that "doesn't hide its labor" (Pollan 73, 238), skeptics will certainly remind us that such private acts of unalienated production can go on without making a significant ripple in the dominant order—without, as Marcuse puts it, "any transformation of the state of fact" (95). Within the contained borders of one's flower and vegetable plots, "subversive" experience is still relegated to a mere preserve, where social and political discontent can be neutralized within zones of private pleasure. Indeed, landowners and industrialists have historically endorsed recreational gardening for precisely this reason, promoting the activity as a way to defuse radical political impulses among laboring classes—whether by offering a sober and "apolitical" weekend activity that might enhance the productivity of factory workers or by expanding rural allotments in nineteenth-century England to "assuage the anger of agricultural workers" (McKay 157).[12] Lefebvre's analysis also highlights this depoliticizing aspect of leisure, noting how readily susceptible it is to being transformed into yet another commodity and industry, an extension of dominated space that answers the demand for qualitative experience while remaining "both an assimilative and an assimilated part of the 'system'" (353).

Granted, the garden may not ultimately serve as genuinely "oppositional" space in such contexts. Yet a certain disruptive potential is surely inherent to the activity; as Cohen and Taylor note in *Escape Attempts*, although leisure practices are generally "licensed by society as safety valves," they must, "like fantasy, . . . be carefully regulated and patrolled. For in these areas, reality may slip away too far, providing glimpses of alternative realities which can have radical consequences" (95–96). Lefebvre echoes this insight in identifying everyday activity as the most significant and pervasive zone where we seek to overcome the divisions enforced by abstract space—rifts between pleasure and work, between the sensory and intellectual, and more. These transgressive tendencies, fantasies, and spaces ultimately reveal where the dominant system's most critical "breaking-points" reside: that is, everyday life and the body. Lefebvre elaborates on this subversive potential by noting that

> The space of leisure bridges the gap between traditional spaces with their monumentality and their localizations based on work and its demands, and potential spaces of enjoyment and joy; in consequence this space is the very epitome of contradictory space. This is where the existing mode of production produces both its worst and its best—parasitic outgrowths on the one hand and exuberant new branches on the other—as prodigal of monstrosities as of promises (that it cannot keep). (385)

Here, Lefebvre's insight might suggest a key reason that gardens and contemporary utopias are so often yoked together. Insofar as leisure or "contradictory" spaces like the garden cultivate desire for an alternative way of being, they serve the very pedagogical function contemporary scholars identify with utopian representation itself. Elaborating on Miguel Abensour's work, E. P. Thompson argues that utopia's most important aim, increasingly, is the "education of desire" and the disruption of prevailing values—"the 'commonsense' of bourgeois society." He invokes Abensour's own remarks to emphasize this point: "This is not the same as 'a moral education' towards a given end: it is, rather, to open a way to aspiration, to 'teach desire to desire, to desire better, to desire more, and above all to desire in a different way'" (*William Morris* 790–91). The heuristic utopia, in other words, would enable readers to experience an alternative structure of feeling and thereby expose the inadequacy and poverty of experience available within the existing system.

So to return at last to *He, She, and It*, and to bring this analysis to bear on our contemporary critical dystopias more generally, it comes as no surprise that Piercy's portrait of the English landscape parks in corporate dystopia are directly countered by the rogue gardens checkered across her pocket utopia, Tikva. Here, tulips and tomatoes are described as growing in "anarchic little plots" (36), while uncaged chickens and turkeys run loose in the gardens. Unlike the manicured and uniform parks of "Y-S," these gardens stage precisely the sort of differential space that Lefebvre imagined would reeducate or restore the body's sensual capacities. In fact, the return of the protagonist (Shira) to this space makes her suddenly aware of "how unstimulated her senses had been all those Y-S years"; she responds to Tikva with surprise and pleasure when "the smells assaulted her: animal smells, vegetable smells, the scent of yellow tulips, the heavier scent of narcissus, cooking odors, the tang of manure, the salty breath of the sea. Everything felt," as she puts it, "unregulated" (36).

Conversely, the garden triggers awareness of pleasures *lost* for the sexually enslaved protagonist (Offred) in Margaret Atwood's 1986 dystopia, *The Handmaid's Tale*. As Offred looks upon the Commander's Wife gardening, she recalls the very sense experiences she is no longer free to enjoy: "I once had a garden. I can remember the smell of the turned earth, the plump shapes of bulbs held in the hands, fullness, the dry rustle of seeds through the fingers" (12). Within Atwood's dystopian future, the corporeal pleasures of gardening, like sex, have been entirely extinguished for women and oppressed classes. Accordingly, Atwood dramatizes a complete dissociation between the garden and the body by having the Commander's Wife perform her yard work with "her knees on a cushion" and "a light blue veil thrown over her wide garden hat" (12). And whereas gardening for Offred had once signified an interpenetration of body and earth (she constantly refers to hands and fingers in this scene), the Commander's Wife never plunges her own arthritic limbs into the dirt. In fact, her hands have been wholly eliminated from the scene and replaced with two manual prostheses—first, a "hired hand" who does the digging, and second, a wand that serves in place of her own fingers. Atwood depicts all this with the economy of a single line: as the worker digs, "the Commander's Wife directs, pointing with her stick" (12).

This strict division of labor in the garden, which fragments the body into so many detachable parts, also prefigures the division of labor to follow in the bedroom. The function of the handmaids, as Offred explains, is to serve as "two-legged wombs . . . sacred vessels, ambulatory chalices" (136), while the Commander's Wife plays a "higher," spiritual role. Like the pair of women, who together make up one half of the sex act, the Commander himself is also disjointed—even absent—from his body. Offred notes that "[i]t's as if he's somewhere else, waiting for himself to come," and thus his thrusting reminds her of someone "drumming his fingers on the table while he waits" (94). While accounts of gardening in utopia provide a figure for integrating with or rediscovering one's own sensorium, the dystopian body is so instrumentalized that (what might otherwise be) excessively and intensively sensual activities—here, gardening and sex—are reduced to a series of automated and alienated actions carried out by disjointed body parts.

Piercy's and Atwood's disparate social orders thus produce radically divergent experiences of cultivated nature. Formerly "cold and inert," Shira ultimately "felt herself loosening" in the space of Tikva's gardens (36); Offred, on the other hand, is distressed by this garden's ability to awaken desires that cannot be acted on. For her, this space seems to "breathe" and emit something she imagines as body heat: Offred complains that "to walk through [the garden] in these days, of peonies, of pinks and carnations, makes my head swim." As a result, she reflects that "winter is not so dangerous. I need hardness, cold, rigidity"—not the abundant but inaccessible temptations conjured by the springtime garden (153–54). However, the gardens in both novels ultimately prove somewhat homologous, extending a kind of mnemonic device for the *possibility* of liberated experience in a society without such oppressions. Whether its pleasures are gratified or withheld, the garden reminds its visitors of the vast distance between spontaneous and emancipated sense experience on one hand and, on the other, the physical and psychological repressions of dystopian society, with its spatial hierarchies and bodily fragmentations, its rigid division of labor and zoning of pleasure from work. In this sense, even the neutered garden of *The Handmaid's Tale*—in which the "swelling genitalia of the flowers" have been "snipped off"—turns out to be an ungovernable space: Offred notes that despite the deformations that patriarchy has produced here, there remains "something subversive about this garden, . . . a sense of buried things bursting upwards" (153). Indeed, the stirrings of desire activated in this space hasten her final act of rebellion. Like the utopian form itself, this garden has, to use Marcuse's words, "planted real longing alongside poor consolidation and false consecration in the soil of bourgeois life" (99).

Toward a Dialectical Utopia

> The war on gardens goes far beyond short-sighted urban planning policies and real estate graft. Community gardens are targets because they are liberated zones, areas free from consumption and mediation, at a time when the very idea of public space is under assault.... In this world ... despite their many benefits, [gardens] are seen as nuisances, obstacles to profit and control, scary pagan groves that threaten the strict fundamentalism of the Market.
> —John Wright (1999)

Beyond the pages of contemporary speculative literature, the city has become the other great arena where garden fantasy and utopian practice have undergone a dramatic transformation. In this final section we will look at political activists, writers, and idealists who use community and guerilla gardening as a form of creative resistance to dominant ideology and culture. Here, the discourse and activism of gardening likewise overturn many of utopia's conventional associations, with growers directly *engaging* (rather than seeking escape from) the urban form, putting a militant spin on the supposedly pacifying effects of gardening, and envisioning the city as a communal project that could challenge the ascendancy of exchange value, private property, and neoliberal governance.

I do not want to suggest that the "activist" gardener is either a new figure or an exclusively American one. In fact, today's politically engaged cultivators hail from a long lineage of historical individuals and groups, from Gerard Winstanley's Diggers (the seventeenth-century English radicals who farmed the commons in defiance of existing social hierarchies) to anyone who has planted seeds on the land of aristocrats or property owners to protest enclosure. Today, however, gardening as an act of protest or reform has become especially visible in the city, where growers take direct action to transform their environment for purposes of food justice, community building, and environmental restoration. Inner-city and low-income neighborhoods in Detroit, Milwaukee, Chicago, and Los Angeles are some of the hotbeds within this movement: here, communities that have historically lacked access to jobs, green space, and often fresh produce have appropriated vacant lots not only for gardening; they also feature fish ponds, chicken coops, and beehives, garden-based education, rehabilitation efforts, job training, and mental health programs. As such, these movements create enclaves of differential value (access to nature, self-determined production, democratic participation, biodiversity, and more) within landscapes otherwise dominated by the single logic of market or exchange value. Moreover, in actively challenging institutions of private property and individualistic domestic arrangements, con-

FIGURE 11. Ron Finley outside his home in South Central Los Angeles. Photo by Stephen Zeigler (2013).

temporary gardeners overturn historical associations that overwhelmingly equate gardens with privacy and retreat. Coalitions of residents, squatters, environmentalists, and community activists have knocked down divisions between backyards to connect and expand formerly private plots. Inspired by these trends, Peter Lamborn Wilson's *Avant Gardening* imagines a utopian future where New Yorkers link entire city blocks by cutting "Fourier-like grand passages" through their houses, combining individual residences into communal gardens (32). In South Central LA, such arrangements clearly confuse observers accustomed to thinking of gardens (and land more generally) in proprietary terms; when growers installed vegetable plots in median strips and along sidewalks, outsiders asked if they were concerned that people would "steal" the food. "Hell no I ain't afraid they're gonna steal it," gardener and organizer Ron Finley responded, "that's why it's on the street!" (Finley).

Such garden-based initiatives also challenge the deeply engrained ways we imagine the city itself. As Raymond Williams famously argues in *The Country and the City*, pastoral fictions have typically produced idealized, nostalgic images of agrarian life that distort or eliminate its realities, while literary and cultural representations of the city—the country's "dark mirror"—have overwhelming highlighted contemporary social problems like poverty, crime, alienation, capitalist exploitation, pollution, and existential loneliness (272–

77). In William Morris's 1890 utopia, *News from Nowhere*, the garden world to which his long-sleeping protagonist awakes is in part an aesthetic rejection of industrial dreariness, while early concepts of the suburb—first popularized by Ebenezer Howard's late nineteenth-century "Garden City" movement—were originally conceived as an antidote to the unsanitary and immoral environs of industrial cities, envisioning each country-style settlement surrounded by a private garden (Hardy). Since the Industrial Revolution, then, urban gardens and parks have generally been regarded as sites of pastoral *relief*—in short, as a kind of "anticity"—within the larger urban landscape.

The gardens discussed in this section, however, are imagined less as modes of *escape* from the city than as instruments to *engage* and *reshape* the urban environment as such. Contemporary community gardeners clearly share Williams's understanding of the traditional city/country divide as misleading and counterproductive, since both rural and urban worlds are produced within and damaged by the same set of capitalist dynamics. This would seem to make any retreatist version of the garden rather futile. Indeed, as community gardening historian Malve von Hassell notes, contemporary urban growers take on the city's spatial regime directly in order to "live with it, confront it, and ... selectively reject and appropriate aspects of its structure and dynamics" (13). What these gardeners oppose is not the urban form itself but rather the administration of the city as a space of pure exchange value and the limiting of residents' roles to that of passive inhabitants rather than architects and creators of those spaces. In thus rejecting dominant versions of the city, growers seek to create a "differential space," what urban historian Iain Borden describes as "a place of nonlabor, joy, and the fulfillment of desires rather than toil; a place of qualities, difference, relations in time and space, contradictory uses and encounters" (20).

Such an approach significantly differentiates today's movement from its predecessors in U.S. history. Urban cultivation campaigns are hardly new, with many contemporary forms having grown out of state-sponsored "victory gardening" practices that aided war efforts earlier in the twentieth century. During World War II, in particular, the American government and business community coordinated massive domestic gardening efforts to free up food supplies for military campaigns, with several million victory gardens eventually producing over 40 percent of the nation's food in both the United States and Canada (McKay, Graham). Yet these efforts largely disappeared after the war's end, with governments withdrawing support and revoking permission for public use of the land. Garden historian Jane Brown also writes of the "digging fatigue" that set in on both sides of the Atlantic, with former gardeners now "want[ing] nothing to do with such symbols of poverty, charity and wartime needs" as allotments, relief gardens, and victory gardens (167).

Yet with renewed economic trouble in the 1970s, particularly within the urban cores of major U.S. cities, large-scale community garden movements reemerged. And as urban gardener and activist Sarah Ferguson argues, this second gardening wave presents a crucial distinction from earlier modes, since the new efforts "were born not out of government support, but rather its neglect" ("Brief History" 83). New York City's garden movements offer an iconic case. When drastic cuts in social services abandoned inner-city neighborhoods of the 1970s to poverty, arson, homelessness, demolition, and decay, local residents—overwhelmingly immigrants and people of color—had to rely solely on their own visions and ingenuity to revitalize their communities, transforming vacant and devastated blocks into productive plots. In the ensuing years, these grassroots efforts grew into a citywide movement that eventually comprised over 750 community garden sites (Raver).

Gardening movements in cities like New York can thus be viewed as a contest over the right to the city. Historian Karen Schmelzkopf notes that in enacting their own visions in and of the city, marginalized residents have mobilized a larger debate "about control over public space, about who has (or does not have) the right to space, and about the right to be a part of the public" (337). Addressing this question is, of course, not only a matter of who but also of what and how—of the shape and nature of the spaces created. In an effort to remain open and amenable to shifting circumstances, desires, and community needs, many urban gardeners today create "nomadic" or "roaming" gardens installed atop mobile platforms that can be moved between sites in order to appropriate the real estate market's temporarily unused or "waste" spaces. As architecture scholar Doina Petrescu explains, each garden's structure "constitutes the floor of a green living-room constructed on the additive principle of horizontal growth," enabling it to accommodate "multiple activities and to shape places for flexible use" (51). Prominent examples include NOMADgardens in San Francisco and ECObox in Paris, where the continually changing topology and configuration of garden experiments highlight their participatory structure and open-ended, situational process.[13]

Moreover, these activities also serve as a kind of experimental template that could potentially give rise to other community-based transformations of urban space beyond gardening itself. The principal function of gardening in these movements may be the production not of spatial objects but of *spatial practices*, the "invention of new tools" for variable and evolving use. As Petrescu points out, since many participatory processes solidify after their goals have been met ("when a contested space is occupied, project built, etc."), urban movements like ECObox and NOMADgardens are defined by "temporary agencies" that "keep the use of space and the process of decision open" (54, 59). In this sense, the nomadic garden serves as a kind of workshop, a "participatory urban laboratory" that explores and tests new ways to democratically reshape the built environment using available materials while tenaciously avoiding closure.

Of course, while flowers and fresh vegetables appeal to many, their pleasantness alone cannot explain why gardening per se has become such a privileged activity within these efforts to reimagine the urban form. Indeed, considering the whole spectrum of "situationist" acts that residents could adopt in appropriated sites like ECObox and NOMADgardens—live performance, community readings, sports, public debate—it hardly seems inevitable that gardening would emerge as a metonym for asserting one's right to the city as such. And yet I argue that there is something singular about the garden's *temporality*—its nature as an exceptionally "processual" space—that uniquely suits it to these acts of appropriation, especially when we consider the increasing attention to "dialectical" utopian forms among scholars and activists today. Whether on wheels or more conventionally rooted in place, the organic, evolving nature of gardens exhibits a dynamic spatiotemporality that requires ongoing maintenance, thus drawing us into its myriad processes of change. Perhaps English author H. E. Bates says it best in his oft-quoted line, "The garden that is finished is dead."

It seems surprising that scholarly attention to the garden has not always emphasized this quality; in fact, Immanuel Kant's *Critique of Judgment*, which lays the foundations for modern aesthetics, categorized landscape gardening not among the "arts of the beautiful play of sensations" but rather among the "formative arts," which include sculpture, architecture, and, above all, painting. More recent scholarship has questioned this taxonomy by highlighting change itself as essential to the garden in ways that do not apply to the other formative arts Kant names here. We might even see the garden as a type of performance—a sequence of events and unfolding experience—that "present[s] the passing of time visually" in ways that are analogous to music, which "presents the passing of time audibly" (Barwell and Powell 136). Indeed, as scholars Ismay Barwell and John Powell go on to point out, because they are living (and also dying) systems, gardens "do not merely *happen* to exhibit time's passing; they must do so" (142). Physical and perceptual change may thus be regarded as the very object of aesthetic pleasure in many sites: "You cannot usually see a mature kauri in a newly established garden nor can you see camellia flowers in summer," Barwell and Powell observe. "You have to wait while the kauri takes its time to grow and you have to wait for the appropriate season to see the camellia in flower" (141). Time, as landscape historian John Dixon Hunt insists, makes a fundamental contribution to the being and experience of the garden: a garden "not only exists in but also takes its special character from four dimensions" (*Greater Perfections* 15).

Together, these unique qualities make the garden a highly suitable figure for the "dialectical utopia," a mode David Harvey offers as a utopian category that would combine both the processual and the spatial. As Harvey has argued, the history of utopian scheming has often been limited by privileging one of these two dimensions at the expense of the other. The "utopia of spatial form," on one hand, immobilizes the processes necessary for its original construction. Thomas More's *Utopia* is a premier example of this mode, where the dialectics of history, as discussed earlier, are suspended or repressed in favor of perpetuating "a happy stationary state." The utopia of *social process*, on the other hand, is figured almost exclusively in temporal terms: these utopias are "bound to no place whatsoever and are typically specified outside of the constraints of spatiality" (Harvey, *Spaces* 160, 174). While Harvey names Marx and Hegel's grand narratives of social and historical process as examples, the version he explores most thoroughly is that of the free-market utopia. And its temporality is troubling to him precisely in its relation to space, since, inevitably, the utopianism of process must materialize, or "come to ground," *someplace*. Indeed, the effects of this collision are the very object of much of Harvey's scholarship, which examines how "capital builds a geographical landscape in its own image at a certain point in time only to have to destroy it later in order to accommodate its own dynamic of endless capital accumulation, strong technological change, and fierce forms of class struggle." That process, of course, receives one of its most succinct expressions in Marx and Engels's characterization of social life within capitalist modernity, where "all that is solid melts into air" (177).

In response to the dilemmas posed by these two models, Harvey proposes a spatiotemporal or "dialectical utopianism" that would negotiate between the endless violence of creative destruction, on one hand, and the problem of closure on the other. And although Harvey does not directly identify the garden as an example of this principle, it hardly seems surprising that gardens figure quite prominently in his own utopian vision, "Edilia," as outlined in the conclusion to *Spaces of Hope* (257–81).[14] Gardens readily lend themselves to both Harvey's notion of the dialectical utopia (defined as that which "operat[es] in relation to both time and space") and to the situationist practices of urban gardening precisely because they are always at once both product and process (Harvey 196). Gardeners with the group ECObox clearly seek this dialectical mode as well, even referring to their appropriated sites as "the gardening" to emphasize the process of "fabrication and becoming" over that of any finished garden object (Petrescu 46).

Yet while many scholars and gardeners may see pronounced utopian possibility in the mobility and protean nature of nomadic gardens like ECObox, surely they also have an element of the dystopian built into their form as well, since the garden's very structure already anticipates its eviction. George McKay notes that the aesthetic of ephemerality in many such projects today is "perhaps itself a comment on [the gardens'] temporary, semi-legal or squatted nature" (173). And even more conventional (nonmobile) community gardens share this precarity: they are often absent from city maps and legal documents (or appear merely as "vacant lots"), an invisibility that makes them especially vulnerable to sudden eradication by landowners and the state. When Manhattan real estate values rebounded in the 1990s, for example, the city moved aggressively to auction those "abandoned lots" for private residential and commercial development (Raver). This led to highly publicized protests with throngs of activist gardeners arrested in the process; similar scenarios have played out across U.S. cities in recent decades, where, for instance, the bulldozing of America's largest community garden (the fourteen-acre South Central Farm in Los Angeles) sparked national media attention, drew high-profile Hollywood celebrities and nationally recognized politicians into the protest movement, and inspired a popular 2008 documentary, *The Garden*, directed by Scott Hamilton Kennedy.

The precarious nature of these plots is especially evident in the intense symbolic value gardeners often attach to ancillary objects and practices surrounding their sites. As von Hassell notes in her ethnographies of New York's Lower East Side gardens, "perception of destruction in the immediate present is acute, as gardeners watch gardens that they have worked on for decades being erased by bulldozers in a matter of minutes" (29). Growers she has interviewed seek to counter the invisibility of these sites by sharing photos of their transformation, telling and retelling stories of their creation, and representing their histories through community museum displays, brochures, quilts, pageants, and even mosaics on neighborhood lampposts created from glass shards and pottery fragments salvaged from razed garden sites.

Not surprisingly, these cycles of eviction and destruction have directly contributed to the radicalization and militant rhetoric of contemporary urban gardening, particularly as seen in the practice of guerilla gardening. Defined as "the illicit cultivation of someone else's land" (Reynolds 5)—from whole urban blocks to empty flower boxes and median strips along streets—guerilla gardening has become a global movement in recent decades, with Richard Reynolds's well-known practical handbook documenting practices in over thirty countries.¹⁵ The rhetoric and imagery of this movement is unambiguously rebellious. Reynolds, for example, calls up images of Che Guevara and Mao Tse Tung in his recipes for "seed bombs" and practical tips for controlling pests unique to the guerrilla garden (namely, landowners and the cops). Meanwhile, street growers in South Central LA recruit inner-city youth by insisting "if you ain't a gardener, you ain't gangsta" (Finley), and London activists wearing green Robin Hood regalia draw inspiration from the Paris Situationists of 1968, promoting ideas of plowing up streets to grow fruit trees and vegetable plots (Downton 122).

These movements' manuals, manifestos, and testimonials also bear striking resemblance to the critical dystopias discussed in the previous section: both draw on the customary repertoire of apocalyptic and war-torn urban tropes as well as figures of social redemption through gardening. Readers of guerilla gardening literature regularly encounter "bombed-out blocks" (Collom 142); "torched buildings tumbl[ing] down," "rubble-strewn lots" that are "magnets for trash, rats, prostitution, drug-dealing, dirty needles, hepatitis" (Will 134); "car skeletons" and human bodies frozen to death in cardboard boxes (Ferguson, "Death" 62–63; "Brief History" 83); incinerators spewing "deadly poisons" (Weinberg 49); police toting M16s and evicting growers (Starr 174); and whole sections of urban America "triaged out of the social contract" (J. Wright 127). Within these devastated landscapes, gardeners are depicted as "armed" with hoes and pickaxes, and pitching "battles . . . with baseball bats and hoes" (Ferguson, "Brief History" 83; "Death" 63). The urban gardening section in Armory Starr's *Global Revolt* (2005) is written in a playfully seditious tone, inviting readers to join this movement "under the cover of darkness" as they "plant seeds and seedlings in all those neglected corners of public space . . . [and] vandalize the city with nature" (181); meanwhile, anarchists' memoirs recount New York gardeners as "bands of night-time raiders, kick-starting the gardening movement with bolt cutters . . . [and] trainings on appropriate trespass tactics" and characterize threatened plots as "forts" protected by "barricades" (Will 135–36).¹⁶ Across these accounts, "seed grenades" (biodegradable packets tossed over fences to scatter herbs and flowers in unreachable zones) have become ubiquitous symbols of the movement. Indeed, nothing could seem less like the innocuous version of gardening represented in older critiques like Keith Thomas's, which hold gardening partially responsible for tranquilizing the "radical and political impulses" of the proletariat.

Like the use of gardens to represent radical terraforming practices in Kim Stanley Robinson's work, the rise of gardening as an urban resistance tactic must also be understood in light of social, political, and scholarly shifts that have reshaped utopian representation more generally. For many contemporary activists, the mere act of displacing the "good life" into some distant future seems like yet another gesture of submission to the dominant order, compelling them to take up more immediate forms of action within the existing system's available or temporarily unclaimed gaps.

From time to time, of course, even the most militant community growers must surely balk at the colossal disparities between the terms of this contest: on one hand, the vast scale of global capitalism, corporate governance, and all the material, ideological, and legal powers at their disposal; and on the other hand . . . growers of turnips and parsley. Even George McKay, the author of *Radical Gardening*, admits that the subversive potential of these efforts must ultimately remain open to question and debate—or at least susceptible to qualification—with "[gardening's] non-threatening nature going some way to explaining its popularity in our apparently post-ideological world" (192). And yet I want to conclude this discussion by noting the historically disproportionate hostility and excessive response of authorities to these practices, which may be reason enough to think twice before writing them off. Many observers, for example, were confounded by the decision to raze Los Angeles's South Central Farm in 2006—the largest community garden in the United States at the time—which had helped revitalize community in a devastated neighborhood better known, prior to the garden's establishment, as the epicenter of uprisings over the Rodney King police abuse verdict. This fourteen-acre garden was not only beloved by the local community (largely low-income people of color) but also became the darling of environmental organizations, major Hollywood celebrities, Los Angeles major Antonio Villaraigosa, and other prominent local and national political figures. And to top it off, the farmers and their allies had even secured $16 million to protect their besieged plot—every penny of the developer's asking price at that time. Yet from a neoliberal perspective, the uncompromising brutality and swiftness with which this project was eradicated—even when funds were raised to protect it—makes good sense. When more than 150 families (mostly Latinx immigrants and their first-generation American children) initially came to garden this vacant lot, they did not ground their claims for land rights in ideologies of property ownership; rather, this was an act of urban usufruct, with growers highlighting the garden's importance in allowing them to feed themselves directly from the land in a self-governed community space. Environmental scholar Janet Fiskio notes that in focusing more directly on food sovereignty (control of the means of production) than on food access per se, the gardeners drew from revolutionary political traditions of land rights for the dispossessed. During public comment sessions on the gardeners' impending eviction, growers invoked Emiliano Zapata's claim that land belongs to those who work it: standing before the City Council, gardener Don Eddie held up his hands, palms out, to announce, "I am a farmer, and here is the proof in my hands! To not allow us to stay on that land that has already been cultivated! For what reason?" Another South Central gardener, Miguel Angel Pérez, cited the mantra of the Mexican revolution, "¡Tierra y Libertad!" (qtd. from subtitles in Kennedy, "The Garden"). As Fiskio argues, the growers' claims here appeal not to individual property rights but rather to "the rights of the community to use the land for sustenance—more similar to the institution of the ejido, which grants communal cultivation rights to landless farmers, than to the independent georgic farmer." Indeed, in deterritorializing this unused space, their practice challenged long-established Jeffersonian narratives of American identity embedded in individual property rights as the basis of liberty and economic development; in its place they presented a counternarrative of land as collective identity and "community and seasonal reproduction" (Fiskio 317–18).

This challenge to the institution of private property—the very cornerstone of capitalist ideology, economics, and society—could not go unanswered, as evidenced by the ultimate response with surveillance helicopters, police in full riot gear, and fleets of bulldozers demolishing every green thing on the fourteen-acre lot. The logic behind that response was made clear in a 2006 *Los Angeles Times* editorial reaffirming the primacy of the developer's claim:

> There are lots of things that would be nice. But the land belongs to Horowitz, and he has every right to kick out the people who have been squatting there for more than a decade. The gardeners . . . have made their plots into a special, almost magical, place. But no magic is so strong that it erases a landowner's right to either his property or its fair value. ("Los Angeles Gothic")

But perhaps the most revealing answer to the question put forward by farmer Don Eddie—"For what reason?"—came from the developer himself, Ralf Horowitz. In the weeks prior to the eviction deadline, Horowitz had stated (clearly in bad faith) that he would accept an offer of $16 million for the property from these disenfranchised, low-income immigrant farmers; yet when the gardeners stunned opponents and supporters alike by actually succeeding in raising the funds, aided in part by the Annenberg Foundation, the Trust for Public Land, and other allies, Horowitz reneged on his offer (Marroquin). In a radio interview run as a voiceover in Kennedy's documentary *The Garden* (just as the film shows bulldozers snapping gorgeous papaya trees in half), the developer explains:

> Even if they raised a *hundred* million dollars, this group could not buy this property. [This is] not about money. It's about, I don't like their cause, and I don't like their conduct; so there's no price that I would sell it to them for.... Is this good for our country, that everybody is owed and nobody is obligated?... What they should have said to the taxpayers of Los Angeles and to me is, "This is a gracious country. Thank you very much for letting us have these gardens here. Thank you. Thank you. Thank you." (qtd. from subtitles in Kennedy)

Horowitz's statement not only racializes and otherizes the farmers, who are counterposed to the "gracious country" hosting them (along with its taxpayers and landowners); as Fiskio points out, his remark also indicates that the right to produce food is not itself a human right but rather "a right derived from property ownership." Outside this legal and ideological arrangement, "the only thing that immigrant and landless communities should hope for is a charity that is easily (even arbitrarily) revoked" (318). Thus, in denying the growers' purchase offer, the developer even allows immediate economic gain to take a back seat to a ritualistic reaffirmation of the broader neoliberal order. He not only refuses to acknowledge the gardeners' land claims but also any form of value external to the market—value added through their labor, the revitalization of community, or the biodiversity now flourishing in an otherwise bleak industrial zone. Indeed, the afterlife of this space underscores the extent to which its destruction served primarily as a symbolic political gesture: evidently, no development had even been planned on the lot, and a full ten years after the eviction, the same parcel remained a desolate expanse of empty dirt—entirely unused and undeveloped.

Conflicts over New York City's community garden efforts have likewise dramatized the threat these grassroots practices pose to neoliberal priorities and to the conception of cities as commodified space. In fact, the draconian policies of Mayor Rudolph Giuliani's administration around the turn of the century suggest that not only activists and utopianists but also city officials and champions of the neoliberal state had begun to reconsider those time-honored assumptions about gardens as apolitical or ameliorative. If one takes into account the sum of all New York lots listed as "vacant" or "blighted" in this period—both gardens and nongardens—it becomes evident that the city's campaign to (re)privatize land in the 1990s actively and disproportionately targeted community gardens. In 1999 the seven hundred identified community gardens made up only a small fraction of the eleven thousand total vacant lots on the city sales inventory, which certainly could have been spared through a whole range of reshuffled development plans (Ferguson, "Death" 73). Yet as Staeheli, Mitchell, and Gibson argue, these gardens were in part singled out because the initial threat of privatization had "called into existence a variety of 'counter publics' seeking to contest the mayor's vision of the city" (204). In its efforts to stamp out those alternative practices, the city's campaign had backfired: endangered gardens effectively became sites in which low-income, marginalized, and racialized groups achieved visibility and mobilized resistance to City Hall and real estate developers (197). As one adolescent activist testified, gardeners no longer worked individually but became a cohesive "force throughout the five boroughs." He concluded: "We're networking. There are people, young kids, who through nothing more than gardening are now becoming activists" (200). Surely the state could no longer afford to think of gardening as a "pastime for the middle-aged retreating from engagement with the world" (Levitas, "Utopia" 146). And while even some garden supporters themselves expressed skepticism that city officials were motivated by anything more than the prospect of immediate economic gain when the garden destruction began, we might do well to keep in mind Henri Lefebvre's observation that

> the quest for a counter-space overwhelms the supposedly ironclad distinction between "reform" and "revolution." *Any proposal along these lines, even the most seemingly insignificant, shakes existing space to its foundations,* along with its strategies and aims—namely, the imposition of homogeneity and transparency everywhere within the purview of power and its established order. (383; italics added)

Apparently, then, these garden practices not only transformed particular spaces; they also transformed growers themselves, along with the larger stakes of their relation to the city and social space as such. Having crossed the threshold from mere "users" to cocreators and cultivators of their city, gardeners were not likely to fall back into thinking of social space as a mere neutral medium. And in the process, they repositioned the time horizon of utopian fantasy itself, reclaiming it from a dim and indefinite future to activate a demand for an alternative here and now. Surely Adam and Eve—along with all their counterparts in those paradise gardens of old—would have been confounded by the magnitude of effort to which this new generation happily commits itself in the garden.

CHAPTER 5

Just Gardens

Uprooting and Recovery in the Postcolonial Garden

> . . . thank you
> the ancestor who loved you
> before she knew you
> by smuggling seeds into her braid for the long
> journey, who loved you
> before he knew you by putting
> a walnut tree in the ground, who loved you
> before she knew you by not slaughtering
> the land; thank you
> who did not bulldoze the ancient grove
> of dates and olives . . .
> —Ross Gay (2015)

Notwithstanding the utopian slant of much garden representation—both historical and contemporary—there also exists a dark underside to the American romance with gardening. Postcolonial writers have long emphasized how dominant Western celebrations of nature are products of imperial legacies and histories of oppression. Indeed, as ecocritic Robert Emmett writes in *Cultivating Environmental Justice*, "nowhere are the ramifications of past environmental injustice and colonialism more evident than in gardening" (171). These include some of North America's most disgraceful legacies—plantation slavery, dispossession, racial violence, and genetic theft—which garden myths and pastoral literature often serve to conceal.

People who have been colonized and displaced know the crime scenes lurking beneath these botanical myths all too well. As Antiguan-born novelist and garden writer Jamaica Kincaid once noted of the pastoral mode, "There is a great tradition of painting agricultural workers, people enjoying the cutting of the weed," people bathed in golden light "[as if] they're in touch with God." But for colonized groups across the Americas, agricultural work is often "associated with enforced labor, with slavery." In Kincaid's birthplace in the West Indies, she notes, "You cannot see any heroic cane-cutting, or any heroic cotton-picking." "It's associated with conquest, it's associated with hell," she writes (*Writing* 91).

Today in the United States, this "hell" of commercial farming and landscape maintenance is overwhelmingly worked by immigrants who toil under conditions of physical pain and environmental illness, the absence of basic legal protections, and fatality rates five times higher than all other workers.[1] After spending two years working the strawberry fields of Washington State with indigenous Triqui and Mixtec berry pickers from Oaxaca, cultural and medical anthropologist Seth Holmes noted that most of those workers declined to share in his appreciation for the striking beauty of their Cascade Valley surroundings; for workers, these picturesque spaces represented *"puro trabajo"* (pure work)—labor requiring them to bend over or pick on their knees seven days a week, often in great pain, exposed to dangerous chemicals, risking detainment and deportation, and living thousands of miles from family and home while barely earning enough to survive. As the typical berry picker's tasks were summarized by a Triqui worker named Abelino, "You suffer a lot in work" (Holmes 89, 93).

Among garden writers secure in their wealth and social position, there is a unique privilege in the act of marveling at hired gardeners who may not enjoy planting and weeding on their grounds. In one of the classic garden books of the twentieth century, Eleanor Perenyi complains of the difficulty of finding "well-trained gardeners who like their work," characterizing those she has hired over the years as a "long procession of incompetents, dumbbells and eccentrics, young and old, foreign and domestic" (*Green Thoughts* 80). Her disappointment in their alleged lack of skill and enthusiasm highlights a blind spot among many affluent and even middle-class garden owners, which Perenyi herself acknowledges at one moment in *Green Thoughts:* "We ... tend to imagine that the people who work for us take the same satisfaction we do in a happy effect achieved, a heavy chore got through," she writes. "Rarely is it so. Why should [the hired worker] have looked forward to taking care of *my* garden, planting *my* fruit trees? To him, it was just a part-time job, a way to earn some extra cash" (82).

Not only do pastoral fantasies in much garden writing distort the hard realities of manual labor; more broadly, the myth of North America as a garden has been used historically to justify the marginalization and exclusion of minorities throughout the United States. Garden imagery featured prominently in nativist writings of the late nineteenth century, including in Thomas

Bailey Aldrich's best-known poem, "Unguarded Gates" (1892), which called for federal restriction on immigration from eastern and southern Europe. Depicting America as a luxurious and unspoiled garden, Aldrich writes of

> A realm wherein are fruits of every zone,
> Airs of all climes, for, lo! throughout the year
> The red rose blossoms somewhere— . . . a rich land,
> A later Eden planted in the wilds.

Yet as his poem warns, this Eden of white European settlers was threatened by immigrants of color entering through America's "Wide open and unguarded" gates, an invasion that would make the Anglo garden over into a multiracial Babel:

> And through them presses a wild motley throng—
> Men from the Volga and the Tartar steppes,
> Featureless figures of the Hoang-Ho,
> Malayan, Scythian, Teuton, Kelt, and Slav,
> Flying the Old World's poverty and scorn;
> These bringing with them unknown gods and rites,—
> Those, tiger passions, here to stretch their claws.
> In street and alley what strange tongues are loud,
> Accents of menace alien to our air,
> Voices that once the Tower of Babel knew! (15–17)

Such nativist sentiments have found expression in real garden plots as well as their poetic representations. Many late nineteenth-century champions of the "old-fashioned" or "grandmother's garden" appealed to nostalgia for pre-Revolutionary America—the fabled golden era before industrialization, labor unrest, and, of course, mass immigration of workers of color (Hill 8). In her 1893 book *Art Out-of-Doors: Hints on Good Taste in Gardening*, Mariana Griswold Van Rensselaer joined a chorus of period garden writers in calling for the exclusive use of native plants to preserve a distinctly "national character" in the landscape. "We want American gardens, American landscapes, American parks and pleasuregrounds," she wrote, "not the features of those of a dozen different countries huddled together" (63). Such sentiments were anticipated a year earlier in Mary Caroline Robbins's glowing portraits of the grandmothers' gardens and country cottages outside Hingham, Massachusetts, a region that had preserved "the American race at its best," allowing visitors to still find gardens, homes, and habits "unadulterated by foreign admixture" (Robbins 167–68).

And predating all this, of course, the myth of a New World Eden served as a pretext to justify the displacement of America's original cultivators. When founding member of the Massachusetts Bay Colony, John Winthrop, called for increased settlement of New England in 1629, he anticipated objections to the displacement of indigenous people by invoking God's charge to the sons of Adam—namely, the English—to till and improve the land. Citing Genesis, his widely influential treatise argued that

> The whole earth is the Lord's garden, and he hath given it to the sons of men with a general commission: increase and multiply, and replenish the earth and subdue it.... Why then should we stand starving here for places of habitation ... and in the meantime suffer a whole continent as fruitful and convenient for the use of man to lie waste without any improvement? (139)

While Winthrop does make concessions for Native people's claim to their cornfields, his framing establishes a binary that defines not Native residents but rather European settlers as cultivators: "As for the natives in New England, they enclose no land, neither have they any settled habitation, nor any tame cattle to improve the land by, and so have no other but a natural right to those countries." Winthrop thus argued that the farming people of England—the true heirs of the Lord's garden—"may lawfully take the rest, there being more than enough for them and for us" (141).

This refusal to fully acknowledge Native people as cultivators in their own right takes different forms across colonial representations of the American garden—sometimes as a willful disregard of obvious fact to justify land seizure, and sometimes as a simple product of Edenic rhetoric and imagery as such. In early European accounts, the very depiction of North America as a garden paradise already implied a certain absence of any labor or effort from cultivators. Historian Jackson Lears notes that a great many seventeenth-century colonial accounts established an imagery of New England that was "more extractive than agricultural" (*Fables* 30). English colonist George Alsop's 1666 promotional treatise depicted Maryland as a "Terrestrial Paradice" bearing the last trace of our "Adamitical or Primitive situation." Here, not the native inhabitants but rather a mystical Edenic power works to "generously fructifie this piece of Earth with almost all the sorts of Vegetables ... Flowers ... Herbes and Rootes," offering "their benefits daily to supply the want of the Inhabitant[s] whene're their necessities shall *Sub-poena* them to wait on their commands" (31–33).

Such characterizations, which cast Native people as gleaners rather than growers, typically resulted from white settlers' own ecological and horticultural ignorance, leading those unfamiliar with the intricacies of Native cultivation techniques to misjudge the practice even when they saw it. Environmental historian William Cronon explains how, for instance, intermittent controlled burning of dense forest floors created conditions favorable to berries and other gatherable foods in New England. Yet English observers lacked the conceptual tools to understand that "Indians . . . were not just taking the 'unplanted bounties of nature'; in an important sense, they were harvesting a foodstuff which they had consciously been instrumental in creating" (*Changes* 51). That same structure of ignorance also led colonists in the Great Lakes region to overlook the careful husbandry involved in wild rice harvesting. Robin Wall Kimmerer, a plant ecologist and member of the Citizen Potawatomi Nation, notes that "Early colonists on Turtle Island were stunned by the plenitude they found here"; in just a few days of harvest, the Ojibwe could fill their canoes with enough wild rice to last all year. Yet

> the settlers were puzzled by the fact that, as one of them wrote, "the savages stopped gathering long before all the rice was harvested." She observed that "the rice harvest starts with a ceremony of thanksgiving and prayers for good weather for the next four days. They will harvest dawn till dusk for the prescribed four days and then stop, often leaving much rice to stand unreaped. This rice, they say, is not for them but for the Thunders. Nothing will compel them to continue, therefore much goes to waste." (181)

White colonists, as Kimmerer notes, construed this practice as "evidence of laziness and lack of industry on the part of the heathens. They did not understand how indigenous land-care practices might contribute to the wealth they encountered," how rice around the lakes was intentionally left for nesting ducks the Ojibwe hunted later in the season, and unharvested grain reseeded itself for sustainable harvests across the years to come (181).

Such myths die hard. Some three and a half centuries later, popular culture continues overwhelmingly to depict Native people hunting and making war, rarely as farming or gardening (Berry, *Enduring Seeds* xiii). Yet the American garden is more than just a fantasy realm constructed to subjugate and exclude the subaltern. Indeed, for many colonized, marginalized, and displaced growers, gardens are a critical site of resistance, an arena for imagining and creating their own visions of the good life, a place to reclaim a just relation to the land and the stories we tell about it. Immigrant growers frequently assert the garden's value as a living connection to memory, childhood, community, and home. Gardening can allow them to resist assimilation by preserving elements of their cultural heritage and identity, while simultaneously helping these immigrants establish a meaningful sense of belonging in unfamiliar new places. Other subordinated social groups acknowledge gardening as a way to experience a unique sense of agency as they reshape their physical surroundings according to personal desires and visions. Garden plots may give visibility to the invisible or voice to those unable to communicate in their native tongues. For those who have experienced trauma, gardening can provide comfort; for prisoners, a space of hope and futurity; for the homeless, a sense of stability, beauty, and home. And above all, perhaps, both real and represented gardens are a place to reimagine a more inclusive and sustainable ethic for our age. Across such accounts, land is understood not as property or resource but as an extended network of community and kin, a source of creative coproduction and a wellspring of diversity—both cultural and biological—that vastly enriches our shared stories.

These multispecies visions of the garden offer a categorical alternative to some of the dominant narratives of nature and humanity in Western culture. In the traditional Iroquois myth of Sky Woman, the mother of humanity receives aid from a community of nonhuman animals as she falls toward their world: seeing her plunge downward after tripping through a hole in the Sky World, geese fly up to break her fall, and while lowering her to a world made entirely of water, the beaver, otter, swan, and fish begin to create a suitable home for this dryland newcomer. Turtle offers his back, and the others dive beneath the water's surface to retrieve mud, spreading it across his shell. Sky Woman has not come without gifts of her own; in her initial tumble from above she attempted to stop her fall by grasping at the Tree of Life beside the hole and thus arrives on Turtle Island still clutching a fistful of seeds, flowers, and fruits. Scattering these in the newly created soil on Turtle's back, Sky Woman gives rise to the earth's food plants, trees, and wild grasses. That green world flourishes both for the unborn children she carries within her and for the helper animals who now come to live with her on Turtle Island (Shennandoah and George; Kimmerer).

As Kimmerer reminds us, such stories are not just relics of the past but also a "compass" that can direct our values toward more reciprocal environmental practices in the present. Unlike the Judeo-Christian Eve, banished from her garden home and instructed to subdue the wilderness into which she is cast, Sky Woman creates a garden for the flourishing of all life—both human and nonhuman creatures. "One story leads to the generous embrace of the living world, the other to banishment," Kimmerer writes: "One woman is our ancestral gardener, a cocreator of the good green world. . . . The other was an exile, just passing through an alien world on a rough road to her real home in heaven" (7). And so as we reaffirm some of the early stories of cultivation on Turtle Island—along with more recent accounts of marginalized growers—new pathways emerge for exploring the significance of American garden writing and its connection to claims for environmental justice.[2] These stories are told by gardeners who are not published writers (immigrant, homeless, imprisoned, and refugee gardeners) as well as by well-known literary figures like Alice Walker, Toni Morrison, Jamaica Kincaid, Leslie Marmon Silko, and Héctor Tobar. Together, their counterfantasies and critical interventions open a space where the menace of the garden with "Unguarded Gates" becomes a garden without any gates or walls at all, a shared place where more inclusive, reciprocal, and collaborative relations might be imagined and experienced.

"Little plots among the Jimson weeds"

> Siento que es mio . . . I feel like it's mine—mine, not like my private property, but mine like my planet. I think it's mine. Just like the sun, I say it's mine too. And like the air is mine. And the stars are mine. That's how I feel about the garden. And then, the people are part of it— of me, of the garden.
> —Monica Sanchez, member of Franklin Community Garden in Los Angeles

Toward the end of John Steinbeck's *The Grapes of Wrath*, displaced sharecroppers gaze over fences at unused and uncultivated private property to imagine what they might do with just "a little piece" of that rich California soil. As Steinbeck writes, some individuals "crept out in the evening . . . to hoe in the stolen earth," and with "a package of carrot seeds and a few turnips," they built "[s]ecret gardens hidden in the weeds." Yet, eventually, landowners—even those with no immediate intention of using these spaces—discover and swiftly crush their attempts. Interpreting the draconian response of police and property owners who evict those landless growers, Steinbeck suggests why these gardens cannot be tolerated: "Land hoed and then carrots eaten—a man might fight for land he's taken food from. Get him off quick! He'll think he owns it. He might even die fighting for the little plot among the Jimson weeds" (259).

For those who are hungry, the ability to grow food is indeed essential. Yet as Steinbeck hints here—and as we see in so many other accounts of gardening on the margins—physical hunger alone cannot explain a grower's intense bond with the land. Indeed, the significance of soil-based attachment may include everything from community belonging and connection with the past to preservation of memory and identity, personal artistic expression, and a redeemed experience of time itself. Survival, after all, is always more than just a metabolic affair.

Throughout American history immigrants have carried seeds to new homes both to preserve material links to places left behind and establish a sense of belonging in new homes. While twenty-first-century immigrants in the United States may have less access to land for food production than previous generations, many still find ways to plant seeds from their homeland in balconies and windowsills, community gardens, backyards, or tiny spaces between apartment buildings. In her study of immigrant gardening in California, *Paradise Transplanted*, Pierrette Hondagneu-Sotelo profiles the Franklin Urban Community Garden in Los Angeles as a powerful antidote to the experience of placelessness and exclusion among some of the city's poorest and most marginalized residents. The majority of these growers come from southern Mexico and Central America, having fled the wreckage of civil war, neoliberal trade policies, and other forms of social and economic violence. Like millions of other undocumented immigrants today, they find themselves cut off from home by an increasingly militarized U.S.-Mexico border. Since the 1990s, in particular, Hondagneu-Sotelo notes that "participating in transnational circuits by traveling back to visit family and home" has become significantly more difficult than it was for earlier generations of Mexicans and Guatemalans who were able to obtain legal status or simply cross a less dangerous border (135). Indeed, many today face the prospect of never visiting home again, and for these immigrants a debilitating *añoranzas*—or "permanent homesickness"—can set in. Planting seeds and nurturing crops from their home countries help establish an element of continuity and familiarity in strange settings, particularly among those who grew up in rural farming communities. Moreover, insofar as gardening involves an intimate engagement with natural cycles of regeneration and growth, it can allow individuals to experience a sense of "belonging" rooted in life and land rather than state institutions. As such, growers claim a relation to community and place that transcends nationality and legal status.

Of course, any number of physical objects or practices may help bridge present realities with elements of one's personal or collective past—a photo, an old keepsake, a familiar custom. Yet insofar as the sensorium triggers memory in some of the most immediate ways, gardening and food (aspects of everyday life that are themselves deeply sensory) offer especially potent links to faraway places, people, and experiences. As Hondagneu-Sotelo writes, Franklin growers who carried bulbs and seeds across the border or found other ways to procure cherished homeland plants like achiote, chiles, sugarcane, epazote, and yerba buena, comment on "the restorative power of being in a garden that looks, feels, and smells like their original homeland" (119). Indeed, as anthropologist Teresa Mares argues, for people throughout the world, food and food customs are immensely powerful material practices that "enact cultural identity and sustain connections" with community back home (335).

Yet sensory connection with the past goes beyond the mere production and consumption of food, and even much younger immigrants with no direct experience of farmwork or food preparation in their home countries can find themselves transported to a remote past through embodied garden experience. Hondagneu-Sotelo's interviews with Franklin growers include a conversation with Fernanda, a young woman originally from Oaxaca City who came to Los Angeles at such a young age that memories of her native land are fleeting and faint: "I forgot, I forgot a lot when I came here," she explains. Yet while unable to recall details of a specific place or scenario from her childhood, a kind of physical memory of Mexico's vegetation—something she perceives as existing "deeply in her bones"—awakens through gardening. "I felt like it was in me or something, I don't know where exactly," Fernanda recalls. And as she grew up in Los Angeles, that nebulous longing for her lost childhood in Mexico found its form in the inner-city garden plots: "I had a craving to plant something, and I did it. I had a craving to just pick a fruit out of the tree. And I finally did it. Or just to sweep, you know, the leaves, the water, [to experience] the smell" (Hondagneu-Sotelo 146–47).

As much as gardening may be a way of linking to the past, it can also reshape a small part of one's world in the present and future, helping individuals claim the right to more just and livable communities. Indeed, the material and symbolic power of making and shaping is so central for growers that Patricia Klindienst, a scholar of American immigrant experiences and ethnic gardens, asks us to wholly reconsider the customary practice of characterizing immigrants as "uprooted" or "transplanted" people.[3] In place of these metaphors, she proposes the immigrant as a gardener—someone who is less a passive object of history than an agent who actively shapes the world. Puerto Rican girls who have taken up gardening through a Latina youth program in South Holyoke, Massachusetts, embody this very promise of heightened agency in describing the garden's importance to them. As they look into the world surrounding them, perhaps for the first time they see their identities and efforts reflected back to them by a physical landscape they've helped create. Hilda Colon, the founder of South Holyoke's Raíces Latinas, notes how the spatial ambitions of these girls expands with their gardening experience, even noting a sense of prerogative more commonly associated with the likes of city planners than inner-city girls of color: as she explains, "Now every time they see a vacant lot, they say, 'That's a big space—can we turn *that* into a garden?'" (Klindienst 203).

For some, gardening efforts can even transform the meaning of brutally repressive and hostile environments. In memoirs of Japanese Americans imprisoned in World War II internment camps, gardens emerge as a kind of anticamp—a refusal of prison life's bleakness and regimentation. Some internees planted species that could not possibly survive in the camps' inhospitable desert climates, but the practice nonetheless allowed them to structure daily life around acts of care. Relationships to the environment once defined by oppression are now redirected toward hope, creation, futurity, and life. In her memoir *Desert Exile*, Yoshiko Uchida remembers internees in her prison block planting willow saplings brought "from somewhere beyond the desert." "The young trees looked too frail to survive in the alkaline soil," she writes, "but we all felt anything was worth trying. We longed desperately for something green, some trees or shrubs or plants so we might have something to look forward to with the approach of spring" (126). Other internees cared for abandoned apple and pear trees they found clinging to life in the Manzanar concentration camp. As Jeanne Wakatsuki Houston explains in her memoir, *Farewell to Manzanar*, she moved with her family to block 28, "right up next to one of the old pear orchards. That's where we stayed until the end of the war, and these trees stand in my memory for the turning of our life in the camp, from the outrageous to the tolerable" (95). Prisoners in southern Idaho also used gardening to defiantly reaffirm the very ethnic and cultural identities for which they had been imprisoned, "bonsai-ing" wild sagebrush that grew around the camp perimeters (Helphand 169).[4]

The history of American gardening is filled with these improbable acts. Even homeless growers manage to reinvent bleak city streets and empty lots through gardening, giving stunning expression to the garden's transformative power. Since 1989, photographer Margaret Morton has extensively documented the homeless street-growers of New York City who create and tend plots of corn, flower patches, and surreal gardens filled with scavenged stuffed animals. One grower, Bernard Isaac, showed Morton the abandoned railroad tunnel beneath Manhattan's Riverside Park where he lived for more than a decade, directing her attention to the frail plants he began tending after sprouts emerged from seeds blown down the shafts. Among these volunteers was an anemic-looking tree that hadn't survived the previous winter; yet as Isaac dreamed of a more secure future, he empathetically linked the tree's dilemma to his own and remained faithful to these seedlings struggling to survive in the darkness. After escaping his predicament, he explained, "I'd like to leave something like a plant or a tree behind, then one day return here and say, 'Look how my tree has grown'" (Morton, "Gardens" 303).

Given the meager resources of growers and the desolation of environments where such gardens are created, their very existence seems so improbable as to border on the miraculous. Indeed, in documenting elaborate fishponds built in bare dirt lots and towering sunflower and corn groves tended along

FIGURE 12. Margaret Morton, *Bernard's Tree*. © OmbraLuce LLC (1995).

trash-strewn alleys, Morton's photos force observers to ask themselves how people lacking basic resources for survival manage to transform devastated zones into spaces of beauty. Yet perhaps such a question misses the larger point. After all, the deficiency of home and security may be less an impediment than the *raison d'être* for these gardens: one might just as convincingly argue that many homeless growers do not simply garden *despite* but rather *because* their lives are continually shattered by displacement, violence, and vulnerability. And while individual plots may prove far from secure (with most of these gardens condemned to abrupt endings beneath the bulldozer's blade, as we have seen in the previous chapter), like a word spoken, even momentary garden "statements" can furnish an opportunity to be seen and heard. Indeed, one might venture that the ultimate power and appeal of these gardens lies in their capacity to make visible some of society's most invisible and voiceless groups.

In interviews with Patricia Klindienst, other voiceless groups—particularly non-English-speaking growers—similarly highlight gardening as an opportunity to "speak." Decades after fleeing Pol Pot's regime, Cambodian refugees in Amherst, Massachusetts, organized the Khmer Growers to cultivate food and flowers on four acres of land while preserving their culture and healing the wounds of genocide, torture, starvation, and forced labor. One of the garden's originators, Sokehn Mao, explains that many of the group's older refugees have never learned English: following the loss of family, friends, and homeland in Cambodia, they now struggle with the inability to be understood in their native tongue—a predicament that Mao equates with a loss of identity itself and a major source of depression and alienation for these elders. Small wonder, then, that these immigrants characterize the Amherst garden as their "spiritual place." As plantings begin to sprout in spring, Mao notes, participants feel "connected": even the oldest members can be found here from sunup to sundown. "They even ask people if they can build a house here," he explains, "because they don't want to go to town, they don't want to see anyone, they just want to talk to their own garden.... It doesn't speak a foreign language. It speak[s] their own language. Whatever they touch, it grows right out" (Klindienst 127).

Speaking, in this case, is not simply an act of individually broadcasting something to the world (in the way tagging a wall with one's name, an image, or a political message may be). Rather, speech acts in the garden are inherently reciprocal and thus closer to a conversation than a singular statement. In his claim that "[w]hatever [the elders] touch, it grows right out," Mao highlights how gardens directly respond to the grower's hands, knowledge, and effort. The practice involves a two-way dialogue arising from physical and intellectual knowledge applied to the living world, along with the response of that world in the form of leaves, blooms, and fruit. As such, Mao notes that older immigrants often feel "paralyzed" and "useless" in Amherst's urban environment, where they can no longer employ farming skills passed down through generations in rural Cambodia. "They want to do something, to be creative or to be useful," he explains:

> So they start to grow their garden.... These are the skills they came with—their hands, their knees, their legs, this knowledge. So as soon as they put the seed on the ground and it grow[s], they feel special. Maybe they're not good at raising their children in America, but this is [the] thing they wanted to show America and their children—this is the thing that they're good at. (qtd. in Klindienst 126)

Of course, not all immigrants who garden freely choose to do so. In tending America's lawns and landscapes, countless hired laborers—many of whom are undocumented and thus excluded from higher-paid work—endure significant physical hardships, exposure to toxic chemicals, poor pay, and no job security. Those workers also remain virtually unseen and unacknowledged as creators of the lush green landscapes around us. That invisibility is the subject of Los Angeles–based artist Ramiro Gomez, the son of Mexican immigrants employed in those very "behind-the-scenes" jobs. Gomez's paintings invert the customary dynamics of background and foreground in everyday domestic life by depicting the armies of workers who maintain Southern California's seemingly "breezy" lifestyle. Gomez also gained national attention for his acrylic-painted cardboard cutouts of immigrant workers, which he has installed on the East Lawn of the Capitol building, outside the White House gates, along busy intersections of Bel Air, and in the private gardens of affluent Hollywood estates—places where domestic workers are largely invisible. The collection of his work in *Domestic Scenes* (2016) offers a striking counterpoint to the typical coffee-table garden book featuring glossy images of unpopulated, "finished" landscapes where the tools and garden creators themselves have been removed from the frame.

This emphasis on documenting the undocumented, both in the work of Gomez and countless other advocates for immigrants' rights, suggests how invisibility itself can be more pernicious even than the physical demands of their work. Indeed, the challenging nature of gardening and landscaping is a source of pride among many laborers who uniquely understand the immense effort and skill it requires. Such dynamics invite several questions. What do gardens mean to those whose work is intimately connected with the land but isolated from basic modes of social, cultural, and political recognition and representation? What kind of insight, knowledge, and meaning arises from the lived experience of landless but highly skilled manual laborers, individuals who directly engage these green landscapes with their hands, muscles, and backs as well as their minds and imaginations?

These are among the questions explored by Héctor Tobar in *The Barbarian Nurseries* (2011), a novel where different garden practices and perceptions highlight deep disparities in America's twenty-first-century caste system. His is a complex and at times ambiguous account in which Latinx immigrants tend gardens for the enjoyment and consumption of their employers, and yet like nannies who form intense attachments to children under their care, those workers also develop forms of knowledge and pride that their employers can hardly appreciate as mere consumers of California's garden landscapes.

FIGURES 13A AND 13B. *Above:* Ramiro Gomez and David Feldman, *Gardeners, Doheny Drive, West Hollywood* (2012), archival pigment print. *Below:* Ramiro Gomez, *A Lawn Being Mowed (after David Hockney's A Lawn Being Sprinkled, 1967)* (2013), acrylic on canvas. Courtesy of the artist and Charlie James Gallery, Los Angeles. Top photo: Michael Underwood. Bottom photo: Osceola Refetoff.

When the Great Recession of the early twenty-first century brings financial trouble to the suburbs of San Diego, an affluent white couple (Scott and Maureen Torres-Thompson) cuts back on domestic expenses by letting their gardener and nanny go. Only the Mexican housekeeper, Araceli, is retained, and this story is told largely through her eyes. With no one but the tender-handed homeowners left to take up landscape maintenance around the house, Araceli mournfully watches the tropical garden out back wither, while Scott focuses instead on ministering to the front lawn (where "public" appearances must still be maintained). Prior to the layoffs, both the front lawn and backyard garden had been tended by Pepe, a talented Mexican gardener whom Araceli regards as "a magician, a da Vinci of gardeners, worth twice what they paid him." With his "thick, smart fingers" he brings stunning variety to life in the miniature jungle out back, a dreamscape that inspires the imaginative playtime adventures of the Torres-Thompson children. Araceli shares the children's love of the garden, marveling at this living thing that "glistened and shimmered like a single dark and moist organism, cooling the air that moved through it." Yet after Pepe is let go, "the leaves of that banana tree [began] cracking and the nearby ferns . . . turn[ed] golden." As is so often the case with invisible domestic workers, the employers only seem to notice the existence of their gardener in his absence. Maureen makes a few brief attempts at tending the garden but is ultimately deterred by the sinister-looking pesticides in the garage—chemicals she has been perfectly content to have hired laborers use over the years (11). Meanwhile, her husband immediately dismisses any such gardening interventions as futile:

> It seemed to him that it would take a village of Mexicans to keep that thing alive, a platoon of men in straw hats, wading with bare feet into the faux stream that ran through the middle of it. Pepe did it all on his own. He was a village unto himself, apparently. Scott wasn't a village and he decided to forget about the tropical garden for the time being because it was in the backyard, after all, and who was going to notice? (15)

But as the garden further deteriorates, it *is* noticed—and indeed becomes a punch line for one of Scott and Maureen's guests during an elaborate house party. This provides the impetus to finally tear the whole thing out and replace it with a garden of cacti and other succulents that "practically take care of themselves." In this way, a space meticulously cultivated by a skillful gardener, and lovingly used by the children, is supplanted by something expressly meant to obviate interaction, contact, care—indeed, even people themselves. In place of Pepe's garden, a team of day-laborers "installs" the succulent garden in the space of a single afternoon, complete with color-coordinated sand, volcanic rocks, and a ten-foot ocotillo cactus that the nursery manager calls the "compositional anchor to the whole garden"—highlighting the new space as an object to look at rather than a lived, interactive *place* for work or play (95). Araceli is painfully aware of this difference, noting all the experiential aspects of the old garden she will miss: the rustling of its broad leaves at the slightest breeze, the movement of the water in the small stream, and "the way the calla lilies changed their shape from early morning to noon" (106).[5]

The garden's "upgrade" thus presents more than just an allegory of replacing manual labor with better and more efficient solutions in our increasingly automated labor market. As Araceli's reflections indicate, a certain sensory experience and knowledge is also lost with the disappearance of bodily engagement from contemporary work. While the homeowners are perfectly content with a garden one merely looks at, Araceli and the children seem less convinced of its virtues. Mentally comparing the "instant" garden with its more labor-intensive predecessor, Araceli reflects that the "new desert garden was a static construction, while the tropical garden was a work of performance art, with Pepe as its star, stepping inside its verdant stage to send streams of water that cascaded over the tops of the plants, catching the sun's rays and making rainbows." When pressed by her *jefa* to say if she likes the new installment, Araceli cannot find the right words in English to express "that something was too still, that [she] preferred plants that you could feel breathing around you." Thus she simply replies, "I like it before. . . . But this is very pretty too" (106).

While this replacement of one garden with another is only a brief episode in a much longer novel, it speaks volumes about the social hierarchies and disposability of low-wage workers at the heart of Tobar's narrative, along with the unrecognized skill inherent in so-called unskilled labor. And Araceli, whose social position affords her a level of insight her employers lack, is just the person to reflect on such seemingly immaterial horticultural whims. As a vulnerable domestic worker and immigrant herself, she reflexively empathizes with the fate of an older, labor-intensive garden that is utterly at the mercy of a privileged family's personal finances and social insecurities, wincing with "pangs of nostalgia" as it is hacked down and fed to a chopping machine. More importantly, her status allows her to acknowledge the garden as something that thrives because of the hands that care for it—and comprehend the social implications of her employer's new preference for a zero-maintenance plot that makes those very hands superfluous. Thus, as the tropical garden is ripped out, Araceli says *adiós* to a place she recognizes as

"Pepe's garden," *adiós* to "the green leaves and flowers that carry the memory of his hands" (91).

These reflections on the meticulous labor inherent in so many domestic gardens—and the unacknowledged artistic talent of workers who create and maintain those vibrant spaces—run across countless biographical as well as fictional accounts of gardening in the shadows. Alice Walker uses her celebrated 1974 essay, "In Search of Our Mothers' Gardens," to identify the survival strategies of black women of the post-Reconstruction South "who might have been Poets, Novelists, Essayists, and Short Story Writers" but instead were sentenced to "toiling away their lives in an era, a century, that did not acknowledge them, except as 'the mule of the world.'" To Walker, a lifetime of brutalizing work that forces soulful individuals to stifle their creative gifts seems enough to drive anyone mad; and yet in investigating these women's strategies for preserving their souls and sanity, she discovers one simple method in the daily practice of her mother. After long days spent toiling in the fields, caring for children, making and mending clothes, housecleaning and preparing meals (activities that "muzzled and often mutilated" her artistic spirit), Walker's mother would slip out to garden at night until it was too dark to see, throwing herself into this "work her soul must have. Ordering the universe in the image of her personal conception of Beauty." It was, as Walker notes, the sole activity in which she could relate to the world as an artist.

Moreover, as Walker's essay suggests, this gardening practice not only constituted an act of spatial creation but also involved a temporal creation within a life where leisure time simply did not exist. Remembering her mother as relentlessly "hindered and intruded upon," Walker reflects that the very existence of these gardens—"with over 50 different varieties of plants that bloom[ed] profusely from early March until late November"—seems to defy basic temporal laws. Thus, as Walker's mother struggles under the extraordinary burdens of a schedule saturated by work and family obligations, where every moment is seized in the totalizing grip of survival, her garden activity seems to magically secrete excess time, like water from a stone.

Those who have always enjoyed ample leisure time for gardening (or ample resources for hiring others to garden) may entirely overlook the sheer luxury those uncolonized hours represent. The "insta-garden" that replaces Pepe's tropical creation in *The Barbarian Nurseries* prompts us to consider the difference between the garden as mere "installation" versus more traditional, labor-intensive versions that represent significant accretions of time. While the affluent white homeowners in Tobar's novel may lack appreciation for this distinction, for many poor and overworked individuals, the garden's very fantasy and appeal lies in the way it signifies a luxurious and excessive time, a slower pacing of everyday life.[6] In her 1997 novel *Paradise*, Toni Morrison profiles the gift of minutes and hours that homemakers suddenly enjoy in the early 1960s when the all-black town of Ruby experiences an unprecedented prosperity:

> In every Ruby household appliances pumped, hummed, sucked, purred, whispered and flowed. And there was time: fifteen minutes when no firewood needed tending in the kitchen stove; one whole hour when no sheets or overalls needed slapping or scrubbing on a washboard; ten minutes gained because no rug needed to be beaten ... two hours because food lasted and therefore could be picked or purchased in greater quantity. (89)

And yet, interestingly, nowhere in this painstaking inventory of minutes saved do we see Ruby's women "liberating" themselves from daily gardening tasks. In fact, the extra time gained is directly reinvested in their gardens:

> The dirt yards, carefully swept and sprinkled in Haven, became lawns in Ruby until, finally, front yards were given over completely to flowers for no good reason except there was time in which to do it. The habit, the interest in cultivating plants that could not be eaten, spread, and so did the ground surrendered to it.... The women kept on with their vegetable gardens in back, but little by little its produce became like the flowers—driven by desire, not necessity. Iris, phlox, rose and peonies took up more and more time, quiet boasting and so much space new butterflies journeyed miles to brood in Ruby. (89–90)

Such garden fantasies underscore the desire to reconfigure daily tasks around joyful, deliberative activity. Of course, unlike the women of Ruby, Alice Walker's mother has no such access to these middle-class comforts or labor-saving devices. Yet it is precisely this limitation that makes her garden all the more radical a figure. It does not emerge within a temporal *opening* in her daily routine; rather, it is imagined as something akin to a green shoot breaking through an endless concrete expanse, appearing within and *actively expanding* the uninterrupted and ubiquitous fabric of time devoted to work and survival. Consequently, when Walker remarks that her mother's gardens "grew as if by magic," she not only communicates the improbability of plant survival in the rocky soil where they lived; rather, she imagines the garden as a kind of violation of temporal law itself, as if its mere existence had somehow added a thirteenth number to the clock.

Crime Scenes in Paradise

> Why must people insist that the garden is a place of rest and repose, a place to forget the cares of the world, a place in which to distance yourself from the painful responsibility of being a human being?
> —Jamaica Kincaid (2001)

Notwithstanding the hopeful tone of such accounts of gardening on the margins, many postcolonial writers remain wary of the temptation to imagine gardens as a simple panacea, an opening into some realm unmarked by the violent legacies of racism and colonialism. Indeed, within works like Jamaica Kincaid's *My Garden (Book)* and Leslie Marmon Silko's *Gardens in the Dunes*, histories of slavery, Euro-American imperialism, biopiracy, and displacement constantly resurface to shatter the fantasies of growers seeking solace from those very injustices in their gardens. Silko's novel traces connections between plundered indigenous lands and lavish colonial gardens across Europe and the Americas, while the beloved botanical garden of Kincaid's Antiguan home becomes a scene of alarming childhood revelations: here among the rubber trees and other exotic specimens, the author discovers herself to be just another transplanted object in the grand pageant of Western empire. Yet as Silko's and Kincaid's works explicitly render these landscapes as a palimpsest and approach gardening as a strategy to *unearth* rather than conceal deeply sedimented histories in North America's soil, their garden writing reopens a space for excluded memories and voices. Although their gardens remain places that are far from safe and whole—sites marked by pain, risk, anger, and uncertainty—they are nonetheless realms these writers can claim and narrate as their own.

In *My Garden (Book)*, Kincaid tenaciously strips the innocence from American gardens by rereading their history through the lens of colonial occupation. Revisiting official botanical literature and other canonical works of Western gardening history, she notes that "[t]here is always a moment when I feel like placing an asterisk somewhere in its texts and at the end of the official story making my own addition," noting, for instance, the theft and transplantation of seeds in plantation economies and the stripping of indigenous names to apply Latin taxonomies to American plants. Yet Kincaid's interventions are not limited to the literary and historical archive; she also revisits her own earliest memories to reveal some rather dark chapters in Antiguan history. Reflecting back on the beloved botanical garden near her childhood home, Kincaid admits she regarded this as a magical space in her youth—the scene where she met lovers and passed afternoons with her stepfather during his illness, surreptitiously gathering herbs for his medicinal teas and resting with him in the shade of a rubber tree (144). Yet like everything else in the botanical garden, that rubber tree "was not present in Antigua through a benign curiosity" (148). At the time Kincaid only knew that it was "part of the economy of some of the people of the mysterious Far East" (145).[7] Within that fact, however, lies a vast, as-yet unapprehended history of plantation agriculture and colonial violence—sugar, cotton, indigo, rubber, tobacco, lumber; the creation of vast slave economies; dispossession and genetic theft—all of which involve Kincaid, her family and ancestors, and indeed everyone and everything in the Caribbean. Both plants and people are part of this grand accumulation strategy; and the botanical garden, as she learns, plays a unique role in these histories by staging a monument to colonial power and its ability to amass and display all the exotic flora of conquered lands. More insidiously, the botanical garden lulls visitors into a state of social and political amnesia by decontextualizing the world's diverse plant life and cultural meanings as mere scientific or aesthetic "specimens." As Kincaid notes, the rubber tree was a "curiosity" when it first came to the island; but eventually the Antiguans "accepted its presence in our midst, even as we accepted our own presence in our midst, for we, too, were not native to the place we were in" (145). In establishing this indeterminate parallel between her people and the history of the tree, Kincaid suggests the perils of naturalizing botanical transplantation. If the garden's history and origins can be overlooked here and simply dissolve into the calming "natural" backdrop it has become for so many Antiguans who enjoy it, perhaps the historical violence of human uprootings—including their own—can also be forgotten.

The botanical wonders of the British and American empires likewise serve as agents of shattered childhood innocence in Leslie Marmon Silko's novel *Gardens in the Dunes* (1999). Set in the 1890s, the narrative begins and ends in a hidden corner of the American Southwest, a tiny and dreamy garden tended by a few surviving members of the fictional Sand Lizard people (whom Silko loosely based on the O'odham and Colorado River people). The two remaining girls, Indigo and Sister Salt, learn subsistence gardening from their grandmother, who teaches them to tend native plants that thrive along the desert floodplain terraces: amaranth, datura, sunflowers, beans, corn, and melons. These gardens enable the Sand Lizard family to preserve—for a short time, at least—their way of life in the remote dune country along the California-Arizona border. Yet while this desert sanctuary initially seems frozen in time and safely secluded in space, the larger arc of Silko's novel takes us across the globe to explore the role of botanical collection and biopiracy in Euro-American colonialism and to expose luxuriant Anglo gardens and lifestyles as the spoils of that conquest.

After the Sand Lizard girls are captured and sent to a missionary school, the younger sister, Indigo, eventually lands in the custody of a white couple, the Palmers. These guardians take her on their travels across the northeastern United States and eventually throughout Europe. Sections told though Indigo's eyes highlight the joint uprooting of Native people and nonhuman life in this colonial process: when the family visits a wealthy relative who is transforming her grounds into a lavish landscape garden, Indigo is stunned to find greenhouses filled with exotics raided from across the globe and perceives two transplanted beech trees as captive beings sharing a fate much like that of her own people. As the trees arrive from Oyster Bay to give the new estate the "appearance of maturity," Indigo perceives the noble giants "lying helpless" in wagons, "wrapped in canvas and big chains," their "leaves shocked limp . . . the stain of damp earth like dark blood seep[ing] through the canvas" (182–83). Indeed, in sharing her own name with the *Indigofera*, a plant that Native Americans were once forced to cultivate on plantations and *encomiendas* up until Europeans shifted to an African workforce, Indigo is similarly depicted as a kind of resource and casualty within this grand colonial pageant. That status is further underscored by the views of her white guardian, the plant smuggler and curiosities trader Edward Palmer, whose primary interest in Indigo seems to hinge on perceptions of this Sand Lizard girl as yet another rare specimen—one of the "last of her tribe." At times, it is hard to tell the difference between Edward's regard for his ward and his broader ambitions to collect plants and seeds with commercial potential and ultimately "discover a new plant species that would bear his name" (78).

Yet despite overlaps in these two postcolonial garden accounts, in one regard Kincaid's experience of lost innocence is significantly more devastating than her fictional counterpart in Silko's novel (which we will revisit at the end of this chapter). Indigo, at least, discovers the malicious forces bound up with American gardens and botanical collection far from her own garden sanctuary still hidden safely in the dunes; Kincaid, on the other hand, discovers that history *within* the very garden that enchanted her childhood—a place that made her youth "bearable," that significantly contributed to her becoming a writer, and that served as the scene for "meet[ing] the great loves of [her early] life" (218, 147). The garden's status as both sacred and malicious in *My Garden* thus produces some odd twists—and occasional narrative contortionism—as Kincaid acknowledges the site's unsavory backstory while simultaneously seeking, somehow, to preserve its integrity within her own memory. In revealing the rubber tree's colonial origins, Kincaid stops short of fully implicating her childhood self in this disclosure. Instead, she displaces the structure of her own ignorance onto her father, casting him as somehow impossibly unaware of the history of conquest that filled Antigua with exotic plants (and people from other lands) and that orphaned him when his own father shipped off to work—and ultimately die—on the Panama Canal. As Kincaid frames it,

> my father, when sitting under the rubber tree in the botanical garden, was in the presence, the atmosphere, the shrine of Possession, and . . . he himself was an object, a mere thing, within it. . . . My father had absorbed all this culture of Possession: the rubber tree, the bamboo tree, the plant from which his medicine was made (this shrub was not native to Antigua . . .) . . . all that was in the botanical garden, including himself and me (and while speaking to his daughter he had removed himself, magically, from being a mere subject in this drama of possessing).

In concluding her anecdote, Kincaid summarizes all these fraught relations as somehow "of no importance to my father." And so as they sit in the garden and talk of the things that shattered his childhood, she notes with a mixture of pity and contempt that the phrase Panama Canal "rolled off his tongue as if he had a rightful and just claim to it" (148).

In deflecting attention away from the speaker as the real ingénue in this exchange, Kincaid's scene suggests deep anxieties around highlighting the conditions of ignorance under which cherished memories have been produced. In light of the larger account, of course, it seems nearly impossible to believe Kincaid's claim that "the botanical garden of my childhood is . . . Edenic in my memory" (143); yet the immensity of her *desire* to remember it as such becomes all the more apparent through her painstaking efforts to preserve some small, unspoiled pockets within this archive of childhood memory.

Of course, even as Kincaid has removed her childhood self into a kind of narrative witness-protection program here (and used her impossibly naïve father as her alibi), she has nonetheless dutifully revealed the tormented histories lurking beneath these splendid scenes. That commitment to disclosing the garden's dark underside later reemerges in the Kew Botanical Gardens Kincaid visits as an adult, where the writer recalls coming upon "the most beautiful hollyhock I had ever seen." No sooner has she allowed herself to be enchanted by this plant than Kincaid discovers her misidentification: the "hollyhock" turns out to be a flowering cotton plant. This time around, Kincaid is equipped with a historical perspective she lacked as a child, and accordingly she fills in the lacunae of the specimen's official field definition: "In the sharp, swift, even brutal dismissive words of the botanist Oakes Ames," she writes, the cotton plant at Kew is reduced to an economic annual, "but the tormented, malevolent role it has played in my ancestral history is not forgotten by me." At the same time, however, Kincaid suggests that the initial moment of misrecognition has allowed a certain aesthetic pleasure. In a line that seems uttered with mantra-like intent—a kind of self-willed reconsideration, perhaps—Kincaid states: "Cotton all by itself exists in perfection, with malice toward none" (149–50). In this wish that the flower could just be enjoyed as a flower, Kincaid reopens the possibility that botanical gardens might have some redeeming function. As literary scholar Rachel Azima has noted, the author's initial misrecognition highlights an essential contrast between the plantation and the botanical garden: "[I]n the former, cotton plants, like slaves, are understood as having only economic value, while the latter emphasizes cotton's aesthetic value" (105–6). In the end, of course, the aesthetic and the economic can never truly be separated, and Kincaid has already exposed the perils of any attempt to do so. Yet she also has trouble squaring her historically informed aversions with this particular experience of the cotton flower's beauty, wanting to indulge the sheer wonder found in a plant "all by itself." Ultimately, these tensions remain unresolved, but readers glimpse a certain possibility that encountering the plant outside its dominant historical and economic context can be something more than just an act of violence. Indeed, perhaps it could furnish the space to reimagine those relations, to attach alternative meanings and values to plants otherwise regarded as mere commodities.

Since the authority to define and conceal the meaning of plants (and our various relations to them) remains so tightly controlled within the botanical garden, Kincaid turns to her personal garden in New England as a more promising realm for reasserting her voice, creating her own aesthetic, and revisiting personal and historical memory on her own terms. Yet even in the controlled space of her backyard, this exercise remains fraught with peril, with both physical and symbolic remnants of America's colonial legacy continually surfacing in her garden. One spring Kincaid happens to be reading William Prescott's *History of the Conquest of Mexico* at planting time and learns that the beloved zinnias and dahlias she grows—flowers originally cultivated by the Aztecs—were plundered by Cortés after his armies slaughtered the people who tended them (6; 117–18). Moreover, after hiring day laborers to help with various tasks, Kincaid finds herself wondering if she herself has now "joined the conquering class," since "who else could afford this garden—a garden in which I grow things that it would be much cheaper to buy at the store?" (123). In seeking to live ethically from this small plot behind her home, Kincaid often finds that she does not even understand her own horticultural impulse—nor can she make sense of the unconventional shape her garden is taking. Eventually, however, her activity gains some clarity:

[I]t dawned on me that the garden I was making (and am still making and will always be making) resembled a map of the Caribbean and the sea that surrounds it, [but] I did not tell this to the gardeners who had asked me to explain the thing I was doing. . . . I only marveled at the way the garden is for me an exercise in memory, a way of remembering my own immediate past, a way of getting to a past that was my own (the Caribbean sea) and the past as it is indirectly related to me. (8–9)

This personal refashioning of an iconic colonial geography is a powerful, albeit unusual, gesture. Here, the colonized subject not only assumes an authorial role over this New World domain but does so through gardening, an activity Kincaid repeatedly identifies as a typically Western habit. At the same time, the colonizing perspective implied in her arrangement—the garden-as-Caribbean map—seems peculiar given the decolonizing intent of Kincaid's efforts. After all, its panoptic aesthetic seems to impose the totalizing view of imperial cartography itself, obliterating the intricate particularities of place and the partial and embodied perspectives of those who live and work in the dense folds of these island landscapes. Yet the very act of laying out a kind of colonizer's map here allows Kincaid to establish the narrative coordinates of her book, priming readers from the outset to recognize all subsequent discussions as an explicit revisiting of colonial history and its devastating legacy. Of course, with Kincaid as author (and place-maker) this time around, a wholly different story will unfold.

Careful that her garden will not be established at the cost of someone else's memories, Kincaid tells layered stories of its contents and production in her adopted home of Vermont (a place where she often relishes her status as "not-the-native"). Like all places, its histories and meanings do not begin and end with the current occupant's arrival; accordingly, Kincaid's account always seems to enter the garden story in medias res. One spring, maroon shoots emerge from the middle of her lawn, and through conversations with Vermont "natives" Kincaid learns of Mrs. McGovern, a woman who lived in the house years earlier and had peony beds in that spot. When Kincaid moves to a new house, she pauses to explain to readers that it was built in 1935 by a man named Robert Woodworth, "for himself and his wife, Helen, and their three children":

I am very conscious of this fact, for almost every day something makes me so . . . those uninteresting evergreens; when something, the plumbing, breaks and has to be repaired; the low cost of heating such a large house (it is well insulated); the room in which I write. He died in the room in which I write. (31)

Kincaid allows others, both past and present, to speak in her book, interlacing the larger narrative with their memories and anecdotes about this small piece of land in Vermont. Someone tells her of Woodworth's time-lapse photography in the garden, and Kincaid wonders if it involved the trilliums and squirrel corn that still grow outside her kitchen window. Another acquaintance relates the difficulty Woodworth faced digging holes in the rocky ground. No detail is treated as insignificant or superfluous. Kincaid also makes a special effort to view the place through the perspective of the youngest Woodworth son, who grew up in this house and occasionally drops by to visit it:

> He remembers when those ordinary, unimpressive evergreens were planted; he remembers how big they were in relation to his own height at the time they were planted. He will look at the trees, the evergreens, and he will place his hand somewhat above his head and say that he remembers them being much taller than he was when they were planted.

Such anecdotes about the Woodworths and other gardeners, both past and present, bring an expanded perspective to Kincaid's persistent refrain that "memory is a gardener's real palette" (218), highlighting the always-collective nature of what might otherwise seem the most "individual" of human faculties. That recognition informs Kincaid's refusal of any act that would uproot long-embedded memories for the convenience of the current occupants. At one point she hosts a guest who "knows a lot about landscape" but evidently little about the value of memories and social histories layered in its soil: when the man suggests that Kincaid improve this site by removing the old evergreens (trees Kincaid herself previously deemed "uninteresting"), she calls us back to the stories she has since learned about the land's former residents. Kincaid notes that the visitor "had never seen the youngest son of Robert Woodworth measure his grown self against the grown tree. To see the top of the grown tree now, the grown man has to arch his head way back until it is uncomfortable to swallow." The offense Kincaid takes is now on behalf of a lineage of human occupants as well as the trees themselves: so when the visitor leaves, Kincaid goes around to apologize to the trees, stating, "I do not find such a gesture, apologizing to trees, laughable" (34). In drawing on these collective narratives and combining them with her own gardening and writing in the present, Kincaid honors multiple pasts and dwells mindfully in a place that, like all gardens, is always deeply historical and richly sedimented with the desires, actions, and stories of other productive agents—human and nonhuman, present and past.

Gardens without Gates

> These stories are like plants, and you are the gardener. Every time you share a story out loud you bring it to life; you help it grow.
> —Caduto and Bruchac, *Native American Gardening* (1996)

> Our relationship to the land cannot heal until we hear its stories.
> —Robin Wall Kimmerer, *Braiding Sweetgrass* (2013)

As Toni Morrison reminds us, a great many historical notions of paradise have been defined through exclusion, "by who is not there as well as who is" ("This Side"). This dynamic gives rise to much of the violence in her novel *Paradise*, a story set in and around the all-black town of Ruby, Oklahoma, which founders established in 1950 as a new Eden for black residents. Morrison's plot centers on a group of women deemed dangerous "outsiders" by townspeople who not long ago came to Ruby to escape racial exclusion and violence themselves. In seeking to break this pattern, the outcast women experiment with radical models of openness and inclusivity in forming their own community in a former convent on Ruby's margins. Even their gardens resist exclusive notions of purity—and gain regional fame and admiration—by producing a "heavenly" strain of "hellfire peppers" (242). This mixing of the sacred and profane may even suggest the profoundly hybrid and inclusive soil *required* for sustainable cultivation, since no plot back in the patriarchal town of Ruby succeeds in transplanting the peppers: "though many customers tried planting the seeds, the peppers grew nowhere outside the Convent's garden" (11).

And yet as our discussion of Kincaid has indicated, "inclusion" is a matter not just of mixing but also about unearthing invisible, buried, or forgotten stories layered in the soil underfoot. Thus, to confront the violent exclusions running through dominant myths of the American garden, postcolonial garden writers put a premium on storytelling as a way to reclaim their place in the historical narrative and imagine more just and inclusive relations to the land. These inclusive gestures are not only multicultural but also multi*species*—acknowledging both human and nonhuman contributions to the making and maintenance of gardens (and indeed *all* natural/cultural landscapes we inhabit). As such, they offer visions of the American garden that radically expand our notions of environmental and ecological justice.

For indigenous people labeled as noncultivators—and accordingly dispossessed of their land—such commitments are of vast importance. Renarrating the American garden is not just a matter of correcting the violent forgeries in our national myth and reasserting Native people's land rights; it can also reconnect displaced communities with a lost heritage of food production and cultural identity. Traditional Iroquois (Haudenosaunee) gardening methods, for instance, have been preserved within stories of "The Three Sisters," a plant trio that thrives on mutual exchange. According to these accounts, the youngest sister in the family is tender and green, able only to crawl and thus dependent on the eldest to support her; the swift-footed middle sister wears a bright yellow frock and is prone to wandering, while the eldest stands erect above the other two, distinguished by her pale green shawl and silky yellow hair. These three sisters represent, respectively, the bean, squash, and corn plants—a group traditionally grown together by Iroquois people in a technique known as intercropping ("Three Sisters" 19–21).[8]

Ironically, as Patricia Klindienst points out, one of the most detailed records of this Iroquois growing practice in colonial New England was penned by John Winthrop Jr., whose own father had justified the displacement of Native people based on their failure to "improve" the land. Presenting his account before the Royal Society in 1662, Winthrop Jr. documented the virtues of intercropping as an exceptionally sustainable method of agriculture. As represented in the Three Sisters stories, cornstalks provide structural support or "poles" for bean vines to climb and access sunlight, while the broad leaves and wandering structure of the squash plants shade the soil, reducing weed growth and maintaining moisture in the ground (Winthrop 128–29). Indeed, the ecological wisdom of this technique was more sophisticated than Winthrop's contemporaries could have known: when planted together, the roots of bean plants fix nitrogen in the soil, which otherwise is quickly depleted by corn plants. And from a nutritional standpoint, the combination of beans, corn, and squash provides a complete balance of amino acids needed for human nutrition (Kimmerer 128–40). Yet as Klindienst notes, Winthrop Jr. somehow failed to see the vast contradiction between his own testament to the efficiency and productivity of intercropped gardens and "his father's claim thirty years earlier that the Indians did not know how to use land and so had no legal claim to it" (231).

Moreover, many European settlers missed the logic of intercropping entirely: accustomed to their own tidy monocultural fields, they were unable to perceive any "method" in the dense tangle of food plants typical of Native plots. As Native people continued to lose land and older modes of cultivation were eventually supplanted by vast monocultures, mechanization, synthetic fertilizers, and pest control, intercropping fell into relative obscurity in many communities. Indeed, by the mid-twentieth century, the once-sacred maize of indigenous North Americans had been transformed into the very cornerstone of an international processed-food industry, with corn constituting the largest single crop in U.S. agriculture and appearing in one out of every four of the nearly forty-five thousand products in the average American supermarket—from hot dogs and ketchup to Pop-Tarts and beef, canned fruit, frozen yogurt, diapers, toothpaste, candy, and soda (Pollan, *Omnivore* 19). In this way, many twentieth-century descendants of people stripped of *land* under Winthrop's logic eventually lost traditional *methods* under the juggernaut of industrial agribusiness as well.[9] Most critically, this legacy of colonial appropriation spread from the more "visible" outward forms to overtake indigenous structures of meaning themselves, with the sacred and storied seed converted to a currency and the rich cosmologies that once included land, water, indigenous wisdom, and a diverse community of life in and above the soil now transformed into mere commodities.

Yet even within periods when many of the gardens themselves disappeared, Iroquois stories preserved this knowledge of intercropping methods. Despite the fact that no one he knew grew a Three Sisters garden, Clayton Brascoupé, a Mohawk and member of the Six Nations of the Iroquois Confederacy, recalls the persistence of the old stories on the Tuscarora Indian Reservation where he grew up. Reflecting back on the 1950s and 1960s, he notes, "I'd never seen it, ever, when I was growing up. People knew about it, people talked about it, people referred to the story, but I never saw one person do it" (Klindienst 7). Motivated by the radical spirit of the 1960s and increasing public alarm over the toxic effects of industrialism, commercial agriculture, and other forms of Western land abuse, Native activists turned to their elders to recover indigenous knowledge, combining those alternative techniques with research in sustainable agriculture practiced throughout the world. The Native American rights movement of the 1970s and 1980s further empowered communities to reclaim their cultural heritage—not only through food production but also in indigenous languages, narrative, dress, and other cultural practices. Today that movement continues to flourish, with Native cuisine, high-profile chefs and restaurants, gardening programs, publications, and other initiatives popularizing a "pre-colonization diet."[10] Brascoupé himself went on to serve as founding director of the Traditional Native American Farmers Association, an intertribal consortium that works to make family-scale farming a viable profession—especially among young people—by educating communities about traditional crops and land-use philosophy, while preserving and distributing heirloom seeds of indigenous foods.

Brascoupé explicitly links his knowledge and philosophy to traditional narratives like the Three Sisters story and Iroquois creation story, in which the world's original garden—actually conceived as a grave—gives birth to the traditional plants of his people: corn, beans, squash, and tobacco. As he recalls of his initial (re)awakening to the spiritual and ethical dimensions of Native methods,

> I listened really carefully, and I began to understand what [those stories] were telling us. If we eat this diet that was described in oral tradition telling how this land was created, how the spirit of the earth—her being—came with the corn, beans, and squash, we're eating a balanced diet. And if we plant these things in the prescribed manner, we are also taking care of the land, our first mother. (Klindienst 8)

As Brascoupé's comments indicate, the stories and rituals are more than just entertainment. Similarly, they are more than practical instructions on food production familiar to many Western garden readers. Rather, these Native gardening stories present full cosmologies that affirm the personhood of nonhuman life and our responsibility to engage nature in a spirit of reciprocity. Such a gardening approach may even be seen as a form of "sacred ecology," a concept that indigenous studies scholar Mascha Gemein describes as "encompass[ing] ecology and spirituality, positing humans as part of and partner within nature. Values and ethics derive from the necessity of empirical knowledge and reciprocity between humans and other natural counterparts to create an inclusive, holistic community" (493). Even popular "instructional" gardening books like Michael Caduto and Joseph Bruchac's *Keepers of Life* and *Native American Gardening* are inextricable from indigenous narrative traditions that promote ethical environmental practices and sacred identification with plants and the broader natural world. These works do not impose lines of separation between practical aspects (how to cultivate and use plants for food, medicine, and ornament); stories about the sacred origin of particular crops; gestures of thanksgiving that attend different harvests; the meaning of various natural phenomena; or creation stories in which Native people themselves originate from plants like maize, the ash tree, or butternut squash. Caduto and Bruchac's works also share Native teachings on giving thanks through song, art, prayer, and ceremony to encourage a spirit of mindfulness and gratitude before one takes life from the soil (whether through gardening or foraging). Above all, the integrated structure of Native garden writing seeks to promote "empathy with and responsible stewardship toward all plants on Earth," as *Keepers of Life* makes explicit (xvii). Because "community" and "kin" go beyond the narrow Western boundaries of "humans-only," this Native gardening practice demands acts of sharing among nonhumans: rather than focusing on chasing off raccoons and deer that may take interest in one's food garden, cultivators are instructed to plant extra seeds so that the harvest is sufficient for all (*Native American Gardening* 65, 80).

While such instructions are likely to be dismissed as absurd by many Western gardeners, they are in fact based on thousands of years of collective indigenous observation and practice, on what Daniel Wildcat calls "multigenerational deep spatial knowledges" in his environmental treatise *Red Alert! Saving the Planet with Indigenous Knowledge* (2009). When integrated with contemporary scientific knowledge and technologies, Wildcat argues, indigenous wisdom may even offer the kinds of "insights into how to live well in the diverse environments of this planet" at a moment of unprecedented ecological crisis and extinction (15-16). Within Native North American gardening narratives, one of the most well-known examples of such practical ecological wisdom is related through the story of the Corn Spirit who abandons people who refuse to honor her—an account suggesting the mutually reinforcing relation between effective husbandry and ethical practice as preserved within storytelling tradition. Robin Wall Kimmerer, a professor of plant ecology and student of her own people's indigenous land practices, explains how versions of the corn myth serve as a cautionary tale among Native people from the Southwest to Northeast. During the good years when harvests were so bountiful that little work was needed to maintain the corn plants, villagers became idle and eventually neglected to observe the prescribed ceremonies or sing songs of gratitude to the plants. They wasted the corn or used it in frivolous ways not intended by the Three Sisters. Feeling dishonored, the Corn Spirit left in search of a community that would value her contributions, and the following season no corn grew in the people's fields, leaving them hungry and in despair (Caduto and Bruchac, *Keepers;* Kimmerer 187-88). "When they abandoned gratitude, the gifts abandoned them," Kimmerer notes (188). Like much traditional myth, these stories need not be "factually" accurate to communicate a deeper truth. Indeed, what might seem like arbitrary narrative custom contains the collective ecological wisdom of people passed down through generations. The corn story, and others like it, promotes an ethos of mindfulness and a spirit of reciprocity in human use of nature's gifts. As a scientist, Kimmerer shows how traditional protocol pertaining to a wide variety of Native subsistence practices—fishing, foraging, hunting, gardening, and the use of plant materials for other everyday purposes—is based on sophisticated environmental observation and ongoing monitoring of populations. "The traditional ecological knowledge of indigenous harvesters is rich in prescriptions for sustainability," she writes. "They are found in Native science and philosophy, in lifeways and practices, but most of all the stories, the ones that are told to help restore balance, to locate ourselves once again in the circle" (181, 179).

Literary fiction similarly acknowledges the intimate link between gardening, traditional storytelling, environmental ethics, and the preservation of Native cultures. In Silko's *Gardens in the Dunes*, stories passed down to the young Sand Lizard girls contain practical instructions for subsistence practices—

and perhaps a path toward self-determination—in the remote dune country beyond encroaching white culture. These narratives and rituals also strengthen a sense of identity and moral accountability toward nonhuman nature that is central to Sand Lizard philosophy. It is surely no accident that Grandma Fleet, the novel's most skilled gardener, is also the most accomplished storyteller. In reciting the old stories to Indigo and Sister Salt, Grandma Fleet prepares these girls to live ethically on the land, telling of the original gardens planted for their people by Sand Lizard, a relative of Grandfather Snake, and passing on ancient instructions for tending their plots. "The first ripe fruit of each harvest belongs to the spirits of our beloved ancestors, who come to us as rain," she explains; "the second ripe fruit should go to the birds and wild animals, in gratitude for their restraint in sparing the seeds and sprouts earlier in the season. Give the third ripe fruit to the bees, ants, mantises, and others who cared for the plants" (14). Here, a multispecies cast is acknowledged as part of the Sand Lizard story and recognized for its contributions to the health and integrity of the gardens. Crucially, then, preserving the Sand Lizard narrative and gardening heritage does not just reflect something past but *actively produces* a broadly inclusive community in the present, one that includes water cycles, seed-carrying birds, pollinating insects, plants as bearers of fruit, reptiles as ancestor figures, and human actors both living and deceased as a source of practical gardening knowledge. Grandma Fleet's stories also include instructions to entrust some of the garden's reseeding to natural agents by leaving a few choice pumpkins and squash unharvested. In this way, animal cultivators take a leading role in the process: "Old Sand Lizard insisted her garden be reseeded in that way," she explains, "because human beings are undependable; they might forget to plant at the right time or they might not be alive next year" (15). In short, nonhuman agents are recognized as gardeners in their own right: after all, the very existence of any plant—whether wild or domesticated—ultimately depends on larger natural processes that play out on vast scales of time and space and involve countless animate and inanimate actors and interdependencies. Meanwhile, in noting the limitations and unreliability of human interventions, our own role in the garden is recast from that of superior "manager" to just another member of nature's community (and beneficiary of its gifts). Humans may be important agents in a given garden, but they are hardly the source of the life principle underlying it.

The Sand Lizard garden ethos thus stands in marked contrast to the exclusivity of both early European myths that cast Native people out of the American garden and the popular style of "Grandmother's Gardens" (in vogue during the 1890s when Silko's novel takes place)—a garden trend that played on racist and anti-immigration sentiments by urging white growers to preserve "native" plants and styles from a colonial era when western European immigration predominated. Whether intentional or fortuitous, Silko's indigenous version of the "grandmother's garden" puts an ironic spin on the commercial version sharing this name in the 1890s. Not only does Grandma Fleet's garden reclaim from European settlers the distinction of the "native"; it also defines the "traditional" American gardens as profoundly integrative. Indeed, Grandma Fleet is a curious experimenter and avid collector of seeds: "The more strange and unknown the plant, the more interested Grandma Fleet was," Silko writes. "[S]he loved to collect and trade seeds. Others did not grow a plant unless it was food or medicine, but Sand Lizards planted seeds to see what would come; ... and Grandma said they never found a plant they couldn't use for some purpose" (83–84). In this way, the key elder in Silko's novel establishes Native garden practice as hybrid and open-ended rather than isolationist or pure. Indeed, as literary scholar Shelley Saguaro points out, "the notion of a static or 'pure' tradition is not accurate nor was it ever desirable or insisted upon by Native communities themselves." Silko insists on sovereignty, respect for ethnic heritage, and the right to maintain Native customs and lifeways; and yet, as Saguaro insists, this "should not be misconstrued as a culture wanting to be a museum piece" (197).

And so when Indigo ultimately returns to the dunes at the novel's end, resuming care for the old gardens according to ancestral teaching, her homecoming is not some doomed attempt at reliving the past nor a retreat from the historical forces reshaping the world at this pivotal turn-of-the-century moment. Combining Sand Lizard philosophy with careful botanical observation and the exchange of seeds via gift giving throughout her European travels, Indigo has become a thoroughly cosmopolitan and integrative gardener, uniquely positioned to hybridize the old gardens with a vast repertoire of new seeds, stories, and horticultural practices. And in contrast to colonial plant-smugglers like Edward Palmer, who seek to plunder, objectify, name, and possess, Indigo has rigorously preserved and honored multiple stories and garden customs during her botanical education and "Grand Tour," learning and retelling the local names, uses, and meanings of the plants she collects and forging intercultural alliances with women who tend these faraway gardens. As such, her practice suggests that these botanical newcomers—European, Mexican, Anglo, and more—will not supplant but rather fortify the already-diverse garden culture Indigo has inherited from her people, thus strengthening its chances of survival into the future.

Lest we forget the profound ethical implications of the stories we tell, Ursula Le Guin reminds us of Western culture's long romance with the Warrior-Hero narrative, a legacy that glorifies violence, patriarchy, possession, and mastery of nature. Of course, the hero narrative is neither recent nor uniquely Western, and in "The Carrier Bag Theory of Fiction" Le Guin traces its history back tens of thousands of years to cave paintings depicting the spear-wielding hunter, the thrill of the chase, and the kill. Yet these are not the only stories that can be told. Imagine how our values might shift, Le Guin suggests, if we turned from the stories of the hunter to those of the gatherer—to stories reflecting the experience of women and other collectors of plants and grains, to activities that seek not the beast but the seed. In light of the challenges facing us today, our survival may even depend on such a narrative refocusing. "It sometimes seems that the story is approaching its end," Le Guin writes. "Lest there be no more telling of stories at all, some of us out here in the wild oats . . . think we'd better start telling another one, which maybe people can go on with when the old one's finished. . . . [I]t is with a certain feeling of urgency that I seek the nature, subject, words of the other story, the untold one, the life story" (168).

Perhaps there is no better place to start than with the stories of life found in postcolonial garden writing. After all, like the Iroquois myth of Sky Woman—the mother of humanity who shares the gift of seeds with all life on earth and acts as cocreator of its gardens—Silko's stories invite us to reconsider some of the foundational narratives of Western thought as such. This reframing extends back to the first biblical garden and the serpent who corrupted it: yet in *Gardens in the Dunes*, the very archvillain of Judeo-Christian paradise is represented neither as invader nor as menace but rather as the guardian of the desert springs that give life to people and plants. After white settlers kill the old rattlesnake in the garden during Indigo and Sister Salt's absence, the girls invite the serpent's daughter to return to the spring at the novel's end, affirming her presence as an honored member of the garden's spiritual and ecological community.

Given the environmental and social crises of our age, it is hard to overstate the importance of this simple act of reintegration. For if the Garden of Eden story is framed by exclusion and expulsion, Indigo's garden comes into being precisely *because* of its diverse cast of contributors—human and nonhuman, indigenous and immigrant, those who are rooted in native soil and those transplanted from other lands. In inviting the snake to also rejoin this family, *Gardens in the Dunes* cultivates a space in which more inclusive stories can regenerate, planting seeds of justice and sustainability to support the flourishing of all members of our shared earthly garden.

EPILOGUE

Garden Writing and the Phenomenology of Dirt

> What an occupation [gardening] is for thought! . . . [Y]ou are not thinking about anything, but are really vegetating, like the plants around you. I begin to know what the joy of the grape-vine is in running up the trellis, which is similar to that of the squirrel in running up a tree. We all have something in our nature that requires contact with the earth. In the solitude of garden-labor, one gets into a sort of communion with the vegetable life, which makes the old mythology possible.
> —Charles Dudley Warner (1870)

When Charles Dudley Warner published his garden account nearly a century and a half ago, he helped set in motion a literary mode touching on many key fantasies and concerns of American life explored throughout this book—issues of labor, leisure, place, food production, consumer culture, public space, the dynamics of belonging and exclusion, and many more.

Our world, of course, has changed considerably since 1870. Today, we face challenges that would have seemed unimaginable to Warner's readers: climate change, ocean acidification, cataclysmic soil loss and water depletion, superstorms and drought, pervasive chemical pollution, and levels of habitat and biodiversity loss that may be ushering in Earth's "sixth mass extinction" event. In the face of these issues, it may seem quaint to imagine that everyday gardening practices or literature hold any useful responses or solutions. And yet perhaps this genre's reflections have more relevance today than ever, providing insights that uniquely speak to our present moment in the Anthropocene.

Garden writing is a genre steeped in embodied practice; as such, it offers an important angle of vision into our physical encounters with nonhuman nature and the reciprocal dynamics connecting humans to wider communities of life. In fact, in calling us back to the sense experiences we share with other forms of life, gardening practice can remind us of our own animal existence, promoting felt and imagined connections (what phenomenologists call "vital sympathies") that are a precondition for extending moral consideration beyond human life.

In opening this book, we visited the gardener in wintertime, trapped indoors amidst stacks of seed catalogs that fuel fantasies of the green world's return. Yet as Czech author Karel Čapek once noted, it is not the visual elements of a completed garden that primarily drive the grower's fantasies in those frozen months, but rather the desire to plunge one's hands into the soil, to "hoe, manure, trench, dig," to "rake, order, water, multiply . . . dung, weed, sow," to "smell the soil," "wipe off sweat," to "eat like a wolf . . . feel hard buds, develop the first spring blisters and altogether live, broadly and vigorously, after the gardener's fashion" (28).[1] Garden writers commonly make distinctions between "mind gardeners" (those who merely design green spaces) and what Julie Messervy calls "dirt gardeners": those who are "gardener[s] of the hands," experiencing the green world with all senses engaged, bodies lowered down close to the roots and the worms (102–3). Indeed, the high priestess of American gardening herself has partly built her empire on the fantasies and desires involving such intimate, earthbound activity: as any of her followers can attest, the iconic image of Martha Stewart shows her with hands plunged in the dirt (Graham 352).

So central is the body to gardening practice that growers even reflect on human anatomical design in terms of the garden's need. In profiling the gardener, Čapek assesses the body's specific intricacies insofar as they are amenable or inconvenient to garden tasks, describing how "legs may be folded in different ways; one may sit on the heels, kneel on the knees, bring the legs somehow underneath, or finally put them round one's neck; fingers are good pegs for poking holes, palms break clods or divide the mould." The human back, unfortunately, "remains an inflexible thing which the gardener tries in vain to bend"—a predicament that leads Čapek to wonder why gardeners should have such a troublesome body part in the first place. These reflections inform his admiration for the backlessness of worms and his conclusion that "[if] gardeners had been developing from the beginning of the world by natural selection, they would have evolved most probably into some kind of invertebrate" (24). His lived experience in the garden even gives rise to whimsical fantasies of a different anatomical design altogether, with Čapek reflecting on how gardeners ideally

> would have legs like beetles, so that they need not sit on their heels, and they would have wings . . . so that they might float over the beds. Those who have had no experience cannot imagine how one's legs are in the way, when there is noth-

ing to stand on; how stupidly long they are if one has to fold them underneath to poke with a finger in the ground; how impossibly short they are if one has to reach the other side of the bed without treading on a clump of pyrethrum. If only one could . . . have limbs telescoping like a photographic stand! (38)

This intensely physical emphasis in gardening reflection arises not only from the embodied experience of *working* in the soil but also from the rich sensuous pleasures of *consuming* its products. George Eliot celebrates garden experience for involving "no monotony of enjoyment for one sense to the exclusion of another; but a charming paradisiacal mingling of all that [is] pleasant to the eye and good for food" (134). In "Giving Good Weight," John McPhee conveys the multisensory delights of consumption in less measured language, narrating the experience of pulling onions from the dirt and being driven wild by the feel of their weight as they're heaved from the ground, the sensation of peeling them sheet by sheet, the wetness and sting and aromatic fullness that fills his mouth at first bite. In engaging their various sensuous features, he admits to becoming "so crazed with the lust for these bulbous herbs—these enlarged, compressed buds—that I run to an unharvested row and pull from the earth a one-pound onion, rip off the membranous bulb coat, bare the flesh, and sink my teeth through leaf after leaf after savory mouth-needling sweet-sharp water-bearing leaf to the flowering stalk [at its] center" (61). Contemporary poet and gardener Ross Gay takes these reflections on the interpenetration between body and biosphere to their ultimate biological conclusion in celebrating the process by which fruit trees build themselves out of decomposed body parts:

> You're right, you're right,
> the fertilizer's good—
> it wasn't a gang of dullards
> came up with chucking
> a fish in the planting hole
> or some midwife got lucky
> with the placenta—
> *oh, I'll plant a tree here!*—
> and a sudden flush of quince
> and jam enough for months—yes,
> the magic dust our bodies become
> casts spells on the roots
> about which someone else
> could tell you the chemical processes,
> but it's just magic to me. ("Burial" 11)

Taken together, the intensely physical desires and urges characterizing these accounts offer extraordinary insight into our particular historical moment, throwing into relief a condition that has become a defining feature of modern life: the proliferation of virtual experience, diminished physical contact with "wild nature," and the rapid disappearance of habitats (including public spaces in cities themselves).

Recent decades have seen a surge in language and concepts expressing both the desire and angst surrounding our relations to the nonhuman world: from E. O. Wilson's *biophilia*, the innate "urge to affiliate with other forms of life"; to Camille Parmesan and Lise Van Susteren's "climate depression," the hopelessness arising from political inaction and social anxieties in the face of projected climate disaster; to Richard Louv's "nature deficit disorder," which links behavioral and psychological problems to the absence of outdoor activity and contact with nature; to lepidopterist Robert Pyle's "extinction of experience" and ecopsychologist Peter Kahn's "environmental generational amnesia," where the loss of intact wilderness areas—and each generation's declining experience of them—dilutes our concern for wild creatures and ultimately shifts humanity's "baseline" for the idea of wilderness as such.[2] Robin Wall Kimmerer, a biologist and member of the Citizen Potawatomi Nation, summarizes much of this anxiety in her reflections on "species loneliness":

> I'm trying to imagine what it would be like going through life not knowing the names of the plants and animals around you. Given who I am and what I do, I can't know what that's like, but I think it would be a little scary and disorienting—like being lost in a foreign city when you can't read the street signs. Philosophers call the state of isolation and disconnection "species loneliness"—a deep, unnamed sadness stemming from estrangement from the rest of Creation, from the loss of relationship. As our human dominance of the world has grown, we have become more isolated, more lonely when we can no longer call out to our neighbors. (208)

And while these responses may often focus on "wild" rather than "domestic" nature, the underlying desire for physical contact with our living world surely lies at the heart of all such expressions, wherever they may come in for landing.

Of course, the general sense of alienation from nature is hardly unique to our moment; that perceived loss, as we have seen, informs biblical accounts of human expulsion from the Garden and arguably goes back to civilization's earliest known literary works.[3] More recently (at least since the Industrial Revolution), narratives of a severed natural bond have been a mainstay of Western environmental writing. Yet today's particular incarnation, with its explicit anxieties about vanishing *embodied* experience, suggests the unique ways that our perceptual capacities are being transformed along with the sensuous landscape that serves as an external counterpart and repository for human sensibilities, memories, and experience. Take, for example, the following passage from Rebecca Solnit's *Wanderlust*, a book on the social history of walking. Near the end of her account Solnit reflects on contemporary gyms as factories for the production of muscles, spaces composed of "isolated figures each absorbed in his or her own repetitive task" (262). The author admits that while lifting weights and pulling machine levers at the gym, she often imagines herself pumping water or lifting hay bales. This imagined simulation of classic farmwork leads her to wonder:

> What exactly is the nature of the transformation in which machines now pump our water but we go to other machines to engage in the act of pumping, not for the sake of water but for the sake of our bodies, bodies theoretically liberated by machine technology? Has something been lost when the relationship between our muscles and our world vanishes, when the water is managed by one machine and the muscles by another in two unconnected processes? (263)

Again, this reflection appears in a book about walking, not cultivation; yet the discussion lands squarely in the midst of garden and farm territory when Solnit takes up the problem of bodily disconnection from meaningfully productive activity. That turn should hardly feel surprising to contemporary readers, emerging as it does from a broader postindustrial gestalt where farmwork and food cultivation are repeatedly, almost reflexively invoked as a touchstone for modes of production that intimately connect our bodies to fundamental processes in the natural world. Michael Pollan's comments are typical here: the activity of gardening, he argues, has merit in its simple power to remind one that "you need not be dependent on specialists to provide for yourself—that your body is still good for something and may actually be enlisted in its own support" ("Why Bother").

Of course, gardening and farming themselves are no guarantee that one will be plunged into a relation of physical intimacy with nature (or, indeed, that one will *relish* such experience); in fact, a certain approach to gardening has increasingly been remade into a kind of "virtual experience" itself. Despite his praise for the immersive, hands-on experience of home food production, Michael Pollan juxtaposes his own practice with his father's quintessential 1960s approach, when gardening amounted to installing a state-of-the-art sprinkler system he could run from his "command center" in the garage. Such a method effectively "replaced laborious, direct involvement with the earth and plants" with mere supervision and "technological tinkering." Little wonder, then, that his father failed to bond with this "remote-controlled" landscape (*Second* 31). Similar concerns run back even earlier in the twentieth century, with John Steinbeck linking our exploitation of farmland, in part, to the mechanization of production: in *The Grapes of Wrath*, corporate agribusiness seizes a once intensely physical vocation and reinvents it as the mere driving of heavy equipment, creating a generation of machine operators who have never crumbled the soil in their hands or "let the earth sift past [their] fingertips," who "could not smell the land as it smelled; [their] feet did not stamp the clods or feel the warmth and power of the earth. [They] sat in an iron seat and stepped on iron petals" (36, 38).

Again, such accounts of lost intimacy with the natural world arise in representations of consumption as well as garden and farm-based production. As we have seen in chapter 3 (and as any reader of contemporary garden writing already knows), recollections of how food *used* to taste, and protests over the standardization of edible and ornamental plants, are ubiquitous in the genre—from depictions of cardboard strawberries and tennis-ball-like tomatoes to the "dusty little Madeleines of commercial florists" and apples that "taste like raw potatoes and look like Jungian archetypes." While some may dismiss these grievances as the trivial carping of gourmands, they offer an important glimpse into the historical transformations of industrial agriculture (with crops standardized to suit industrial priorities and horticultural biodiversity dramatically reduced across the world), along with their impact on the human sensorium itself.

Yet if garden writing were merely an obituary for lost embodied experience and discarded sensory landscapes, it would hardly have the massive appeal it enjoys today; indeed, while expressions of loss may be a common subtext in many narratives, what magnetizes readers, ultimately, are the scenes of rich sensuous engagement with our more-than-human world. These encounters span the natural and built environment: the kitchen counters where Eleanor Perenyi luxuriates in sliced tomatoes "slippery as an eel" (219); the urban gardens where Ross Gay feeds his soil shovel-loads of cow shit and spent beer grains that "make the compost writhe giddy and lick its lips" ("Catalog" 83); the streets of Philadelphia where dazed pedestrians gather beneath a fig tree "looking into it like a constellation," pointing at the fruit and "reaching into giddy throngs of yellow-jackets sugar stoned" to gather figs (3, 4); and Katharine White picking wild lilies by canoe in remote mountain ponds, a vivid physical experience that involves interlinked sensations like "plung[ing] her arm ... into the cool water [to] break off the rubbery stem," intricately balancing her body to keep the canoe from tipping when she leans out, the feel of the dripping plants lifted over her bare legs, and the "heavenly fragrance mounted all around [them]" while paddling back in a boat filled with lilies (129). Indeed, garden writing can easily stand beside the very best nature writing from the past century, despite the fact that it has so often been excluded from its traditional canon. One doesn't have to be a garden enthusiast to delight in Čapek's portraits of spring, which draw the full sensorium into a world teeming with life and forego an exclusively visual emphasis on blooms (a more conventional approach to celebrating spring) to probe the physical intricacies of the buds preceding them:

> There are buds deep scarlet and rosy with cold; others are brown and sticky like resin; others are whitish like the felt on the belly of a rabbit; they are also violet, or blond, or dark like old leather. Out of some pointed lace protrudes; others are like fingers or tongues, and others again like warts. Some swell like flesh, overgrown with down, and plump like puppies; others are laced into a tough and lean prong; others open with puffed and fragile little plumes. I tell you, buds are as strange and varied as leaves and flowers. There will be no end to your discoveries. But you must choose a small piece of earth.... You must stand still; and then you will see open lips and furtive glances, tender fingers, and raised arms, the fragility of a baby, and the rebellious outburst of the will to live; and then you will hear the infinite march of buds faintly roaring. (34)

This complex, multisensory appeal cannot be reduced to a mere rhetorical strategy or literary frill in the genre; rather, it proceeds directly from the gardener's practice. As renowned twentieth-century landscape gardener Russell Page once remarked, his expertise developed by directly handling plants, "getting to know their likes and dislikes by smell and touch." "'Book learning' gave me information," he explained, "but only physical contact can give any real knowledge and understanding of a live organism" (16). Perhaps no facet of garden writing better exemplifies this point than its accounts of the muscle memory developed by working in the soil—the very medium and condition of all garden practice. Indeed, the grower's kinetic experience of subterranean realms defies our common disregard for the dynamic world beneath our feet; as Čapek writes, "you will see that not even clouds are so diverse, so beautiful, and terrible as the soil under your feet." Yet unlike cloud watching, soil "watching" would yield little of value. As Čapek insists, you must have a garden and work it actively; then, and only then, "[y]ou will know the soil as sour, tough, clayey, cold, stony and rotten; you will recognize the mould puffy like pastry, warm, light, and good like bread, and you will say of this that it is beautiful," just as others may comment on the beauty and variety of the clouds:

> You will feel a strange and sensual pleasure if your stick runs a yard deep into the puffy and crumbling soil, or if you crush a clod in your fingers to taste its

airy and tepid warmth. And if you have no appreciation for this strange beauty, let fate bestow upon you a couple of rods of clay—clay like lead, squelching and primeval clay out of which coldness oozes; which yields under the spade like chewing-gum, which bakes in the sun and gets sour in the shade; ill-tempered, unmalleable, greasy, and sticky like plaster of Paris, slippery like a snake, and dry like a brick, impermeable like tin, and heavy like lead. (87–88)

This perceptual attunement to the fullness and intimacy of embodied contact with the earth not only registers the rich variety of our living landscape but also gives rise to a startling recognition of the body as a highly sophisticated instrument of ecological intelligence, one that can detect soil composition through the taste of an herb, predict changes to humidity and pressure in the joints and muscles, or feel with the hands the maturity of roots buried away from our eyes. Indeed, these moments of "concrete reflection," as philosopher Maurice Merleau-Ponty calls them—a mode of "plung[ing] into the world instead of surveying it" (39)—may suggest how gardening practice has come to rival our national love affair with municipal and national parks, spaces that, historically, have often denied nature to the senses by emphasizing its "scenic" aspects and organizing visitor experience along roads or pathways governed by rules that discipline the body: keep off, do not climb, do not pick, eat, or feed. In fact, if we consider garden writing within the broader oeuvre of traditional American nature writing, it deserves much credit for unsettling the privileged status of vision (and the reduction of nature to an optical artifact) within that canon.

Admittedly, gardening's promise of restored contact may not include wild rivers or remote landscapes and animals. And yet it can be argued that the modes of experience Čapek and other garden writers describe are more intimate—and certainly more readily available—than many nature experiences requiring time and travel to designated wilderness areas. Indeed, many today still only recognize encounters with the "natural world" as those distinctly marked off from everyday practice: a visit to the beach, a weekend hike on a trail we drive to, a vacation to a national park or other remote destination. Such one-off or intermittent encounters make it difficult to foster the kind of ongoing, intimate, and reciprocal relations with nature distinctive to gardening. Growers, on the other hand, may walk through their garden every morning on the way to work or sit in its midst with a drink in the evening. The garden is a place we touch, smell, shape, weed, water, plant, and eat for lunch. Reciprocally, the garden produces blisters, sore muscles, and flavor sensations; it may trigger our allergies in spring or keep us up at night with worry during a dry spell. We identify with it, invest ourselves in it. We may love a particular national park and return there year after year, but we do not relate to it through continuous acts of care—or, indeed, belong to it—in the same way. The garden, in short, is a world we experience as *ours*.

Such acts of care, moreover, are central to the distinctive appeal of contemporary gardening practices; after all, cultivating plants and soil is not just an opportunity for natural contact but, more specifically, for a mode of contact that directly contributes to the increase and well-being of life. Čapek comes to understand this role when gardening moves him from the position of a "remote and distracted onlooker of the accomplished work of gardens" to the position of someone responsible for enhancing *conditions* that are conducive to the flourishing of life. This ultimately leads him to recognize that "a real gardener is not a man who cultivates flowers; he is a man who cultivates the soil" (23). Laura Bodey, the protagonist of Richard Powers's novel *Gain* (whom we met in this book's introduction), has a similar epiphany as she lies dying from cancer toward the end of the novel. At one level, focusing on the garden outside her window helps turn her thoughts from cancer back to life: "The ripples in her plaster ceiling deepen into furrows as she studies them. She drifts from visualizing her T cells, finds herself getting the visualized poppies in. She decides to do all blooms this year, to leave the vegetables for another life" (318). Yet on another level Laura also perceives the unique importance of the garden in the fact that it is not a natural process taking place entirely independent of her. Here, each plant is encountered as something that needs to be watered, tended, and nourished. That relationship becomes especially apparent as she finally begins to let go of her life: "Everything else, she learns how to shed. It's weight off her . . . a spring cleaning. . . . Things will do their work without her. Things will do their work without her." This final phrase is repeated with a mantra-like intent, attempting to secure comfort in the thought that, insofar as Laura purportedly plays no part in supporting the broader life of things, her passing will not interrupt its continuation. That notion, however, is at once interrupted by the thought of her garden:

> . . . Things will do their work without her. Things will do their work without her.
> All except her one good thing. [Laura] can no more relinquish it than she can leave her own children. If she could just get the soil ready again, sink her hands in wrist deep, she might be all right. She lies in bed, twelve feet away from that plot. She obsesses over that perfect ground, the richest soil in the world, lying there going to waste. (318)

Unlike all other things, which "will do their work without her," Laura's garden comes into being and thrives through and because of her effort. Indeed, the final line makes it hard to distinguish the fate of the garden from that of her own body; both, it suggests, are left "lying there going to waste." Yet Laura's epiphany here is not, I would argue, an unredeemed tragedy, since the scene also reveals how her garden has offered Laura a unique opportunity to experience fulfillment in being a source of flourishing for something beyond herself. In short, gardening has recast Laura as a partisan and source of life—certainly no small gesture in a novel where it is otherwise massively profitable (at least for multinational corporations) to deal in death, to perpetuate a system that produces not just consumer goods but also illness, inequity, and environmental devastation.

At the same time, to highlight the garden as something we encounter through acts of care is not to infantilize nature or to deny its radical otherness and agency. Indeed, garden writing endlessly returns to the ways this practice manifests our utter dependence on soil, plants, and other "source-of-life" elements. Philosopher David Cooper describes the attitude of the veteran gardener—one who has had to renounce, time and again, the claim to having the power to make the things and conditions on which she depends—as one of "creative receptivity": a sense of wonder and gratitude for that which "is granted to us as a gift," for an elemental world that "by no device of our own, comes to presence for us" (146). Such recognition leads garden writer Amy Stewart to reflect that "[a]part from fire-building or stone-cutting, gardening may well be our oldest human enterprise," an activity "so primitive" that it seems farcical to lump it together with other pastimes. "It is not golf or tennis," she insists; "It is not, despite what backyard makeover television shows would have us believe, a type of home décor. No, gardening is how we interact with the plant kingdom. The one that makes the air we breathe and the food we eat and the medicine we take when we're sick" ("Universal" 138–39). Of course, it may be expected that devotees of any number of activities—hiking, cooking, music, chess—will similarly hold up their commitment as fundamentally distinct from all others. Yet insofar as these refrains in garden writing emerge from various urges to communicate our bodies' fundamental embeddedness in the living world, the convention cannot easily be dismissed. As predictable—even cliché—as such expressions have become in the genre, they lie at the heart of larger ethical and ecological impulses behind the desires and fantasies of gardening.

This ecocentric orientation is also evident in writings linking the singularity of garden practice with lived experience of nature's rhythms and demands, with the way gardening's process draws us in and actively reshapes our priorities and behaviors. In joining the familiar chorus about gardening's distinction from other hobbies, David Cooper emphasizes that the practice cannot be picked up and left off like stamp collecting or painting, since gardens involve agents and conditions that are not of our making and that proceed according to their own imperatives; thus "the specific demands and development of the 'materials'—the need, say, of certain plants to be pruned at a certain time of the year—constrain and shape the gardener's life" (75). Growers must enter a voluntary submission to the discipline of the garden—and nowhere, perhaps, does that relationship become more apparent than in the moment of its interruption. When midcentury garden writer Ruth Stout is laid up for weeks after throwing out her back, she epitomizes this dynamic in a single, comical image: unable to rise, she has her bed moved to the second-floor screened porch where she uses opera glasses to monitor the garden's activity just forty yards away. Readers cannot help but laugh at the sheer torment of this vigil, with Stout watching helplessly as crops go to seed like fireworks displays, weeds arrive and multiply like mutant party-crashers, and in defiance of her tidy schemes, nature runs wild below (52).

Such moments, however, are also occasions for curiosity and wonder, recalling us to the fact that even the most meticulously controlled gardens are ever subject to nature's process and unpredictability. Entangled with a multitude of living, organic things that are not human, gardens shift, flow, and transform in astonishing ways. While serving as a fellow at Dumbarton Oaks gardens, Eric MacDonald noted this uncertainty as perhaps the "fundamental source of enchantment" in gardens, where

> moments of wonder may occur as glimpses of previously unseen or new components of the assemblage: a strange insect, or an enveloping fog. Or they may arise from encounters with entities that behave in surprising ways: a bird performing a curious "dance," a once-solid hillside that is now saturated with gurgling water, on the verge of melting into the streambed below.... The sudden appearance of any one of these things—the bug, the bird, the fog, and the dissolving hillside—highlights the sheer complexity of the assemblage that envelops us. The garden is not just complicated—that is, made of many parts—it is complex, meaning that the individual components are related in ways that make the garden's "performance" something that can never be entirely predicted. (129–30)

As our participation in this process draws our attention beneath the visible surface of living things, we encounter what Robert Pogue Harrison describes as "the depths in which they stake their claims on life and from which they grow into the realm of presence and appearance" (30). Karel Čapek, once again, vividly dramatizes the very phenomenological conversion described here in defining the gardener as one who "lives buried in the ground," one who becomes "a creature who digs himself into the earth," "leav[ing] the sight of what is [merely] on it" to those who inhabit a narrower stratum of our infinitely complex lifeworld (23). Indeed, Čapek speculates that after death "the gardener does not become a butterfly, intoxicated by perfumes of flowers, but a garden worm tasting all the dark, nitrogenous, and spicy delights of the soil" (25). Ross Gay's postmortem garden reflections place even further emphasis on these soil-based intimacies—and on nature's agency as such—by flipping the dynamic of creatures-consuming-plants. In "Burial," the ashes of Gay's deceased father are fed to the soil beneath a plum tree, whose

> ... roots curled around him
> like shawls or jungle gyms, like
> hookahs or the arms of ancestors,
> before breast-stroking into the xylem,
> riding the elevator up
> through the cambium and into the leaves where,
> when you put your ear close enough,
> you can hear him whisper
> *good morning*[.] (12–13)

These reflections and concrete perceptions return us, finally, to the body itself, illuminating why, at this particular moment in history, our immersive encounters in the garden matter so much. Humans may be the only species to write gardening books, but we are not the only species that depends on the nutrients of our soils and the microcommunities that comprise them, on plants, water, air, or light. In experiencing ourselves as embodied beings with immutable organic needs, we experience precisely that which connects us to all other organisms with which we share this planet. Indeed, it is largely through this lived body consciousness that we are able to recognize ecological or "vital values" more broadly—those values related to the existence and flourishing of life, along with the animate and inanimate processes that maintain it. As phenomenologists like Merleau-Ponty and Max Scheler argue, such an appreciation can hardly arise from intellectual effort alone; rather, it requires a "profound *feeling* of the meaning and value of organic life" inherent in the experience of one's creaturely being and needs (J. White, "Person" 234). Scheler specifically frames this phenomenon in the context of "feeling-states" inherent to embodied life: "feelings of 'quickening' and 'declining' life, the feelings of health and illness, the feeling of aging and oncoming death, the feelings of 'weakness,' 'strength,' etc." (106–7). If our everyday lives and practices inhibit, devalorize, or cut us off from the experience of our own vital values, we are less likely to cherish and promote the values of a living world populated with other creaturely existence. These carnal perceptions are thus a precondition for developing the kind of "vital sympathy" that allows us to "enter into another's vital world"—in short, to extend moral consideration beyond our own species (J. White, "Lived Body" 182–83, 187).

Gay's *Catalog of Unabashed Gratitude* provides a powerful twenty-first-century testimony to the garden's agency in nurturing these sympathies. After years of intimate work in the soil, a reciprocal transformation takes place that gives rise to both the general sense of gratitude suffusing Gay's collection and the specific act of love and vital sympathy characterizing a single moment of eating a fig in his poem "Sharing with the Ants." Initially believing that he alone has discovered the tree's last piece of fruit, Gay chomps into the fig to learn his mistake: here, he finds an ant already at work on it from the inside. Yet the poet declines either to discard the fig or to brush the insect away, leaving both creatures nibbling toward each other until the ant's waving antennae come directly up against Gay's own whiskered chin. This encounter gives rise to a vision of cosmic continuity,

> our mouths sugared
> and shining both of us
> twirling beneath the fig's
> seeds spinning like a newly
> discovered galaxy
> that's been there forever. (58)

Far from being some trendy new ecocentric emphasis, recognitions like these lie at the heart of American garden writing going back to Charles Dudley Warner, who likewise found himself "[entering] into a sort of communion with the vegetable life" as gardening moved him from states of "thinking" to "vegetating"—a mode of concrete reflection through which one might "begin to know what the joy of the grape-vine is in running up the trellis, which is similar to that of the squirrel in running up a tree" (54). As gardening activities and reflections thus reaffirm our membership in the larger community of life, they also invite us to reaffirm the organic foundation of all intelligence and action, opening a space in which we might take seriously the vibrancy of matter and the infinite forms of nonhuman agency around us.

Notes

Introduction. "Gardens of the Mind"

1. Katharine White even reviewed seed catalogs in the *New Yorker* as a distinct literary genre, insisting "[t]hey are as individualistic—these editors and writers—as any Faulkner or Hemingway, and they can be just as frustrating or rewarding. They have an audience equal to the most popular novelist's, and a handful of them are stylists of some note" (21).

2. While many readers and scholars see Candide's final actions as a gesture of disillusionment (unable to improve the world, the individual withdraws to cultivate "a private island of order" [Finney 52]), alternative readings have interpreted the declaration "*Il faut cultiver notre jardin*" as either a call to concrete action (a commitment to creation, maintenance, and care of the world we inherit [Harrison x]) or as a rejection of the metaphysical reasoning of theologians by redirecting our focus toward the concerns of everyday life ("the 'garden' here being seen as a metaphor for such 'common life' reasoning" [O'Brien 9]).

3. These "costs" within *Gain* manifest as cancer, environmental depletion, meaningless work, offshored jobs, and a general sense of social alienation. In a significant scene early in the novel, Jephthah Clare (father of the founders of Clare Soap & Chemical) wonders at early nineteenth-century networks of exchange that do not appear to enrich any one party at another's expense, arrangements where "[h]e, the Oregon trapper, the Chinese Hong, . . . everyone prospered. Each of them thought he'd gotten the better end of the deal. Now, how could that be? Where had the profit come from? Who paid for their mutual enrichment?" (10). Powers ultimately resolves these speculations by paying the balance in the form of a toxic twentieth-century landscape and Laura Bodey's poisoned body.

4. Even Whitman's reflections are predated by thousands of years in the writings of Cicero: in celebrating the delights of horticulture and the "power of the soil," the Roman philosopher argued that its "pleasures have an account in the bank of Mother Earth who never protests a draft, but always returns the principal with interest added, at a rate sometimes low, but usually at a high per cent" (63).

5. See Lawson, *City Bountiful;* and Steinglass, "The Machine in the Garden."

Chapter 1. American Garden Writing and the Reinvention of Work as Play

1. See Finney (2–12); Conlogue (1–15); Sweet (1–11); and Buell (*Environmental* 31–52).

2. The pastoral approach was, however, less common in accounts produced by colonists and explorers themselves, whose lived experience could not possibly match the romanticized New World–paradise myth. William Bradford's 1620 characterization of New England is hardly gardenlike, instead describing a "hideous and desolate wilderness, full of wild beasts and wild men." This wilderness portrait typifies the second prevailing metaphor of the American continent (see Nash for further discussion of early wilderness metaphors in environmental ideology). Yet despite the plentiful contradictions presented by the likes of Bradford, the Edenic version was ultimately the most widely reproduced—and, as it turns out, the most resonant—among Europeans from the Elizabethan period until well into the nineteenth century (also see Hoyles 263–65; and chapters 2–3 in L. Marx).

3. In his description of the "New World" cultures encountered during expeditions in this period, Montaigne also asserted that "[t]hese people are wild in the same sense that fruits are, produced by nature, alone, in her ordinary way" (63).

4. In 1589 English explorer and writer Richard Hakluyt similarly depicted indigenous people living in lands "so full of grapes, as the very beating and surge of the Sea overflowed them," and described them effortlessly gathering sustenance from a soil that surpassed even "the most plentifull, sweete, fruitfull, and wholesome of all the worlde" (298, 304). This erasure of indigenous cultivation practice remained a fixture in the popular imagination well into the twentieth century (see Saguaro 191–95). Leslie Marmon Silko's *Gardens in the Dunes*, discussed here in chapter 5, directly overturns such views of Native American food production as a mere matter of "gleaning."

5. As Lewis Simpson has argued, southerners of the "post–Virginia Company era" represented their historical legacy in a markedly different fashion from their counterparts to the north. In contrast to New Englanders, southern writers defined their mission "not as an errand in a howling wilderness, in the midst of which as God's regenerate band they would make a pleasure garden for Him, but as an errand in the open, prelapsarian, self-yielding paradise, where they would be made regenerate by entering into a redemptive relationship with a new and abounding earth" (15).

6. Jefferson's original "Garden Book" was an unpublished diary recording horticultural experiments, observations, and reflections dating from 1766 to 1824. The published version I draw on here, *Thomas Jefferson's Garden Book* (1944), is a compilation annotated by Edwin Morris Betts that also includes garden-related discussions from different sources, including Jefferson's written correspondence and memorandum books (like the *Farm Book* and the *Weather Memorandum Book, 1776–1820*). Jefferson *does* mention his slaves in some of the supplemental documents Betts added to this compilation, but no such references appeared in the original garden memorandum itself.

7. Also see Graham, *American Eden*; and Martin, *The Pleasure Gardens of Virginia*.

8. Also see Gibbs, "Little Spots Allow'd Them"; and McDonald, "Independent Economic Production by Slaves."

9. See complete discussion in Hatch, "African American Gardens at Monticello."

10. George London and Henry Wise were a well-known team of eighteenth-century English landscape designers who incorporated a Baroque style in their gardens, including radial avenues, parade courts, and stately fountains.

11. For further discussion see Mickey, *America's Romance with the English Garden;* and Demaree, *American Agricultural Press.*

12. In Jefferson's view, such unsightliness proceeded directly from the unique character of American labor dynamics: "We have so little labor in proportion to our land," he explained, "that although perhaps we make more profit from the same labor, we cannot give our grounds that style of beauty which satisfies the eye of the amateur" (461). Indeed, apart from slaveholding or otherwise wealthy landowners like himself, Americans in the colonial and early republican periods lacked both the necessary workforce and wealth required to build and maintain the elaborate gardens featured across the Atlantic (Hugill 408).

13. To clarify, existing horticultural literature did include discussion of ornamental planting and landscaping, but U.S. writers before Downing had not published any specialized works devoted *exclusively* to this topic. Garden historian Thomas Mickey argues that Bernard McMahon, author of *The American Gardener's Calendar* (1806), was the "first early American garden writer to address the issue of landscape design" (91), although his discussions were integrated throughout with instructional discussion of practical kitchen gardening. Additionally, as Charles Wood argues, the *Horticultural Register* ran an article in 1835 that might technically qualify as the first published work of American landscape design. Yet it was likewise one entry among a whole company of assorted gardening articles in this same edition, which included pieces on the "Best Mode of Destroying Caterpillars" and "Blanching Vegetables" as well (Teschemacher 157).

14. The *Treatise* became the most influential of all Downing's works, appearing in more that fifteen editions over some forty years.

15. There are other fascinating approaches to women's writing in this period that suggest alternative ways to read the bifurcated structure I analyze here. Literary scholar Dorri Beam argues that florid and sensuous styles in women's writing—what she terms "highly wrought" language—have an "aesthetic and feminist rationale" and cannot simply be reduced to a sentimental mode for "emotional outpourings or irrational excesses" (2, 1). In exploring associations of femininity with flowers, she explores uses of "flower language" in the nineteenth century as examples of highly wrought style that present an "alternative language" in themselves (rather than serving as a mere "code" for transgressive sexualities, for example) (38). Margaret Fuller's 1841 essay "The Magnolia of Lake Pontchartrain," for instance, resists the common one-on-one correlation of flowers with particular feminine sentiments by presenting them as a language of "outer complexity that embodies an untranslatable excess that is both sensual and suprasensual" (53). As such, Fuller's flower language "preserve[s]

the hieroglyphic essence of the flower [in order to] preserve the complexity, interest, and fullness of nature's alterity" (57). Along with many other discussions of women writers in this work, Beam's analysis here suggests new ways of regarding style as a medium through which gender might be represented and reshaped.

While Beam does not analyze garden writing per se, her analysis suggests a different approach to the one I take in discussing gardening literature as overwhelmingly split between beauty versus utility. For Beam, rather than reinscribing the division between "ethereal spirituality" and "earthly embodiment," much flower language of the nineteenth century could be read as offering a glimpse of the "potential entwinement of the bodily and the spiritual" in discourses of feminism (104). For a detailed discussion of these possibilities, see Beam's *Style, Gender, and Fantasy*.

16. However, even Johnson's work remains divided on this matter, to some degree. Despite claims to gardening independence in her title (along with identifying her book as "A Handy Manual" of gardening), Johnson goes on to state in the introduction that "[t]o be sure, Pat O'Shovelem's aid is needed to prepare the ground, lay out the beds, and harden the walks." Women could then take up lighter tasks: "gentler, smaller hands can plant the seeds and roots, can keep down the weeds, tie up, stake, train, water and prune." Finally, Johnson insists that no one should extrapolate from garden to farmwork, where it would be absurd to recommend women "holding the plow—wielding the spade or the shovel" (6–7).

17. As such, these works seemed to return to earlier trends in the genre: as art historian May Brawley Hill notes, despite growth in mid-nineteenth-century gardening manuals specifically for women following the American reprinting of two English titles (Louisa Johnson's 1832 *Every Lady Her Own Flower Gardener* and Mrs. Loudon's 1843 *Gardening for Ladies* and *Ladies' Companion to the Flower Garden*), "none had encouraged women to do the work themselves" (27).

18. This declaration is repeated almost verbatim by nurseryman Roland Shumway, who appealed to customers in the introduction to his 1887 seed catalog by writing, "From the beginning of the new year, until after spring planting, my industrious employees work 16 hours, and myself and family 18 or more hours a day. Are we not surely knights at labor? How can we do more? Do we not deserve the patronage of every planter in America?" (qtd. in Mickey xx).

19. For further discussion of the elements of play in Warner's writing, see Allan Gurganus, introduction to *My Summer* (vii–xxxvii).

20. Coverdale juxtaposes Blithedale's "earthen cups" with the "pictured porcelain" and "silver forks" to which he and Zenobia are accustomed, and he watches in horror as Silas eats his dinner "on the flat of his knife-blade" and uses the wrong utensil to serve his ham (23).

21. Unskilled labor rates for gardeners in Central Park during these very same years, for example, were around $1.60 per day (see Rosenzweig and Blackmar 275–76). In fact, Warner has already admitted to paying $2.25 per day for hired assistance with his gardening tasks—the actual going rate, we are to assume, for such work in his region of New England (Warner 80).

22. Indeed, garden writers and critics who take issue with Thoreau's misgivings about upsetting weeds and parasites may overlook the lighthearted manner in which those very scenes are staged. For more discussion of tongue-in-cheek performance in *Walden*, see Gross, "The Great Bean Field Hoax."

23. After the first summer's end, Thoreau abandons his bean project, and in one of his last published works, he comes down definitively on the side of wilderness, pledging, "[I]f it were proposed to me to dwell in the neighborhood of the most beautiful garden that ever human art contrived, or else of a dismal swamp, I should certainly decide for the swamp" ("Walking" 98–99).

24. For further discussion of the economy of Thoreau's bean production, see Bromell (216–24).

25. Even as the last of the garden's autumn decay is being raked and cleared away, a certain disregard for solemnity (and order itself) prevails; the rites go on "with the hilarity of a wake, rather than the despondency of other funerals" (97).

Chapter 2. Lost at Home

1. "Locavore" was also designated as 2007's "word of the year" by the *Oxford American Dictionary*.

2. Many other books in this cohort of postmodern food exposés follow a corresponding pattern. Deborah Barndt's *Tangled Routes* (2002) repeatedly employs diagrams and maps that delineate the social, natural, political, and economic dimensions of the transnational tomato chain from Mexico to Canada. Similarly, a reviewer calls Jay Weinstein's *The Ethical Gourmet* (2006) "an excellent roadmap to socially conscious eating" and a necessary guidebook for "navigating the relative morality of buying local, buying organic or buying fairly traded food." Freidberg's *French Beans and Food Scares* (2004) claims to "tak[e] the reader on a fascinating tour of [European] foodways," tracing this bean from farms in Africa to French and English dining tables.

3. A generation earlier when interest spiked in rural communes, the American counterculture produced its own flurry of exposés on our industrial food system: 1972–75 saw the publication of Judith Van Allen's *Food Pollution* (1972), Jim Hightower's *Eat Your Heart Out* (1975), Jaqueline Verret and Jean Carper's *Eating May Be Hazardous to Your Health* (1974), Ross Hume Hall's *Food for Nought* (1974), and E. F. Schumacher's *Small Is Beautiful* (1973). For a detailed discussion, see Belasco, *Appetite for Change*.

4. Jackson Lear's *No Place of Grace* (1981) remains an influential account of the origins of turn-of-the-century American antimodernism, examining period desires for "authentic" physical or spiritual experience, skilled craftsmanship, and the search for cultural self-sufficiency through the Arts and Crafts movement.

5. After finishing the description, Wyckoff asks to "be set to work immediately," and "a minute later" he is off to the barn to fetch a broad hoe (555).

6. As is true with my focus on the wheat fields of California and the Dakotas later in this chapter, the present evaluation of Wyckoff's and Baker's articles is clearly limited

to regionally specific accounts. As such, it cannot possibly represent the wide diversity of experiences distinctive of different classes or regional farming cultures and economies across the United States in this period. However, in emphasizing responses to the advent of large industrialized farm operations, I hope to identify a pattern that is structurally repeated across a significant part of the period's agricultural literature—from southern accounts of decaying plantations to those of family farms in Nebraska and the mid-Atlantic.

7. As Harvey goes on to explain, property-owning classes adopted Enlightenment representational technologies to advance their interests, while the state, with its "concern for taxation of land and the definition of its own domain of domination and social control," availed itself of the power to administer areas increasingly defined by "fixed spatial co-ordinates" (*Condition* 254). For a more extensive history of this succession of spatial regimes (from "absolute" to "abstract" space), see Lefebvre (48–53).

8. One illuminating index of this trend was the rise of tenancy rates in the years following the Homestead Act: for example, Henry Nash Smith documents that "Eighteen per cent of the farms in Nebraska were operated by tenants in 1880, the first year for which records are available; in 1890 the figure had risen to twenty-four per cent. By 1900 more than thirty-five per cent of all American farmers had become tenants, and the ratio was increasing rapidly" (190). Thus, despite the lofty predictions of the movement's more socialist champions, political economist Henry George warned in 1871 that the Homestead Act would eventually culminate in a distribution of land that was the very opposite of Jefferson's vision: "Our whole policy is of a piece—everything is tending with irresistible force to make us a nation of landlords and tenants—of great capitalists and their poverty-stricken employees" (Smith 96).

9. T. Byard Collins was one of the earliest writers to use this expression in his book *The New Agriculture* (1906). For a more detailed discussion of the literary history of these bonanza farms and the industrialization of agriculture in general, see Conlogue (2001) and Carruth (2013).

10. Much of the discussion in this chapter is deeply indebted to William Conlogue's scholarship, particularly his analysis of industrialism's impact on farming and American literature in *Working the Garden: American Writers and the Industrialization of Agriculture*.

11. Before the turn of the century, as David Danbom points out in *The Resisted Revolution*, most American farms were generalized operations that produced a wide variety of the goods they consumed: "In addition to laboring on the commercial crops . . . the general farmer also worked in the vegetable gardens, poultry yards, dairy barns, orchards, woodlots and smokehouses which helped the family minimize its economic dependence on the outside world" (5). Moreover, as William Conlogue notes, few growers kept records of their farms "in any systematic, businesslike manner" prior to this period; home production still remained widespread in mid-nineteenth-century America, despite the fact that subsistence practices were in decline, and bartering activities commonly existed alongside cash and credit economies in many regions. In fact, barter practices even predominated in certain regions, with

farmers regularly "exchang[ing] foodstuffs for manufactured goods and often swapp[ing] labor and machinery with neighbors" (Conlogue 13–14). Meanwhile, among Illinois farmers it was unusual to find individuals with sufficient cash for use at local markets; instead, as William Cronon documents, "they brought with them the produce of their farms—sacks of wheat or corn, frozen hog carcasses, potatoes, onions, eggs, butter, anything that might be of value—and expected to purchase groceries, dry goods, and hardware in return" (*Nature* 319).

12. Such observations became legion among commentators reporting on the New Agriculture: as the *Daily Argus* went on to report, rather than using the land to support residents, workers, and animals, bonanza managers bought provisions from other farms: "They did not even raise oats for their horses, figuring they could buy oats cheaper than they could raise them" (qtd. in Drache 69). In 1880 Poultney Bigelow similarly noted that everywhere he visited, "fruit growing appeared to be neglected, and vegetable gardens and poultry were scarce" (36). Even as late as 1939, John Steinbeck's characters had not ceased to wonder at this exclusively commercial and hyperspecialized arrangement: one displaced farmer puzzles aloud as he and fellow migrants confront California's agricultural empire: "Notice one thing? They ain't no vegetables nor chickens nor pigs at the farms. They raise one thing—cotton, say, or peaches, or lettuce. . . . They buy the stuff they could raise in the dooryard" (258).

13. As Thrift sees it, "it was the great cities . . . that witnessed the most spectacular effects of the new electric lighting, that saw the most rapid and most extensive development of their transport and communications systems . . . and where cinemas and galleries were concentrated. It was these cities too where the implications of any change in either the nature or experience of time and space were most fervently discussed (by an urban intelligentsia and bourgeoisie) and where the most sustained attempts were made to represent those changes." Meanwhile, he argues that "outside of the great metropolises change proceeded only much more slowly" and was experienced much less intensely (17). This may be true of many small farms and homesteads, but bonanza farms were just as bound up with international market forces as any urban-based business and became utterly dependent on emerging communication and transportation technologies. And so the collapse of time and space, I argue, has a comparable impact in this realm.

14. W. A. White employs a single expression to discuss all the unique and various instances of grain cultivation addressed in his article: "The *world's wheat-crop*," as he calls it, "might as well lie in one great field, for the scattered acres are wired together in the markets" (547; italics added).

15. On the same page Baker describes the process of shipping grain from American fields to overseas buyers, where he happens to mention that "without comparisons it is difficult to form any conception of the immensity of a cargo this size" (135).

16. Pollan opens *The Omnivore's Dilemma* by announcing that "the best way to answer the questions" surrounding the changes in agriculture and eating was to go into the field and physically "follow the food chains that sustain us, all the way from the earth to the plate" (6).

17. Poultney Bigelow's piece for the *Atlantic Monthly* that same year begins in similar fashion, claiming that "[f]or the purpose of obtaining the data necessary to a more correct understanding of the operations of what are known as the 'bonanza farms' . . . the writer went upon the ground to make a study" (33).

18. As Edward Casey suggests, "place is not entiative—as a foundation has to be—but eventmental, something in process, something unconfinable to a thing" (*Fate* 337).

19. Clearly this was true of certain farm tasks more than others and would have been more significant on emerging bonanza ranches than smaller or low-tech farms where cultivation remained labor intensive and often quite arduous.

20. See also Coffin (531).

21. Moreover, as Laurence Buell argues, inquiries into "official geography as the site of clashing political or cultural systems" may be less instructive than approaches receptive to the way our minds oscillate between mental maps and "scientific" geographies ("both procrustean, yet both having their own explanatory power"), since a critical awareness of those tensions themselves may ultimately produce richer forms of environmental sensibility. From this perspective, he argues, "official maps look more complexly productive than when seen merely as agents of cartographical imperialism." Indeed, individuals in unfamiliar territory often find maps to be an indispensable bridge as they progress beyond the most basic stages of disorientation and slowly begin to apprehend "the subtler navigational clues" that may seem intuitive to long-term residents (*Environmental* 270–71).

22. See in particular "The Goophered Grapevine" and "The Gray Wolf's Ha'nt" in *The Conjure Woman*.

23. Cather's novel is, of course, published nineteen years after Chesnutt's work, yet the narrative action occurs during roughly the same period: if Jim's childhood in Nebraska overlaps with that of Cather's own, his early story would span from the 1880s to the early 1890s; in *The Conjure Woman*, John presumably moves to North Carolina just a few years prior to this period.

24. Casey describes the personal experience of returning to his hometown after years of absence, noting that "[i]n my presence, it releases these memories, which belong as much to the place as to my brain or body. . . . [E]ven when I recall people and things and circumstances in an ordinary place, I have the sense that these various recollecta have been kept securely in place, harbored there, as it were" ("How to Get" 25).

25. Such a fate may also explain why it takes Jim twenty years to visit his old friend Ántonia again: as he notes, "I did not want to find her aged and broken; I really dreaded it. In the course of twenty crowded years one parts with many illusions. I did not wish to lose the early ones. Some memories are realities, and are better than anything that can ever happen to one again" (211).

26. According to Frank Luther Mott, roughly 7,500 new magazines were launched in the United States between 1885 and 1905 (4, 11).

27. The garden oasis Latour discovers at the beginning of *Death Comes for the Archbishop* is only the first in a series of gardens that perform place-making functions in the novel: Latour later encourages his priests to plant gardens in order to stave off

homesickness, and at the novel's end we discover that he and Vaillant have laid out a garden when they first arrived in Santa Fe to maintain contact with the tastes, smells, and visual features of their youth on the other side of the Atlantic. Moreover, Cather shows significant interest in both formal and vernacular gardens across her major works, including *My Ántonia*, *O Pioneers!*, and *The Professor's House*.

28. Although the farm to which Jim moves as a child does not yet qualify as the mechanized soil-factory featured in other accounts, Cather's story traces a historical trajectory of agricultural modernization that ultimately dooms the farms she knew from her own childhood to this modern industrial form.

29. This same motif reemerges in the final scene of Jim and Ántonia's reunion (discussed in this chapter's previous section). When Jim returns to Ántonia's farm, the garden imagery of this earlier scene flashes before him as he approaches the farmhouse porch: here he finds white cats "sunning themselves among yellow pumpkins" as he had done so many years earlier, a perfect reproduction of this original tableau that confirms Ántonia's success in preserving the old ways across the intervening years (213).

30. This is especially true of farms worked by seasonal laborers who traveled great distances for harvests in California and the Dakota territories. Susan Stewart explains that historically, tall tales are overwhelmingly produced by those whose experiences "involve considerable distance between the workplace and the home" and perform "solitary outdoor labor." Since the narrator serves as firsthand witness in such circumstances, the otherwise implausible stories carry an added credibility; yet at the same time they also seem "all the more incredible" precisely because they remain "beyond the range of the audience's experience" (98).

31. Various expressions of miniaturization continue across twentieth-century garden writing, where the comical subgenre of "disaster gardening" effectively links horticultural catastrophe to errors in scale as such. Ruth Stout, who documents her 1930 move from New York City to the countryside in *How to Have a Green Thumb*, disregards entreaties of family and friends to scale back on the acreage she cultivates, learning the hard way as she spends multiple seasons in frenzied activity, anxiety, and finally exhaustion. As she concludes: "it was the unnecessarily large size of my project that made me ridiculous and a legitimate object of pity" (45). Eleanor Perenyi discovers that for literally the only time in her life she cannot bear to work in a particular garden—a "grotesquely sized plot"—on account of its excessive dimensions (243). William Alexander's more recent tales of gardening gone wrong (an undertaking that consumes his life and costs a fortune, produces marital strain, a compromised social life, and a ruined back) proceed entirely from the author's single original sin: in attempting to enact his rural fantasies he installs a two-thousand-square-foot kitchen garden. As a neighbor warns him while the groundwork is still being laid for these massive garden schemes, Alexander risks "crossing the line from gardener to gentleman farmer" (35, 196, 36).

32. One of the more popular works of garden fiction from the period, *Elizabeth and Her German Garden* (1898), attracted ridicule from other garden writers like Pauline

Leonard, who mocked the heroine for being too "proper" to do her own weeding or manual labor. Such aristocratic sensibilities, she wrote in an *Atlantic Monthly* piece, were now "out of place in a garden" (715).

33. In fact, William Morris, one of the leading figures of the Arts and Crafts movements, built one of the first and most famous replicas of these cottage gardens.

Chapter 3. Resensualizing the Garden

1. As Kathryn Dolan points out in *Beyond the Fruited Plain*, such developments were not without precedent: Thoreau himself anticipated many elements of the locavore movement a century earlier in celebrating a sustainable, local, and largely plant-based diet.

2. "Market gardening" refers to relatively small-scale production of fresh fruit, produce, and flowers for direct sale to consumers or restaurants. In contrast to larger, industrialized farms that often specialize in a single crop, market gardens (also called "truck farms") grow a greater variety of seasonal produce on smaller plots (usually a few acres or less), which they distribute through on-site farm stands, farmers' markets, community-supported agriculture, or local restaurants. Compared with large-scale mechanized farms, they also rely more heavily on manual labor and gardening techniques.

3. Barry Benepe's first-year report on the Greenmarket notes that "[p]rices were somewhat less than those typically found in groceries and supermarkets, with three pounds of tomatoes or peppers or a dozen ears of corn selling for one dollar" (7). Also see discussion of the market's accessibility to low-income New Yorkers in Kornfeld, "Bringing Good Food In."

4. This transition has profoundly impacted biodiversity as well, with 75 percent of plant genetic diversity in agriculture lost over the past century (Jackson 71; FAO "Agrobiodiversity").

5. Some of the most sweeping changes emerged from the Nixon administration's cheap food policy, which dismantled the New Deal practice of protecting farmers through subsidized crop limits and instead encouraged growers to maximize production via government reimbursements for the difference between "target prices" and the actual, much-reduced market price. The resulting overproduction drove down prices and rewarded growers who planted enormous quantities of the basic crops used by food processors (corn, soy, and wheat). By the end of the twentieth century, 70 percent of the farmland in the Midwest has been converted into "single-crop farms" devoted either to corn or soybeans, "each one of them now, on average, the size of Manhattan" (Kingsolver, *Animal* 13). The immense supply of cheap staple crops that could be reassembled into value-added products proved a windfall for industrial food processors.

6. See also Pentecost, "What Did You Eat"; and Pollan, *Omnivore*.

7. Also see Pollan's "The Futures of Food" for additional discussion of this literary tradition.

8. This midcentury focus on the ascendance of the image in agriculture and horticulture—crops as pure simulacrum—marks it as qualitatively different from older grumblings about the blandness of commercialized crops, which may be found throughout American literature: in 1862, for example, Thoreau wrote that domesticated apples, in contrast to their wild cousins, were selected "not so much for their spirited flavor, as for their mildness, their size, and bearing qualities," making them "very tame and forgetable. They are eaten with comparatively little zest, and have no real *tang* nor *smack* to them" ("Wild" 521).

9. As Seremetakis frames it, "commensality" is "the exchange of sensory memories and emotions, and of substances and objects incarnating remembrance and feeling" (37). Central to her analysis of modernity and its political, economic, and cultural formations is Seremetakis's observation that the history of the senses within this period "can be understood as the progressive effacement of commensality; that is, of a reflexive cultural institution that produced and reproduced social knowledge and collective memory through the circulation of material forms as templates of shared emotion and experience. In modernity, commensality is not absent but is rendered banal, functional or literal" (37–38).

10. As he ponders this phenomenon, Pollan discovers himself within the company of a significant line of thinkers who have marveled at the same process, including seventeenth-century Flemish scientist Jan Baptist van Helmont. Helmont documents an experiment in which he planted a willow sapling in a tub containing exactly 200 pounds of soil, and as Pollan reports, "for five years, gave it nothing but water. At the end of that time, the tree was found to weigh 169 pounds, and the soil 199 pounds, 14 ounces—from just two ounces of soil had come 169 pounds of tree" (*Second* 171).

11. This fascination with the soil's prodigious output crops up across fictional reflections as well. In Gloria Naylor's novel *Mama Day*, an exceedingly brief exchange between the protagonist and a truck farmer includes no less than three references to the heaviness characterizing this world of soil and fruit, with the farmer sifting black dirt through his fingers, "the weight, the texture, the smell, telling him of possibilities [others] couldn't begin to understand"; his visitor noting the "heaviness" of a tomato handed to her; and the farmer observing that no scale can accurately weigh and compensate growers for "what really goes into one of those" (200).

12. I borrow this phrase from environmental writer Robert Michael Pyle, who examines the social and psychological effects of our disappearing daily contact with wild plants, animals, and landscapes in *The Thunder Tree* (1998).

13. See the discussion of race and class dynamics in contemporary food politics in Guthman, *Weighing In* (2011); Zukin, "Consuming Authenticity" (2008); and Guthman, "Bringing Good Food to Others" (2008). Possibilities for a more inclusive green economy are explored in Alkon's study of Oakland's farmers' market: *Black, White, and Green: Farmers Markets, Race, and the Green Economy* (2012). Also, a good overview and varied discussion of food-justice movements in low-income communities of color is available in *Cultivating Food Justice: Race, Class, and Sustainability*, edited by Alkon and Agyeman (2011).

14. In light of the fuzzy utopian associations often attached to these social spaces, we must remain wary of any assumption that intense affective experience is *in and of itself* progressively transformative. Indeed, in their research on the culture and politics of farmers' markets and other "Slow Spaces," Parkins and Craig reiterate Lauren Berlant's warning against the inadequacy of theories/practices of social transformation that appeal to "feeling good" as "evidence of justice's triumph" (2001). In addition, they caution against a politics of place where the local automatically stands for the good and emotionally nourishing, while the global is cast as bad, unfeeling, abstract, and remote. Instead, they advocate for a "reflexive localism" that, "while not dismissing the value of positive feelings or affects," would not rely on "predetermined responses to familiar localities and subjects. Such a reflexive localism would constitute a shift in emphasis from 'the politics of place to politics in place.'" As such, these scholars are careful to specify that the goal of such projects "is not simply an enriched emotional life but one that fosters forms of ethical reflexivity that cultivate our capacities to imagine, desire and practice more just and equitable ways to be" (91).

15. As Parkins and Craig note, almost all their survey respondents reported that they stayed considerably longer at the farmers' market than needed simply to make their purchases, and "over 60 percent of respondents said they spent an hour or more on an average visit" (93).

16. Even as public demand for alternatives to standardized forms of mass consumption have benefited many small local producers, those same desires to "consume a special kind of authenticity," as Sharon Zukin puts it, have also been co-opted by big business selling its own corporate version of "organic," "artisanal," "ethical," and the like. When Whole Foods opened a massive, three-story supermarket across from the Greenmarket's Union Square site in 2005, farmers reported a significant loss of business as shoppers found it "easier to consume the supermarket's more familiar [and convenient] form of authenticity" (737). Similar challenges run back to the 1970s farmers' markets in New York and neighboring regions. As Hightower noted, supermarket chains played on the nostalgia of Massachusetts farmers' markets in setting up their own "ersatz" versions in store parking lots, where they simply relocated industrial fruits and vegetables in wooden crates under colored umbrellas (234).

17. See Geertz 29–32.

18. Such exchanges exemplify Geertz's argument that the relative absence of product uniformity and prescribed exchange partners within a bazaar compels intensified consumer effort to investigate the quality of items on individualized terms (29–32).

Chapter 4. Against the Grain

1. Similarly, the English word "garden" (from Old Norse *gard*) originally denoted an "enclosure" for flowers, fruit, or vegetable production.

2. Even within Utopia itself, animal slaughter is outsourced to noncitizen slaves to spare citizens from its brutalizing effects.

3. As it appears in the original Latin text: "... quam plurimum temporis ab seruitio corporis ad animi libertatem cultumque ciuibus uniuersis asseratur." Original Latin version of *Utopia*, available online at www.thelatinlibrary.com/more.html.

4. See Wegner, *Imaginary Communities* (11–12).

5. In his youth, Shevek does participate in an "afforestation project," but he considers this more of a distraction from the "important work" than a meaningful activity in and of itself, something indistinguishable from any of the other rotating work postings in which Annares's citizens contribute to the necessary "*kleggich*" or drudgework of their society (46).

6. See Darko Suvin on "cognitive estrangement" as the central formal framework of science fiction (372–82).

7. Roderick Nash traces the history of the term "wilderness" back to early Norse *wild-dêor*, meaning any animal not under human control. As he explains, one of the earliest uses was in *Beowulf*, "where wild-dêor appeared in reference to savage and fantastic beasts inhabiting a dismal region of forests, crags, and cliffs." Etymologically, then, the term came to be *wild-dêor-ness*, literally "the place of wild beasts" (1).

8. See Suzuki, *The Sacred Balance* (183–226); and Eisenberg, *Ecology of Eden*.

9. However, even as these policies worked to undermine and marginalize gardening as a practical matter of everyday living, visitors continued to appropriate the park in various nonsanctioned ways, picking roots, fishing in the lakes, even turning out animals to graze. In fact, it was not uncommon for low-income New Yorkers to earn a small living in the late nineteenth century by selling dandelion greens gathered from park lawns. As late as 1930, Michael Gold's *Jews without Money* testifies to the endurance of such "outdated" garden practices, with the novel's central episode featuring a family excursion to the city park to forage for wild mushrooms.

10. This distinction between "public" and "common" forms of land use was central to the foundational policies governing behavior in Central Park. Since "common" property is traditionally "land or resources to which all members of a community have unrestricted access," it differs from public property in that the right to control the latter "is vested in government officials who determine who has access to it and under what conditions" (Rosenzweig and Blackmar 5, 243).

11. Within the span of just a few years, what had been an arena of production and survival found itself transformed into a revered cultural artifact, what Olmsted Jr. once dubbed a "great work of art" akin to "a Titian or a Rembrandt"—in short, an object for viewing (qtd. in Rosenzweig and Blackmar 428). And so, despite the progressive impulse behind Central Park's creation—a site meant to democratize access to nature and public space and bring people from different classes and backgrounds together in a shared love of the outdoors—the process of the park's production and the conditions of its use often contradicted these democratic ideals, replacing the existing site's multiple gardens, histories, and forms of production with a single, unified garden, one whose conception was entrusted to the master vision of a sole pair of landscape professionals.

12. See also M. B. Hill (145); von Hassell (31–3); Crouch and Ward (27).

13. As it is used here, the root "eco" carries its original Greek meaning of *oikos* or "house, domestic property, habitat, natural milieu" (Petrescu 44).

14. Another likely reason for gardening's privileged status in "Edilia" is that it is already characterized by what Harvey identifies as the most socially gratifying feature of his utopia: the "dissolution of the boundary between work and play" (273).

15. While perhaps the most visible instance, Reynolds's work is hardly the first expression of this movement, with other prominent examples including David Tracy's "manualfesto" *Guerilla Gardening;* Chris Carlsson's *Nowtopia;* and antiglobalization publications like *We Are Everywhere.*

16. For additional images of gardening as an insurgent practice, see Mikalbrown (229–33).

Chapter 5. Just Gardens

1. Immigrant laborers make up over 80 percent of agricultural workers; 52 percent are undocumented (Holmes 99). Statistics available through the U.S. Department of Labor's National Agricultural Workers Survey (NAWS) at www.doleta.gov/agworker/naws.cfm. As Seth Holmes notes, agricultural workers also experience increased rates of illnesses and nonfatal injuries like musculoskeletal pain, heart disease, cancer, and increased risk of stillbirth and congenital birth defects (88–101).

2. See Emmett's *Cultivating Environmental Justice*, which traces many of the seeds of contemporary environmental-justice movements to mid-twentieth-century U.S. garden writing.

3. Klindienst cites the influence of two classic studies of the American immigrant experience—Oscar Handlin's *The Uprooted* (1951) and John Bodnar's *The Transplanted* (1985)—in establishing this common metaphor.

4. For a fuller discussion of internment camp gardens, see Helphand (155–200).

5. Environmental factors make the tension between these two gardens more complicated still, since Pepe's tropical garden requires an abundance of water—a scarce resource in the desert climate of Southern California, which experienced recurring cycles of drought in the late twentieth and early twenty-first centuries. From a sustainability perspective, then, the succulent and cactus garden would actually be a more appropriate choice.

6. For further discussion of the garden as a "slow space," see Cooper's *A Philosophy of Gardens* and Hill and Stewart's "Time."

7. In her discussion of nineteenth-century plant smugglers, Joy Porter traces some of the botanical relocations that gave rise to major colonial economies, with the latex-producing *Hevea brasiliensis* prominent among these: removed from the Amazon in 1876, it "facilitate[ed] the subsequent rise of rubber plantations in Ceylon, Malaya and Sumatra" (62).

8. See also "Traditional Native American Gardening," in Caduto and Bruchac's *Native American Gardening.*

9. For many Native farmers and gardeners, another primary threat came from contamination of their lands by heavy industry. In "Local Food Production and Community Illness Narratives," Elizabeth Hoover extensively documents the environmental plight of communities like the Akwesasne in upstate New York and Ontario—a group that relied almost exclusively on farming, gardening, and fishing for their subsistence well into the 1950s. As pollution from aluminum plants contaminated their lands, and three Superfund sites were created upstream along the St. Lawrence River, environmental illness, crop failure, and livestock death became epidemic. When the EPA advised the Akwesasne not to plant gardens because of the health risks, community members suffered a major psychological impact, since, as Hoover explains, garden cultivation represented a vital connection to their relatives, culture, and personal childhood memories.

10. For further discussion of the precolonization diet (foods eaten before European settlers came to the Americas), visit *From Garden Warriors to Good Seeds: Indigenizing the Local Food Movement*, an online resource maintained by Elizabeth Hoover, Native gardener and ethnic studies professor at Brown University: www.gardenwarriorsgoodseeds.com. Also see Autumn Spanne, "Native American Tribes Tackle Diet and Health Woes with Businesses Built on Traditional Foods," *Guardian*, June 13, 2015, www.theguardian.com/sustainable-business/2015/jun/13/native-american-tribes-diet-health-traditional-foods-business-entrepreneur; and Paul Wachter, "Nephi Craig, Farm to Table Food, and the Movement to Rediscover Native American Cooking," *Newsweek*, August 8, 2013, www.newsweek.com/2013/08/23/nephi-craig-farm-table-food-and-movement-rediscover-native-american-cooking-237856.html.

Epilogue. Garden Writing and the Phenomenology of Dirt

1. While discussions in this book have overwhelmingly focused on American writers, I reach beyond the United States in this final section. What happens in American gardens happens in other gardens, of course. Moreover, the global nature of the environmental issues addressed here opens our inquiry beyond arbitrary national boundaries.

2. As Pyle writes in a well-known passage from *The Thunder Tree*, "As cities and metastasizing suburbs forsake their natural diversity, and their citizens grow more removed from personal contact with nature, awareness and appreciation retreat. This breeds apathy toward environmental concerns and, inevitably, further degradation of the common habitat. . . . So it goes, on and on, the extinction of experience sucking the life from the land, the intimacy from our connections. . . . [P]eople who don't know don't care. What is the extinction of the condor to a child who has never known a wren?" (146–47).

3. See, for example, Robert Pogue Harrison's discussion of *The Epic of Gilgamesh* in *Forests: The Shadow of Civilization* (1992).

Bibliography

Addison, Joseph. *The Spectator* 477 (vol. 7). London: Printed for A. and B. Tonson and T. Draper, 1766.
Agee, James, and Walker Evans. *Let Us Now Praise Famous Men*. 1939. Reprint, Boston: Houghton Mifflin, 1960.
Aldrich, Thomas Bailey. *Unguarded Gates: And Other Poems*. Ann Arbor, Mich.: University of Michigan Library, 2005.
Alexander, Shana. "Requiem for Vestigial Organ." *Newsweek*, Feb. 18, 1974.
Alexander, William. *The $64 Tomato*. Chapel Hill: Algonquin Books, 1997.
Allen, Lewis. *Rural Architecture*. New York: Moore, 1852.
Alsop, George. *A Character of the Province of Maryland*. 1666. Reprint, Freeport, N.Y.: Books for Libraries Press, 1972.
Amazon.com review of *The Constant Gardener: A Novel*. Retrieved Apr. 20, 2015, from www.amazon.com/The-Constant-Gardener-A-Novel/dp/1416503900.
Atwood, Margaret. *The Handmaid's Tale*. New York: Anchor Books, 1998.
Atwood, Margaret. *The Year of the Flood*. New York: Doubleday, 2009.
Azima, Rachel. "'Not the Native': Self-transplantation, Ecocriticism, and Postcolonialism in Jamaica Kincaid's *My Garden (Book)*." *Journal of Commonwealth and Postcolonial Studies* 13–14, no. 2-1 (2006): 101–19.
Baccolini, Raffaella. "Gender and Genre in the Feminist Critical Dystopias of Katherine Burdekin, Margaret Atwood, and Octavia Butler." In *Future Females, the Next Generation: New Voices and Velocities in Feminist Science Fiction Criticism*, ed. Marleen S. Barr, 13–34. Lanham, Md.: Rowman & Littlefield, 2000.
Bachelard, Gaston. *The Poetics of Space*. Boston: Beacon Press, 1994.
Baker, Ray Stannard. "The Movement of Wheat." *McClure's Magazine* 14, no. 2 (Dec. 1899): 124–37.
Barndt, Deborah. *Tangled Routes: Women, Work, and Globalization on the Tomato Trail*. Lanham, Md.: Rowman & Littlefield, 2002.
Barwell, Ismay, and John Powell. "Gardens, Music and Time." In *Gardening: Philosophy for Everyone*, ed. Dan O'Brien, 135–47. Malden, Mass.: Wiley-Blackwell, 2010.
Bataille, Georges. *The Accursed Share*. New York: Zone Books, 1991.

Beam, Dorri. *Style, Gender, and Fantasy in Nineteenth-Century American Women's Writing*. New York: Cambridge University Press, 2010.

Beecher, Henry Ward. *Plain and Pleasant Talk about Fruits, Flowers and Farming*. New York: Derby & Jackson, 1859.

Belasco, Warren. *Appetite for Change*. Ithaca: Cornell University Press, 2007.

Belasco, Warren. *Meals to Come: A History of the Future of Food*. Berkeley: University of California Press, 2006.

Benepe, Barry. *Greenmarket: The Rebirth of Farmers Markets in New York City*. New York: Council on the Environment, 1977.

Berlin, Ira, and Philip Morgan. Introduction to *The Slaves' Economy: Independent Production by Slaves in the Americas*, ed. Berlin and Morgan, 1–30. Portland: Frank Cass, 1991.

Berry, Wendell. Foreword to *Enduring Seeds: Native American Agriculture and Wild Plant Conservation*, by Gary Paul Nabhan, xiii–xiv. Tucson: University of Arizona Press, 2001.

Beverley, Robert. *The History and Present State of Virginia*. Ed. Louis B. Wright. Chapel Hill: University of North Carolina Press, 1947.

Bigelow, Poultney. "The Bonanza Farms of the West." *Atlantic Monthly* (Jan. 1880): 33–44.

Blane, William Newnham. *An Excursion through the United States and Canada During the Years 1822–23: By an English Gentleman*. London: Baldwin, Cradock, and Joy, 1824.

Bloch, Ernst. *The Principle of Hope*. Trans. Neville Plaice, Stephen Plaice, and Paul Knight. 3 vols. Cambridge, Mass.: MIT Press, 1986.

Bluestone, Daniel. "The Pushcart Evil." In *The Landscape of Modernity: Essays on New York City, 1900–1940*, ed. David Warn and Oliver Zunz, 287–312. New York: Russel Sage Foundation, 1992.

Boccardi, Mariadele. "Beyond the Garden: Liminality and Politics in the Twenty-first Century Historical Novel." Paper presented at "The Twenty-First Century Novel: Reading and Writing Contemporary Fiction," Lancaster University, Sept. 2–3, 2005.

Borden, Iain, Joe Kerr, Jane Rendell, and Alicia Pivaro. *The Unknown City: Contesting Architecture and Social Space*. Cambridge, Mass.: MIT Press, 1998.

Bralove, Mary. "Most People Have No Taste: It's Been Lost in the Process. Fresh Foods Taste Peculiar If You Grew Up Eating Instant, Frozen or Canned." *Wall Street Journal*, Apr. 30, 1974.

"Brief Mention." *Hartford Courant*. Dec. 17, 1870.

Brobeck, Florence. "Outdoor Food Markets Are Moving Indoors: The Pushcart Vendor, Who Lends Color to the City's Streets, Feels the Hand of Progress." *New York Times*, Oct. 11, 1936.

Bromell, Nicholas K. *By the Sweat of the Brow: Literature and Labor in Antebellum America*. Chicago: University of Chicago Press, 1993.

Brook, Isis. "The Virtues of Gardening. In *Gardening: Philosophy for Everyone*, ed. Dan O'Brien, 13–25. Malden, Mass.: Wiley-Blackwell, 2010.

Brown, Bill. *A Sense of Things: The Object Matter of American Literature*. Chicago: University of Chicago Press, 2004.
Brown, Jane. *The Pursuit of Paradise: A Social History of Gardens and Gardening*. London: HarperCollins, 1999.
Buell, Laurence. *The Environmental Imagination*. Cambridge, Mass.: Harvard University Press, 1995.
Buell, Laurence. *The Future of Environmental Criticism*. Malden, Mass.: Blackwell, 2005.
Butler, Octavia. *Parable of the Sower*. New York: Warner Books, 1993.
Butler, Octavia. *Parable of the Talents*. New York: Warner Books, 1998.
Byrd, William. "Letter to Mr. Beckford" (Dec. 6, 1735). *Virginia Magazine of History and Biography* 9 (Jan. 1902): 234–35.
Caduto, Michael, and Joseph Bruchac. *Keepers of Life: Discovering Plants through Native American Stories and Earth Activities for Children*. Golden, Colo.: Fulcrum, 1994.
Caduto, Michael, and Joseph Bruchac. *Native American Gardening: Stories, Projects and Recipes for Families*. Golden, Colo.: Fulcrum, 1996.
Čapek, Karel. *The Gardener's Year*. Trans. M. and R. Weatherall. New York: Modern Library, 2002.
Carlsson, Chris. *Nowtopia*. Oakland, Calif.: AK Press, 2008.
Carruth, Allison. *Global Appetites: American Power and the Literature of Food*. Cambridge: Cambridge University Press, 2013.
Casey, Edward. *The Fate of Place: A Philosophical History*. Berkeley: University of California Press, 1997.
Casey, Edward. *Getting Back into Place: Toward a Renewed Understanding of the Place-World*. Bloomington: Indiana University Press, 1993.
Casey, Edward. "How to Get from Space to Place in a Fairly Short Stretch of Time." In *Senses of Place*, ed. Steven Feld and Keith H. Basso, 13–52. Santa Fe: School of American Research Press, 1996.
Cather, Willa. "Nebraska: The End of the First Cycle." *The Nation* (5 Sept 1923): 236–38.
Cather, Willa. *Death Comes for the Archbishop*. New York: Vintage Books, 1990.
Cather, Willa. *My Ántonia*. New York: Houghton Mifflin, 1995.
Cather, Willa. *O Pioneers!* New York: New American Libraries, 1988.
Cather, Willa. *The Professor's House*. New York: Vintage Books, 1990.
Certeau, Michel de. *The Practice of Everyday Life*. Trans. Steven Rendall. Berkeley: University of California Press, 1984.
"Charles Dudley Warner." *Public Opinion* 29, no. 18. (Nov. 1, 1900): 564.
Cheney, Barbara. "Garden Blights." *Atlantic Monthly* 157 (June 1936): 767–68.
Chesnutt, Charles W. "The Conjure Woman." In *Selected Writings*, ed. SallyAnn H. Ferguson, 118–88. Boston: Houghton Mifflin, 2001.
Cicero, Marcus Tullius. "On Old Age." In *On Old Age. On Friendship. On Divination*. Trans. William Falconer. Cambridge, Mass.: Harvard University Press, 1923.

Clayton, Virginia. *The Once and Future Gardener*. Boston: David R. Godine, 2000.
Coffin, C. C. "Dakota Wheat Fields." *Harper's Monthly Magazine* 60, no. 358 (Mar. 1880): 529–36.
Cohen, Stanley, and Laurie Taylor. *Escape Attempts: The Theory and Practice of Resistance to Everyday Life*. New York: Penguin, 1978.
Collom, Jack. "A Few Crumbs from the Houston Street Median-Stripe Naturewalk." In *Avant Gardening*, ed. Peter Lamborn Wilson and Bill Weinberg, 142–56. Brooklyn: Autonomedia, 1999.
Conlogue, William. *Working the Garden: American Writers and the Industrialization of Agriculture*. Chapel Hill: University of North Carolina Press, 2001.
Cooper, David. *A Philosophy of Gardens*. Oxford: Oxford University Press, 2008.
Copeland, Robert. *Country Life: A Handbook of Agriculture, Horticulture, and Landscape Gardening*. Boston: Dinsmoor, 1866.
Cronon, William. *Changes in the Land: Indians, Colonists, and the Ecology of New England*. New York: Hill & Wang, 2003.
Cronon, William. *Nature's Metropolis: Chicago and the Great West*. New York: W. W. Norton, 1990.
Crouch, David, and Colin Ward. *The Allotment: Its Landscape and Culture*. London: Faber & Faber, 1988.
Danbom, David B. *The Resisted Revolution*. Ames: Iowa State University Press, 1979.
Davenport, Eugene. "Scientific Farming." *Country Life*. American Academy of Political and Social Science (Mar. 1912): 45–50.
Demaree, Albert Lowther. *The American Agricultural Press, 1819–1860*. New York: Columbia University Press, 1941.
Dolan, Kathryn Cornell. *Beyond the Fruited Plain: Food and Agriculture in U.S. Literature, 1850–1905*. Lincoln: University of Nebraska Press, 2014.
Donawerth, Jane L., and Carol A. Kolmerten. *Utopian and Science Fiction by Women: Worlds of Difference*. Syracuse, N.Y.: Syracuse University Press, 1994.
Downing, Andrew Jackson. "Essay on Landscape Gardening." 1841. In *American Garden Writing: An Anthology*, ed. Bonnie Marranca, 245–53. Lanham, Md.: Taylor, 2003.
Downing, Andrew Jackson. *Rural Essays*. New York: G. P. Putnam, 1853.
Downing, Andrew Jackson. *A Treatise on the Theory and Practice of Landscape Gardening, Adapted to North America*. 4th ed. New York: G. P. Putnam, 1853.
Downton, Paul F. *Ecopolis: Architecture and Cities for a Changing Climate*. New York: Springer, 2009.
Drache, Hiram M. *Day of the Bonanza*. Fargo: North Dakota Institute for Regional Studies, 1964.
Duncan, Francis. "Planting Your Own Vine and Fig Tree." *Garden Magazine* 15 (Apr. 1912): 158–60.
Dyer, Walter A. "The Humble Annals of a Back Yard: Morning Chapel." In *The Once and Future Gardener*, ed. Virginia Clayton, 285–87. Boston: David R. Godine, 2000. Originally published in *The Craftsman* 26 (June 1914): 270–71.

"E. 59th Street Farmers' Market Thrives." *New York Times*, Aug. 1, 1976.
Earle, Alice Morse. *Old Time Gardens*. Hanover, N.H.: University Press of New England, 2005.
Edgington, Ryan H. "'Be Receptive to the Good Earth': Health, Nature, and Labor in Countercultural Back-to-the-Land Settlements." *Agricultural History* 82.3 (2008): 279–308.
Eisenberg, Evan. *Ecology of Eden*. New York: Vintage Books, 1999.
Eliot, George. *Scenes of Clerical Life*. Vol. 2 of *The Works of George Eliot*. Edinburgh and London: William Blackwood and Sons, 1878.
Emmett, Robert. *Cultivating Environmental Justice*. Amherst: University of Massachusetts Press, 2016.
Federico, Giovanni. *Feeding the World: An Economic History of Agriculture, 1800–2000*. Princeton, N.J.: Princeton University Press, 2005.
Feeley, Lynne. "Tilling After Dark." Paper presented at "Earth Perfect Symposium," University of Delaware, Newark, June 2013.
Feldberg, Robert. "A Defense Is Offered for Lemon Cream Pie." Interview with Robert Weiss, President, Morton Frozen Foods Division of ITT. *The Bergen (New Jersey) Record*, Aug. 13, 1971.
Ferguson, Sarah. "A Brief History of Grassroots Greening on the Lower East Side." In *Avant Gardening*, ed. Peter Lamborn Wilson and Bill Weinberg, 80–90. Brooklyn: Autonomedia, 1999.
Ferguson, Sarah. "The Death of Little Puerto Rico." In *Avant Gardening*, ed. Peter Lamborn Wilson and Bill Weinberg, 60–79. Brooklyn: Autonomedia, 1999.
Finley, Ron. "A Guerrilla Gardener in South Central L.A." TED lecture, Feb. 2013. Retrieved from www.ted.com/talks/ron_finley_a_guerilla_gardener_in_south_central_la.
Finney, Gail. *The Counterfeit Idyll: The Garden Ideal and Social Reality in Nineteenth-Century Fiction*. Tubingen: M. Niemeyer, 1984.
Fiskio, Janet. "Unsettling Ecocriticism: Rethinking Agrarianism, Place, and Citizenship." *American Literature* 84, no. 2 (June 2012): 301–25.
Fite, Gilbert. *American Farmers*. Bloomington: Indiana University Press, 1981.
Fitzgerald, F. Scott. *The Great Gatsby*. New York: Simon & Schuster, 1995.
Flores, Heather. *Food Not Lawns: How to Turn Your Yard into a Garden and Your Neighborhood into a Community*. White River Junction, Vt.: Chelsea Green, 2006.
Foderaro, Lisa W. "Enjoy Park Greenery, City Says, but Not as Salad." *New York Times*, July 29, 2011.
Food and Agriculture Organization (FAO) of the United Nations, Statistics Division. "Staple Foods: What Do People Eat?" Retrieved July 14, 2017, from www.fao.org/docrep/u8480e/u8480e07.htm.
Food and Agriculture Organization (FAO) of the United Nations, Statistics Division. "What Is Happening to Agrobiodiversity?" Retrieved July 14, 2017, from www.fao.org/docrep/007/y5609e/y5609e02.htm.
Foucault, Michel. "Of Other Spaces." *Diacritics* 16, no. 1 (Spring 1986): 22–27.

Francis, Mark, and Randolph T. Hester. *The Meaning of Gardens: Idea, Place and Action*. Cambridge, Mass.: MIT Press, 1990.

Freidberg, Susanne. *French Beans and Food Scares: Culture and Commerce in an Anxious Age*. New York: Oxford University Press, 2004.

Freidberg, Susanne. *Fresh: A Perishable History*. Cambridge, Mass.: Belknap Press, 2010.

Freyfogle, Eric. "Introduction: A Durable Scale." In *The New Agrarianism: Land, Culture, and the Community of Life*, ed. Eric Freyfogle. Washington, D.C.: Island Press, 2001.

Galaxy. A Magazine of Entertaining Reading 6, no. 2 (Feb. 1871): 309.

Gardener's Magazine and Register of Rural and Domestic Improvement. Ed. John C. Loudon. London, 1826–44.

Garfinkel, Harold. *Studies in Ethnomethodology*. Englewood Cliffs, N.J.: Prentice Hall, 1967.

Garland, Hamlin. "Up the Coolly." In *Main Travelled Roads*. Lincoln: University of Nebraska Press, 1995. 45–87.

Gay, Ross. "Burial." In *Catalog of Unabashed Gratitude*. Pittsburgh: University of Pittsburgh Press, 2015. 11–14.

Gay, Ross. "Catalog of Unabashed Gratitude." In *Catalog of Unabashed Gratitude*. Pittsburgh: University of Pittsburgh Press, 2015. 82–98.

Gay, Ross. "Sharing with the Ants." In *Catalog of Unabashed Gratitude*. Pittsburgh: University of Pittsburgh Press, 2015. 55–58.

Geertz, Clifford. "The Bazaar Economy: Information and Search in Peasant Marketing." *American Economic Review* 68, no. 2 (May 1978): 28–32.

Gemein, Mascha N. "'Seeds Must Be Among the Greatest Travelers of All': Native American Literatures Planting the Seeds for a Cosmopolitical Environmental Justice Discourse." *Interdisciplinary Studies in Literature and Environment* 23, no. 3 (Summer 2016): 485–505.

Genesee Farmer. "Kitchen Garden." Vol. 6 (May 1845): 67.

George, Henry. *Our Land and Land Policy*. New York: Doubleday, 1904.

Gernsback, Hugo. *Ralph 124C 41+*. 1911. Reprint, Lincoln: University of Nebraska Press, 2000.

Gibbs, Patricia. "'Little Spots Allow'd Them': Slave Garden Plots and Poultry Yards." *Colonial Williamsburg Interpreter* 20, no. 4 (1999): 9–13.

Gilman, Charlotte Perkins. *Herland*. Minneola, N.Y.: Dover, 1998.

Graham, Wade. *American Eden: From Monticello to Central Park to our Backyards*. New York: HarperCollins, 2011.

Grant, Doris. *Your Bread and Your Life*. London: Faber & Faber, 1961.

Graves, Richard. "The Hermitage." In *Euphrosyne: Or, Amusements on the Road of Life*. London: Printed for J. Dodsley, 1776. 261–62.

Gross, Robert A. "The Great Bean Field Hoax: Thoreau and the Agricultural Reformers." In *Critical Essays on Henry David Thoreau*, ed. Joel Myerson, 193–202. Boston: G. K. Hall, 1988.

Gurganus, Allan. "Sketch in Evergreen: Toward the Resurrection of Charles Dudley Warner." Introduction to *My Summer in a Garden,* by Charles Dudley Warner, xi–xxvi. New York: Modern Library, 2002.

Guthman, Julie. "Bringing Good Food to Others: Investigating the Subjects of Alternative Food Practice." *Cultural Geographies* 15, no. 4 (2008): 431–47.

Hakluyt, Richard. "The First Voyage to Virginia." In *The Principal Navigations, Voyages, Traffiques and Discoveries of the English Nation,* vol. 8, 297–310. Glasgow: James MacLehose & Sons, 1904.

Hardy, Dennis. "Plots of Paradise: Gardens and the Utopian City." In *Earth Perfect? Nature, Utopia and the Garden,* ed. Annette Giesecke and Naomi Jacobs, 172–89. London, UK: Black Dog, 2012.

Harrison, Robert Pogue. *Gardens: An Essay on the Human Condition.* Chicago: University of Chicago Press, 2008.

Harvey, David. *The Condition of Postmodernity.* Cambridge, Mass.: Blackwell Press, 1990.

Harvey, David. "The Nature of the Environment: The Dialectics of Social and Environmental Change." In *Real Problems, False Solutions: Socialist Register,* ed. Ralph Miliband and Leo Panitch, 1–51. London: Merlin Press, 1993.

Harvey, David. *Spaces of Hope.* Berkeley: University of California Press, 2000.

Hatch, Peter J. "African-American Gardens at Monticello." *Twinleaf Journal,* www.twinleaf.org, Jan. 2001.

Hawthorne, Nathaniel. *The Blithedale Romance.* Norton Critical Edition. Ed. Seymour Gross and Rosalie Murphy. New York: W. W. Norton, 1978.

Hawthorne, Nathaniel. "Letters and Journals, 1841." In *The Blithedale Romance,* Norton critical edition, ed. Seymour Gross and Rosalie Murphy, 236. New York: W. W. Norton, 1978.

Heinberg, Richard. *Memories and Visions of Paradise: Exploring the Universal Myth of a Lost Golden Age.* Wheaton, Ill.: Quest Books, 1995.

Heller, Joseph. *Something Happened.* New York: Alfred A. Knopf, 1974.

Helphand, Kenneth. *Defiant Gardens: Making Gardens in Wartime.* San Antonio, Tex.: Trinity University Press, 2008.

Henderson, Peter. *Gardening for Profit: A Guide to the Successful Cultivation of the Market and Family Garden.* 1867. Reprint, New York: O. Judd, 1893.

Hess, John. Preface to *Greenmarket: The Rebirth of Farmers Markets in New York City,* by Barry Benepe. New York: Council on the Environment, 1977.

Hess, John L., and Karen Hess. *The Taste of America.* New York: Grossman, 1977.

Higginson, Thomas Wentworth. "Charles Dudley Warner." *Scribner's Monthly* 7 (1874): 333–34.

Hightower, Jim. *Eat Your Heart Out: Food Profiteering in America.* New York: Crown, 1975.

Hill, May Brawley. *Grandmother's Garden: The Old-Fashioned American Garden, 1865–1915.* New York: Harry N. Abrams, 1995.

Hill, Susan, and Rory Stewart. "Time." In *The Writer in the Garden*, ed. Jane Garmey, 231–35. Chapel Hill, N.C.: Algonquin Books, 1999.

Holloway, Lewis, and Moya Kneafsey. "Producing-Consuming Food: Closeness, Connectedness and Rurality in Four 'Alternative' Food Networks." In *Geographies of Rural Cultures and Societies*, ed. Lewis Holloway and Moya Kneafsey, 262–82. London: Ashgate, 2004.

Holmes, Seth. *Fresh Fruit, Broken Bodies: Migrant Farmworkers in the United States*. Berkeley: University of California Press, 2013.

Hondagneu-Sotelo, Pierrette. *Paradise Transplanted: Migration and the Making of California Gardens*. Berkeley: University of California Press, 2014.

Hoover, Elizabeth. "Local Food Production and Community Illness Narratives." PhD diss., Brown University, 2010.

Houston, Jeanne Wakatsuki, and James D. Houston. *Farewell to Manzanar: A True Story of Japanese American Experience during and after the World War II Internment*. Boston: Houghton Mifflin, 1973.

Hoyles, Martin. *The Story of Gardening*. Concord, Mass.: Journeyman Press, 1991.

Hugill, Peter. "English Landscape Tastes in the United States." *Geographical Review* 76, no. 4 (Oct. 1986): 408–23.

Hunt, John Dixon. *The Figure in Landscape: Poetry, Painting, and Gardening During the Eighteenth Century*. Baltimore: Johns Hopkins University Press, 1976.

Hunt, John Dixon. *Greater Perfections: The Practice of Garden Theory*. Philadelphia: University of Pennsylvania Press, 2000.

Huxley, Aldous. *Brave New World*. 1932. Reprint, New York: Perennial, 1969.

Ish, Lyx. "Peeing on a Lily Pad (and Other Musings on Gardens and Art)." In *Avant Gardening*, ed. Peter Lamborn Wilson and Bill Weinberg, 123. Brooklyn: Autonomedia, 1999.

Jackson, Wes. "Farming in Nature's Image: Natural Systems Agriculture." In *The Fatal Harvest Reader*, ed. Andrew Kimbrell, 65–75. Washington: Island Press, 2002.

Jameson, Fredric. *Archaeologies of the Future*. New York: Verso, 2005.

Jameson, Fredric. "Cognitive Mapping." In *Marxism and the Interpretation of Culture*, ed. Cary Nelson and Lawrence Grossberg, 347–57. Urbana: University of Illinois Press, 1988.

Jameson, Fredric. *Postmodernism, or, The Cultural Logic of Late Capitalism*. Durham, N.C.: Duke University Press, 1991.

Jefferson, Thomas. *Thomas Jefferson's Garden Book, 1766–1824: With Relevant Extracts from His Other Writings*. Annotated by Edwin Morris Betts. Philadelphia: The American Philosophical Society, 1944.

Johnson, Hildegard. *Order Upon the Land*. New York: Oxford University Press, 1976.

Johnson, Sophia Orne. *Every Woman Her Own Flower Gardener: A Handy Manual of Flower Gardening for Ladies*. New York: Henry T. Williams, 1874.

Kamp, David. *The United States of Arugula: How We Became a Gourmet Nation*. New York: Broadway Books, 2006.

Kennedy, Scott Hamilton (dir.). *The Garden*. Black Valley Films, 2008.

Kimmerer, Robin Wall. *Braiding Sweetgrass: Indigenous Wisdom, Scientific Knowledge and the Teachings of Plants*. Minneapolis: Milkweed, 2013.
Kincaid, Jamaica. *My Garden (Book)*. New York: Farrar, Straus & Giroux, 1999.
Kincaid, Jamaica. "Sowers and Reapers." *The New Yorker*, Jan. 22, 2001, 41–45.
Kincaid, Jamaica, with Gerald Dilger. *Writing across Worlds: Contemporary Writers Talk*. Ed. Shusheila Nasta. New York: Routledge, 2004.
King, Francis. *The Well-Considered Garden*. New York: Charles Scribner's Sons, 1915.
Kingsolver, Barbara. *Animal, Vegetable, Miracle: A Year of Food Life*. New York: HarperCollins, 2007.
Kingsolver, Barbara. *Prodigal Summer: A Novel*. New York: HarperCollins, 2000.
Kirkland, Winifred Margaretta. "Discontent in the Garden." *Atlantic Monthly* 117 (June 1916): 852–54.
Klein, Naomi. *This Changes Everything: Capitalism Versus the Climate*. New York: Simon & Schuster, 2014.
Klindienst, Patricia. *The Earth Knows My Name: Food, Culture, and Sustainability in the Gardens of Ethnic Americans*. Boston: Beacon Press, 2006.
Kornfeld, Dory. "Bringing Good Food In: A History of New York City's Greenmarket Program." *Journal of Urban History* 40, no. 2 (2014): 345–56.
Kosinski, Jerzy. *Being There*. New York, Harcourt Brace Jovanovich, 1971.
Lanman, Susan W. "Color in the Garden: 'Malignant Magenta.'" *Garden History* 28, no. 2 (Winter 2000): 209–21.
Latour, Bruno. *We Have Never Been Modern*. Cambridge, Mass.: Harvard University Press, 1993.
Lawrence, Elizabeth. *Gardening for Love: The Market Bulletins*. Durham, N.C.: Duke University Press, 1987.
Lawson, Laura. *City Bountiful*. Berkeley: University of California Press, 2005.
Le Carré, John. *The Constant Gardener*. New York: Scribner, 2001.
Le Guin, Ursula. "The Carrier Bag Theory of Fiction." In *Dancing at the Edge of the World*. New York: Grove Press, 1989.
Le Guin, Ursula. *The Dispossessed*. 1974. Reprint, New York: EOS, 2001.
Lears, Jackson. *Fables of Abundance: A Cultural History of Advertising in America*. New York: Basic Books, 1994.
Lefebvre, Henri. *The Production of Space*. Trans. Donald Nicholson-Smith. 1974. Reprint, Malden, Mass.: Blackwell, 1991.
Leonard, Pauline G. Wiggin. "The Contributor's Club: Democracy and Gardening." *Atlantic Monthly* 85 (May 1900): 714–16.
Levitas, Ruth. "Utopia Here and Now." In *Midlertidige utopier*, ed. Siri Meyer, 142–48. Oslo: Museum of Contemporary Art, 2003.
Levitas, Ruth. *The Concept of Utopia*. London: Philip Allan, 1990.
Linklater, Andro. *Measuring America: How an Untamed Wilderness Shaped the United States and Fulfilled the Promise of Democracy*. New York: Waller, 2002.
Lopez, Barry. *Arctic Dreams*. New York: Vintage, 1991.

"Los Angeles Gothic." Editorial. *Los Angeles Times*, Mar. 11, 2006. Retrieved from http://articles.latimes.com/2006/mar/11/opinion/ed-farm11.

Lovett, Laura. "Land Reclamation as Family Reclamation." *Social Politics: International Studies in Gender, State and Society* 7, no. 1 (2000): 80–100.

MacDonald, Eric. "Hortus Incantus: Gardening as an Art of Enchantment." In *Gardening: Philosophy for Everyone*, ed. Dan O'Brien, 121–34. Malden, Mass.: Wiley-Blackwell, 2010.

Marambaud, Pierre. *William Byrd of Westover, 1674–1744*. Charlottesville: University Press of Virginia, 1971.

Marcuse, Herbert. "The Affirmative Character of Culture." In *Negations: Essays in Critical Theory*. Trans. Jeremy Shapiro. 1937. Reprint, Boston: Beacon Press, 1968.

Mares, Teresa M. "Tracing Immigrant Identity through the Plate and the Palate." *Latino Studies* 10, no. 3 (2012): 334–54.

Marranca, Bonnie, ed. *American Garden Writing: An Anthology*. Lanham, Md.: Taylor, 2003.

Marroquin, Art. "Deputies Evict Farmers, Supporters from South Central Farm." *City News Service*, June 13, 2006.

Martin, Peter. *The Pleasure Gardens of Virginia: From Jamestown to Jefferson*. Princeton: Princeton University Press, 1991.

Marx, Karl. *Capital*. 3 vols. New York: International Publishers, 1967.

Marx, Karl. *Theories of Surplus Value*. Moscow: Progress Publishers, 1963.

Marx, Leo. *The Machine in the Garden: Technology and the Pastoral Ideal in America*. New York: Oxford University Press, 2000.

McAdam, Thomas. "Gardening Books for Christmas Presents." *Garden Magazine*, Dec. 1905, 229–30.

McDonald, Roderick A. "Independent Economic Production by Slaves on Antebellum Louisiana Sugar Plantations." In *The Slaves' Economy: Independent Production by Slaves in the Americas*, ed. Ira Berlin and Philip Morgan, 182–208. Portland: Frank Cass, 1991.

McKay, George. *Radical Gardening: Politics, Idealism and Rebellion in the Garden*. London: Frances Lincoln, 2011.

McPhee, John. *Giving Good Weight*. New York: Farrar, Straus and Giroux, 1979.

Merleau-Ponty, Maurice. *The Visible and the Invisible*. Evanston, Ill.: Northwestern University Press, 1968.

Messervy, Julie Moir. "The Dirty-Minded Gardener." In *The Roots of My Obsession: Thirty Great Gardeners Reveal Why They Garden*, ed. Thomas Cooper, 101–7. Portland: Timber Press, 2012.

Mickey, Thomas. *America's Romance with the English Garden*. Athens: Ohio University Press, 2013.

Mikalbrown, Kerstin. *From ACT UP to the WTO: Urban Protest and Community Building in the Era of Globalization*. New York: Verso, 2002.

Miller, Mara. *The Garden as an Art*. Albany: State University of New York Press, 1993.

Montaigne, Michel de. *On Cannibals*. 1580. In *Reading about the World*, ed. Paul Brians and Mary Gallwey, 2: 63–65. Orlando: Harcourt College, 1999.
Moore, Charles, William J. Mitchell, and William Turnbull Jr. *The Poetics of Gardens*. Cambridge, Mass.: MIT Press, 2000.
More, Thomas. *Utopia*. 1516. Reprint, Mineola, N.Y.: Dover, 1997.
Morris, Elisabeth Woodbridge. "The Contributors' Club: Escaped from Old Gardens." *Atlantic Monthly* 101 (June 1908): 859.
Morris, William. *News from Nowhere, or An Epoch of Rest*. 1890. Reprint, Mineola, N.Y.: Dover, 2004.
Morrison, B. Y. "A Three-Tier Herbaceous Border." *Garden Magazine* 21 (Feb. 1915): 15.
Morrison, Toni. *Paradise*. New York : A. A. Knopf, 1998.
Morrison, Toni. "This Side of Paradise," interview by James Marcus. *Amazon.com*. Jan 1998. Retrieved July 18, 2016, from www.amazon.com/gp/feature.html?ie=UTF8&docId=7651.
Morton, Margaret. "The Gardens of Those Called 'Homeless.'" In *The Good Gardener: Nature, Humanity and the Garden*, ed. Annette Giesecke and Naomi Jacobs, 290–303. London: Artifice Books on Architecture, 2015.
Mott, Frank Luther. *A History of American Magazines*. 5 vols. Cambridge, Mass.: Harvard University Press, 1939–68.
Moylan, Tom. *Scraps of the Untainted Sky*. Boulder: Westview Press, 2000.
Nabhan, Gary Paul. *Coming Home to Eat: The Pleasures and Politics of Local Foods*. New York: W. W. Norton, 2002.
Nash, Roderick Frazier. *Wilderness and the American Mind*. New Haven: Yale University Press, 2001.
National Education Television. "The Great American Dream Machine." Segment on Morton's Lemon Cream Pie, by Marshall Efron and Penny Berstein. Jan. 6, 1971. Transcript.
Naylor, Gloria. *Mama Day*. New York: Vintage Books, 1993.
Norris, Frank. "Letter to Isaac F. Marcosson" (Sept. 13, 1900). In *The Merrill Studies in The Octopus*, ed. Richard Allan Davidson, 5–6. Columbus, Ohio: Charles E. Merrill, 1969.
Norris, Frank. *The Octopus*. New York: Penguin Books, 1994.
O'Brien, Dan. *Gardening: Philosophy for Everyone*. Malden, Mass.: Wiley-Blackwell, 2010.
Obama, Michelle. *American Grown: The Story of the White House Kitchen Garden and Gardens across America*. New York: Crown, 2012.
Olmsted, Frederick Law. *Forty Years of Landscape Architecture: Central Park*. Ed. Frederick Law Olmsted Jr. and Theodora Kimball. Cambridge, Mass.: MIT Press, 1973.
Olwig, Kenneth. "Reinventing Common Nature." In *Uncommon Ground*, ed. William Cronon, 379–408. New York: W. W. Norton, 1996.
Orwell, George. "Some Thoughts on the Common Toad." In *Facing Unpleasant Facts: Narrative Essays*. Ed. Peter Davison. Orlando: Houghton Mifflin Harcourt, 2008.

Otter, Chris. "Industrializing Diet, Industrializing Ourselves: Technology, Food and the Body, Since 1750." In *The Routledge History of Food*, ed. Carol Helstosky, 220–46. New York: Taylor & Francis, 2015.

Ozeki, Ruth. *All Over Creation*. New York: Penguin, 2003.

Page, Russell. *The Education of a Gardener*. New York: New York Review Books, 2007.

Parkins, Wendy, and Geoffrey Craig. *Slow Living*. Oxford: Berg, 2006.

Parsons, Russ. *How to Pick a Peach: The Search for Flavor from Farm to Table*. Boston: Houghton Mifflin, 2008.

Pearson, Edmund Lester. *The Librarian at Play*. Boston: Small, Maynard, 1911.

Pentecost, Claire. "What Did You Eat and When Did You Know It?" Annual Conference of the Society of Photographic Educators (SPE), Las Vegas, Mar. 2002.

Perenyi, Eleanor. *Green Thoughts: A Writer in the Garden*. New York: Modern Library, 2002.

"Pergolas in American Gardens." *The Craftsman* 20 (Apr. 1911): 33.

Petrescu, Doina. "Losing Control, Keeping Desire." In *Architecture and Participation*, ed. Peter Blundell Jones, Doina Petrescu, and Jeremy Till, 43–63. New York: Spon Press, 2005.

Piercy, Marge. *He, She, and It*. New York: Fawcett Crest, 1991.

Piercy, Marge. *Woman on the Edge of Time*. New York: Knopf, 1976.

Pohl, Frederik, and C. M. Kornbluth. *The Space Merchants*. New York: Ballantine Books, 1953.

Pollan, Michael. "The Futures of Food." *New York Times Magazine*, May 4, 2003.

Pollan, Michael. *In Defense of Food: An Eater's Manifesto*. New York: Penguin, 2008.

Pollan, Michael. "Introduction to the Modern Library Gardening Series." In *Green Thoughts*, by Eleanor Perenyi, vii–ix. New York: Modern Library, 2000.

Pollan, Michael. *The Omnivore's Dilemma*. New York: Penguin Books, 2006.

Pollan, Michael. *Second Nature*. New York: Delta, 1991.

Pollan, Michael. "Why Bother?" *New York Times Magazine*, Apr. 20, 2008.

Pope, Alexander. *The Correspondence of Alexander Pope*. Ed. George Sherburn. Oxford: Clarendon, 1956.

Pope, Alexander. "Epistle IV to Earl of Burlington." In *The Correspondence of Alexander Pope*, ed. George Sherburn, vol. 4. Oxford: Clarendon, 1956.

Pope, Alexander. "Essay from *The Guardian*" (1713). In *The Genius of the Place: The English Landscape Garden, 1620–1820*, ed. John D. Hunt and Peter Willis. Cambridge, Mass: MIT Press, 1988.

Pope, Alexander. *Poems*. Ed. John Butt. New Haven: Yale University Press, 1939.

Porter, Joy. "History in *Garden in the Dunes*." In *Reading Leslie Marmon Silko*, ed. Laura Coltelli, 57–71. Pisa, Italy: Pisa University Press, 2007.

Powers, Richard. *Gain*. New York: Picador USA, 1998.

Pyle, Robert Michael. *The Thunder Tree: Lessons from an Urban Wildland*. New York: Houghton Mifflin, 1993.

Raver, Anne. "Houses Before Gardens, City Decides." *New York Times*, Jan. 9, 1997: C-1.

Reynolds, Richard. *On Guerrilla Gardening: A Handbook for Gardening Without Boundaries*. New York: Bloomsbury, 2008.
Ricoeur, Paul. *Lectures on Ideology and Utopia*. Ed. George Taylor. New York: Columbia University Press, 1986.
Rion, Hannah. "What My Garden Means to Me" (1912). In *The American Gardener: A Sampler*, ed. Allen Lacey, 33–35. New York: Farrar Straus and Giroux, 1988.
Robbins, Mary Caroline. *The Rescue of an Old Place*. Boston: n.p., 1892.
Robinson, Kim Stanley. *Blue Mars*. New York: Bantam Books, 1996.
Robinson, Kim Stanley. *Green Mars*. New York: Bantam Books, 1994.
Robinson, Kim Stanley. *Red Mars*. New York: Bantam Books, 1993.
Rogers, Elizabeth Barlow. *Writing the Garden: A Literary Conversation across Two Centuries*. Boston: David R. Godine, 2011.
Rosenberg, Jay. "18th and Rhode Island Community Garden." Message to Jennifer Atkinson. Apr. 11, 2009. Email correspondence.
Rosenzweig, Roy, and Elizabeth Blackmar. *The Park and the People: A History of Central Park*. Ithaca: Cornell University Press, 1992.
Rosin, Jacob, and Max Eastman. *The Road to Abundance*. New York: McGraw-Hill, 1953.
Ross, Stephanie. "Ut Hortus Poesis—Gardening and Her Sister Arts in Eighteenth-Century England." *British Journal of Aesthetics* 25, no. 1 (Winter 1985): 17–32.
Rossi, Peter H. *Down and Out in America: The Origins of Homelessness*. Chicago: University of Chicago Press, 1989.
Ryden, Kent. *Mapping the Invisible Landscape: Folklore, Writing, and the Sense of Place*. Iowa City: University of Iowa Press, 1993.
Saguaro, Shelley. *Garden Plots: The Politics and Poetics of Gardens*. Burlington, Vt.: Ashgate, 2006.
Sanchez, Monica. "Siento que es mio." In *Paradise Transplanted: Migration and the Making of California Gardens*, ed. Pierrette Hondagneu-Sotelo, 153. Berkeley: University of California Press, 2014.
Sargent, Irene. "John Ruskin." *Craftsman* 1 (Nov. 1901): 9.
Schauman, Sally. "The Garden and the Red Barn: The Pervasive Pastoral and Its Environmental Consequences." *Journal of Aesthetics and Art Criticism* 56, no. 2 (Spring 1998): 181–90.
Scheler, Max. *Formalism in Ethics and Non-Formal Ethics of Values*. Trans. Manfred Frings and Roger Funk. Evanston, Ill.: Northwestern University Press, 1973.
Schlosser, Eric. *Fast Food Nation: The Dark Side of the All-American Meal*. Boston: Houghton Mifflin, 2001.
Schmelzkopf, Karen. "Incommensurability, Land Use, and the Right to Space: Community Gardens in New York City." *Urban Geography* 23, no. 4. (2002): 323–43.
Scott, Frank J. *The Art of Beautifying Suburban Home Grounds of Small Extent*. New York: D. Appleton, 1870.
Seaton, Beverly. "Gardening Books for the Commuter's Wife." *Landscape* 28, no. 2 (1985): 41–47.

Seremetakis, C. Nadia. *The Senses Still*. Boulder, Colo.: Westview Press, 1994.

Shennandoah, Joanne, and Douglas M. George. *Skywoman: Legends of the Iroquois*. Santa Fe, N.M.: Clear Light, 1988.

Silko, Leslie Marmon. *Gardens in the Dunes*. New York: Simon & Schuster, 1999.

Simmel, Georg. "The Metropolis and Mental Life." 1903. Reprinted in *On Individuality and Social Forms*. Ed. Donald N. Levine. Chicago: University of Chicago Press, 1971.

Simo, Melanie. *Forest and Garden: Traces of Wildness in a Modernizing Land, 1897–1949*. Charlottesville: University of Virginia Press, 2003.

Simpson, Lewis. *The Dispossessed Garden: Pastoral and History in Southern Literature*. Athens: University of Georgia Press, 1975.

Smith, Henry Nash. *Virgin Land*. Cambridge, Mass.: Harvard University Press, 1978.

Soja, Edward. *Thirdspace: Journeys to Los Angeles and Other Real-and-Imagined Places*. Cambridge, Mass.: Blackwell, 1996.

Solnit, Rebecca. *Storming the Gates of Paradise*. Berkeley: University of California Press, 2007.

Solnit, Rebecca. *Wanderlust: A History of Walking*. New York: Penguin Books, 2001.

Sprang, Rebecca. *The Invention of the Restaurant: Paris and Modern Gastronomic Culture*. Cambridge, Mass.: Harvard University Press, 2000.

St. John de Crèvecoeur, J. Hector. *Letters from an American Farmer*. Oxford: Oxford University Press, 1997.

Staeheli, Lynn A., Don Mitchell, and Kristina Gibson. "Conflicting Rights to the City in New York's Community Gardens." *GeoJournal* 58 (2002): 197–205.

Starr, Armory. *Global Revolt: A Guide to the Movements against Globalization*. New York: Zed Books, 2005.

Steinbeck, John. *The Grapes of Wrath*. New York: Bantam Books, 1969.

Steinglass, Matt. "The Machine in the Garden." *Metropolis Magazine*, Oct. 2000.

Stewart, Amy. "The Universal Itch." In *The Roots of My Obsession: Thirty Great Gardeners Reveal Why They Garden*, ed. Thomas Cooper, 138–42. Portland: Timber Press, 2012.

Stewart, Susan. *On Longing: Narratives of the Miniature, the Gigantic, the Souvenir, the Collection*. Baltimore: Johns Hopkins University Press, 1984.

Stout, Ruth. *How to Have a Green Thumb without an Aching Back*. New York: Cornerstone Library, 1976.

Suvin, Darko. "On the Poetics of the Science Fiction Genre." *College English* 34, no. 3 (Dec. 1972): 372–82.

Suzuki, David. *The Sacred Balance: Rediscovering Our Place in Nature*. New York: Greystone Books, 2009.

Sweet, Timothy. *American Georgics: Economy and Environment in Early American Literature*. Philadelphia: University of Pennsylvania Press, 2002.

Taylor, Dorceta. "Central Park as a Model for Social Control: Urban Parks, Social Class and Leisure Behavior in Nineteenth-Century America." *Journal of Leisure Research* (Fourth Quarter 1999): 420–77.

Teschemacher, J. E. "On Horticultural Architecture." *Horticultural Register* 1 (May 1835): 157.
Thacker, Christopher. *The History of Gardens*. Berkeley: University of California Press, 1985.
Thaxter, Celia. *An Island Garden*. 1894. Reprint, Boston: Houghton Mifflin, 1988.
Thomas, Keith. *Man and the Natural World*. New York: Pantheon Books, 1983.
Thompson, Edward P. "Romanticism, Moralism, and Utopianism: The Case of William Morris." *New Left Review* 99 (Sept.–Oct. 1976): 83–111.
Thompson, Edward P. *William Morris, Romantic to Revolutionary*. New York: Pantheon Books, 1977.
Thoreau, Henry David. *Walden*. New York: Modern Library, 2000.
Thoreau, Henry David. "Walking." Reprinted in *Nature* and *Walking*. Ed. John Elder. Boston: Beacon Press, 1991.
Thoreau, Henry David. *A Week on the Concord and Merrimack Rivers*. Reprinted in *Walden and Other Writings*, 313–40. New York: Modern Library, 2000.
Thoreau, Henry David. "Wild Apples." *Atlantic Monthly*, vol. 10, Nov. 1862.
"The Three Sisters" (Mohawk). Recorded by Lois Thomas of Cornwall Island, Canada, in *Indian Legends of Eastern Canada*, Canadian Department of Indian Affairs and Northern Development, 19–21. Toronto: Centennial College, 1969.
Thrift, Nigel. Introduction to *TimeSpace: Geographies of Temporality*. Ed. Jon May and Nigel Thrift. London: Routledge, 2001.
Tobar, Héctor. *The Barbarian Nurseries*. New York: Farrar, Straus and Giroux, 2011.
Tracy, David. *Guerilla Gardening*. Gabriola Island, B.C.: New Society, 2007.
Trollope, Anthony. *North America*. New York: St. Martin's Press, 1986.
Trollope, Fanny. *Domestic Manners of the Americans*. New York: Whittaker, Treacher, 1832.
Tuan, Yi-Fu. *Space and Place: The Perspective of Experience*. Minneapolis: University of Minnesota Press, 1977.
Tucker, David. *Kitchen Gardening in America*. Ames: Iowa State University Press, 1993.
Twain, Mark. "Letter to Joseph H. Twichell. January 3, 1871." In *Mark Twain's Letters, Volume 4: 1870–1871*, ed. Victor Fischer, Michael Barry Frank, and Lin Salamo, 294. Berkeley: University of California Press, 1995.
Uchida, Yoshiko. *Desert Exile: The Uprooting of a Japanese American Family*. Seattle: University of Washington Press, 2015.
United States Department of Agriculture Economic Research Service. "National Count of Farmers Market Directory Listings Graph: 1994–2016." USDA-AMS Local Food Research & Development Division. Retrieved June 15, 2017, from www.ams.usda.gov/services/local-regional/farmers-markets-and-direct-consumer-marketing.
Van Dyke, Henry. "The Red River of the North." *Harper's New Monthly Magazine* 60, no. 360 (May 1880): 801–18.
Van Rensselaer, Mariana. *Art Out-of-Doors: Hints on Good Taste in Gardening*. New York: Charles Scribner's Sons, 1893.

Veblen, Thorstein. *The Theory of the Leisure Class*. 1899. Reprint, New York: Dover, 1994.

Verne, Jules. "In the Twenty-Ninth Century: The Day of an American Journalist in 2889." In *Yesterday and Tomorrow*. 1898. Reprint, London: Arco 1965.

Viele, Egbert. "Topography of New-York and Its Park System." In *The Memorial History of the City of New-York, From Its First Settlement to the Year 1892*, ed. James Grant Wilson, 551–60. New York: New York History Co., 4: 1892–93.

von Hassell, Malve. *The Struggle for Eden: Community Gardens in New York City*. Westport, Conn.: Bergin & Garvey, 2002.

Walker, Alice. "In Search of Our Mothers' Gardens: The Creativity of Black Women in the South." *Ms. Magazine*. 1974. Retrieved July 18, 2016, from www.msmagazine.com/spring2002/walker.asp.

WALL-E. Dir. Andrew Stanton. Pixar Animation Studios, 2008.

Walpole, Horace. Preface to William Mason's *Satirical Poems*. Ed. Paget Toynbee. Oxford: Oxford University Press, 1926.

"War on Pushcarts Pressed by Mayor." *New York Times*, Jan. 10, 1940.

Warner, Charles Dudley. *My Summer in a Garden*. 1870. Reprint, New York: Modern Library, 2002.

We Are Everywhere: The Irresistible Rise of Global Anti-Capitalism. Ed. Notes from Nowhere. New York: Verso, 2003

Wegner, Phillip. *Imaginary Communities: Utopia, the Nation, and the Spatial Histories of Modernity*. Berkeley: University of California Press, 2002.

Weinberg, Bill. "¡Viva Loisaida Libre!" In *Avant Gardening*, ed. Peter Lamborn Wilson and Bill Weinberg, 38–56. Brooklyn: Autonomedia, 1999.

Weinstein, Jay. *The Ethical Gourmet*. New York: Broadway Books, 2006.

Wells, Patricia. "Best Buys." *New York Times*, Aug. 1, 1979.

Wendt, Gerald. *Science for the World of Tomorrow*. New York: W. W. Norton, 1939.

Weschler, Lawrence. *Domestic Scenes: The Art of Ramiro Gomez*. New York: Harry N. Abrams, 2016.

Whatley, Thomas. *Observations on Modern Gardening*. 5th ed. London: G. Stafford, 1793.

White, John R. "Lived Body and Ecological Value Cognition." In *Merleau-Ponty and Environmental Philosophy: Dwelling on the Landscapes of Thought*, ed. Suzanne Cataldi and William Hamrick, 177–89. Albany: State University of New York Press, 2007.

White, John R. "Person and the Environment: Vital Sympathy and the Roots of Environmental Ethics." In *Ethics and Phenomenology*, ed. Mark Sanders and J. Jeremy Wisnewski, 221–40. Plymouth, UK: Lexington Book, 2012.

White, Katharine. *Onward and Upward in the Garden*. Ed. E. B. White. Boston: Beacon Press, 2002.

White, Trumbull, and William Ingleheart. *The World's Columbia Exposition, Chicago 1893*. Philadelphia: P. W. Ziegler, 1893.

White, William Allen. "The Business of a Wheat Farm." *Scribner's Magazine* 22, no. 5 (Nov. 1897): 531–48.
Whitman, Alden. "I Can Still Taste It". *Newsweek*. May 28, 1973.
Whitman, Walt. "This Compost." In *Leaves of Grass*. Ed. Bradley Sculley and Harold Blodgett, 368–69. New York: W. W. Norton, 1973.
Wildcat, Daniel R. *Red Alert! Saving the Planet with Indigenous Knowledge*. Golden, Colo.: Fulcrum, 2009.
Wilder, Louise Beebe. "Magenta the Maligned." In *The American Gardener: A Sampler*, ed. Allen Lacy, 94–99. New York: Farrar, Straus and Giroux, 1988. Originally published in *Colour in My Garden*. Garden City, N.Y.: Doubleday, Doran, 1918.
Will, Brad. "Cultivating Hope: The Community Gardens of New York City." In *We Are Everywhere: The Irresistible Rise of Global Anti-Capitalism*, ed. Notes from Nowhere, 134–39. New York: Verso, 2003.
Williams, Raymond. *The Country and the City*. New York: Oxford University Press, 1973.
Williams, Raymond. *Keywords: A Vocabulary of Culture and Society*. New York: Oxford University Press, 1976.
Williams, Raymond. *Problems in Materialism and Culture: Selected Essays*. London: Verso, 1980.
Wilson, Peter Lamborn. "Avant Gardening." In *Avant Gardening*, ed. Peter Lamborn Wilson and Bill Weinberg, 7–34. Brooklyn: Autonomedia, 1999.
Winthrop, John, Jr. "Indian Corne" (1662). In Fulmer Mood, "John Winthrop, Jr., on Indian Corn," *New England Quarterly* 10 (1937): 125–33.
Winthrop, John, Jr. *Winthrop Papers: Vol. 2, 1623–1630*. Boston: Massachusetts Historical Society, 1931.
Wood, Charles B. "The New 'Pattern Books' and the Role of the Agricultural Press." In *Prophet with Honor: The Career of Andrew Jackson Downing, 1815–1852*, ed. George B. Tatum and Elisabeth Blair MacDougall, 165–89. Philadelphia: Athenaeum of Philadelphia, 1989.
Wright, John. "Clearcutting the East Village." In *Avant Gardening*, ed. Peter Lamborn Wilson and Bill Weinberg, 127–31. Brooklyn: Autonomedia, 1999.
Wright, Mabel Osgood. *Flowers and Ferns in Their Native Haunts*, 1907 (excerpt). In *The American Gardener: A Sampler*, ed. Allen Lacy, 195–96. New York: Farrar, Straus and Giroux, 1988.
Wright, Mabel Osgood. *The Garden of a Commuter's Wife*. Norwood, Mass.: Macmillan, 1901.
Wright, Richardson. "Little Gardens." In *The Gardener's Bed-Book*, 46–47. New York: Modern Library, 2003.
Wyckoff, Walter A. "The Workers: IV—A Farm Hand." *Scribner's Magazine* 22, no. 5 (Nov. 1897): 549–60.
Wyman, Carolyn. *Better Than Homemade: Amazing Foods That Changed the Way We Eat*. Philadelphia: Quirk Books, 2004.

Zoh, Kyung-Jin. "Reinventing Gardens: A Study in Garden Theory." PhD diss., University of Pennsylvania, 1994.
Zukin, Sharon. "Consuming Authenticity: From Outposts of Difference to Means of Exclusion." *Cultural Studies* 22, no. 5 (2008): 724–48.

Index

Abensour, Miguel, 153
Accursed Share, The (Bataille), 12–13
activist gardener, lineage of, 156–57
Addison, Joseph, 29
advertising, 104
"Affirmative Character of a Culture, The" (Marcuse), 23
African American women, 5, 26, 28, 143, 168–69, 184–85, 193
Agee, James, 9–10
Aldrich, Thomas Bailey, 169–70
Alexander, William, 112, 223n31
Allen, Lewis, 35
All Over Creation (Ozeki), 75
Alsop, George, 171
American Grown (Obama), 28
Animal, Vegetable, Miracle (Kingsolver), 12–13
apples, 100–101, 107–8
Army and Department of Agriculture, 99
Art of Beautifying Suburban Home Grounds of Small Extent, The (Scott), 37
Art Out-of-Doors (Van Rensselaer), 170
Arts and Crafts movement, 82, 89–92
Atwood, Margaret: *The Handmaid's Tale*, 154–55; *The Year of the Flood*, 15, 143–46
"Avant Gardening" (Wilson), 107–8, 114, 130–33, 157

back-to-land movements, 95
Bacon, Francis, 103
Baker, Ray Stannard, 87–88; "The Movement of Wheat," 63, 69–70, 71

Barbarian Nurseries, The (Tobar), 151, 180–85
bargaining, 125–26
Barndt, Deborah, 219n2
barter systems, 220n11
Bataille, Georges, 12–13
Beecher, Henry Ward, 1, 39, 54
Being There (Kosinski), 129
Belasco, Warren, 103
Benepe, Barry, 95–97
Beverley, Robert, 25
Bigelow, Poultney, 73
Blane, William, 34
Blithedale Romance, The (Hawthorne), 22–23, 28–33, 40–41, 46
Bloch, Ernst, 6; *The Principle of Hope*, 2
body, 202–3, 204–10, 212–13
bonanza farms: cartography of, 71–81; class struggle and, 87–88; definition of, 59, 65–67; globalization and, 67–69; illustrations of, 71; market economy, integration into, 66–67; monocultures and, 67; scale of production, 70–75, 86; subsistence farming, decline of, 66–67
botanical relocations, 187–89, 190–91
Boyd-Orr, John, 102
Bradford, William, 216n2
Brascoupé, Clayton, 195–96
Brave New World (Huxley), 105
Brooks-Smith, Derryck, 122–23
Brown, Bill, 112
Brown, Lancelot, 147–48
Bruchac, Joseph, 196

"Burial" (Gay), 203, 212
"Business of a Wheat Farm, The" (White), 68
Butler, Octavia, 143
Byrd, William, II, 25

Caduto, Michael, 196
Cambodian immigrants, 179
Candide (Voltaire), 5, 130
"Capability" (L. Brown), 147–48
Čapek, Karel, 2, 202, 207–8, 209, 211–12
Carnival, 124
"Carrier Bag Theory of Fiction, The" (Le Guin), 200
cartography, 71–81
Catalog of Unabashed Gratitude (Gay), 206, 213
Cather, Willa: *Death Comes for the Archbishop*, 82–83; *My Ántonia*, 69, 79–81, 84–85
Center on the Environment, 118
Central Park, 35, 148–50, 218n21
cheap food policy, 224n5
Chesnutt, Charles, 77–79
Cicero, 215n4
City Beautiful Movement, 120
civilization, 134–35
class: "culture" and, 23; etiquette and, 46
Cohen, Stanley, 4–5, 6, 153
commensality, 109
commodity ticker, 68
commodity value, 125–26
communes, 22, 219n3
community gardens: control of public space, 159; invisibility of, 162; property rights and, 164–67; real estate market and, 162; spatial practices, 159–64; victory gardens and, 158–59; waste and, 14–15
"Compost, The" (Whitman), 14
Conjure Woman, The (Chesnutt), 77–79
Constant Gardener, The (Le Carré), 129
consumption, 203–4, 213
contamination, industrial, 229n9
Copeland, Robert, 37, 39
corn, 98, 194–97
cottage gardens, 90–92
cotton, 9–10, 189–90
Country and the City, The (Williams), 146, 157
Country Life (Copeland), 37, 39
Crèvecoeur, Hector St. John de, 57–58

Critique of Judgment (Kant), 160
Cultivating Environmental Justice (Emmett), 168
cultivation, Native American exclusion from, 24–25, 51, 170–72, 193–95, 198
culture, 23, 134

Day of the Bonanza, The (Drache), 86
death, 209–10, 211–12
Death Comes for the Archbishop (Cather), 82–83
de Certeau, Michel, 62, 77
Department of Public Markets, 119
Desert Exile (Uchida), 177
diets, consolidation of biodiversity in, 99–101
dirt gardeners, 202
"Discontent in the Garden" (Kirkland), 91–92
Dispossessed, The (Le Guin), 137–38
Domestic Scenes (Gomez), 180
Downing, Andrew Jackson, 34–37
Drache, Hiram, 86
Duncan, Frances, 89
Dwyer, Thomas, 119

Earle, Alice Morse, 84, 90
Eat Your Heart Out (Hightower), 107
ECObox, 159–60, 161–62
Eddie, Don, 165
Efron, Marshall, 103
Eliot, George, 203
Emmett, Robert, 168
Escape Attempts (Cohen and L. Taylor), 4–5, 6, 153
Ethical Gourmet, The (Weinstein), 219n2
Every Woman Her Own Flower Gardener (Johnson), 37–38

Farewell to Manzanar (Houston), 177
Farm Book (Jefferson), 26
farmers, population of, 65
Farmer's Almanac, 23, 33
farmers' markets, 118–19, 121; New York City Greenmarket, 95–97, 109–13, 115–18, 121–24, 125–26, 226n16
Farm Journal, 66
Ferguson, Sarah, 159
Finley, Ron, 157
Fiskio, Janet, 164–65

Fitzgerald, F. Scott, 151
Flowers and Ferns (M. O. Wright), 41
food analogs, in science fiction, 104–6
food critics, 97. *See also* Hess, Karen
food exposés, rise of, 58–59
"Food not Lawns," 150
Foucault, Michel, 136
Franklin Urban Community Garden, 175
Freidberg, Susanne, 219n2
French Beans and Food Scares (Freidberg), 219n2
Freyfogle, Eric, 58
Fuller, Margaret, 217n15

Gain (Powers), 7–8, 20, 209–10
Garden, The (Kennedy), 162, 165–66
Garden Book (Jefferson), 25–28
"Garden City" movement, 158
gardening: as apolitical, 5–6, 152; labor of (*see* labor, outsourcing of); political, 129–30; popularity of, 2–3; as radical, 128–30, 143, 146, 162–67, 172–74; sexuality and, 154–55
Gardening by Myself (A. B. Warner), 37
Gardening for Love (Lawrence), 106
Gardening for Profit (Henderson), 39–40
Garden of a Commuter's Wife (M. O. Wright), 38
gardens: American compared with European, 33–34; without cultivation, 24–28; definition of, 3; as enclosed, 84–86, 135, 145; etymology of, 84, 139, 226n1; literary knowledge and, 28–30; meanings of, 82–92; as paradise, 132–35 (*see also* utopias); as place, 92–93; as site of resistance, 172–74; temporality and, 160–62
—as foil to industrialized farms: artisanal labor, 89–93; enclosed, 84–86; small scale, 86–89
Gardens in the Dunes (Silko), 186, 187–88, 197–99, 200, 216n4
"garden writing," 3–4
Gay, Ross: "Burial," 203, 212; *Catalog of Unabashed Gratitude*, 206, 213
Genesee Farmer, 37
geographies of cultivation, 23–24
Georgics (Virgil), 24
Gernsback, Hugo, 105
Gilman, Charlotte Perkins, 152
Giuliani, Rudolph, 166–67

"Giving Good Weight" (McPhee), 95, 109–10, 116, 203. *See also* farmers' markets: New York City Greenmarket
globalism, 202
Global Revolt (Starr), 163
Gold, Michael, 227n9
Gomez, Ramiro, 180
grain elevators, 87
Grant, Doris, 95
Grapes of Wrath, The (Steinbeck), 9, 174, 206
Graves, Richard, 31
Great Depression, 9
Great Gatsby, The (Fitzgerald), 151
Greenmarket, New York City. *See under* farmers' markets
Green Thoughts (Perenyi), 169
guerrilla gardening, 14, 162–64. *See also* community gardens

Hakluyt, Richard, 216n4
Handmaid's Tale, The (Atwood), 154–55
Harvey, David, 64, 75, 161–62
Hawthorne, Nathaniel, 22–23, 28–33, 40–41
He, She, and It (Piercy), 137, 143, 146–47, 153–54, 155
heirloom produce, 99, 106
Helmont, Jan Baptist van, 225n10
Henderson, Peter, 39–40
Herland (Gilman), 152
"Hermitage, The" (Graves), 31
hermitages, 30–32
Hess, John, 97, 101, 107; *The Taste of America*, 105–6
Hess, Karen, 97, 101, 107; *The Taste of America*, 105–6
Hightower, Jim, 97–98; *Eat Your Heart Out*, 107
History and Present State of Virginia (Beverley), 25
History of the Conquest of Mexico (Prescott), 190
Hodson, Rich, 123
hollowness, 109
Holmes, Seth, 169
homelessness, 177–79
Homestead Act, 220n8
homogenization of landscape, 75
Horowitz, Ralf, 165–66
Houston, Jeanne Wakatsuki, 177

How to Have a Green Thumb (Stout), 10, 223n31
Hoyles, Martin, 5
Hunt, John Dixon, 30
Huxley, Aldous, 105

immigrants: exploitation of, 169; food customs of, 175; gardens, meaning of, and, 172; garden writers and, 169; as hired laborers, 180–85; as invisible, 180; land, views on, 169; non-English-speakers, 179; physical health of, 228n1; restrictions on immigration, 169–70; seeds and, 174–76; as uprooted or transplanted peoples, 176
industrial farms, 9–10, 59, 63, 83, 85–86, 88–89. *See also* bonanza farms
industrialization, 59
"In Search of Our Mothers' Gardens" (Walker), 184–85
intercropping, 194–96
Isaac, Bernard, 177
Island Garden, An (Thaxter), 38

Japanese-American internment camps, 176–77
Jefferson, Thomas: on American gardening, 33–34; and Land Ordinance, 65
—works: *Farm Book*, 26; *Garden Book*, 25–28
Jews without Money (Gold), 227n9
Johnson, Sophia Orne, 37–38

Kant, Immanuel, 160
Keepers of Life (Caduto and Bruchac), 196
Keillor, Garrison, 10–12
Kennedy, Scott Hamilton, 162, 165–66
Kew Botanical Gardens, 189–90
Khmer Growers, 179
Kimmerer, Robin Wall, 204
Kincaid, Jamaica, 5, 168–69; on Jefferson, 26; *My Garden (Book)*, 186–92
Kingsolver, Barbara, 12–13
Kirkland, Winifred, 91–92
Klein, Naomi, 130; *This Changes Everything*, 5
Kosinski, Jerzy, 129

labor: class struggle and, 87–88; erasure of, 146–47; as heroic, 168–69; immigrants and, 169; itinerant workers, 61, 69–70, 223n30; outsourcing of, 88–89, 154, 169, 190–91; rates for, 49; scale of industrial farms and, 87–88; shortage of, 217n12; as "unskilled," 180–85. *See also* slavery
"Lady Does Her Own Work, The" (Stowe), 37
La Guardia, Fiorello, 120
Land Ordinance (1785), 64–65
landownership: private use versus commercial gain, 77–79; views of, 164–67, 170–73
Latinx immigrants, 174–76, 180–85
lawns, 84, 147–48, 150–52, 180–82
Lawrence, Elizabeth, 106
Lears, Jackson, 124
Le Carré, John, 129
Lefebvre, Henri, 167; *The Production of Space*, 136–37
Le Guin, Ursula: "The Carrier Bag Theory of Fiction," 200; *The Dispossessed*, 137–38
Letters from an American Farmer (Crèvecoeur), 57–58
Let Us Now Praise Famous Men (Agee), 9–10
Levitas, Ruth, 6
Librarian at Play, The (Pearson), 38–39
London, George, 217n10

MacDonald, Eric, 211
magenta, 90–91
"Magnolia of Lake Pontchartrain, The" (Fuller), 217n15
mail service, 81
Mama Day (Naylor), 225
Mao, Sokehn, 179
Marcuse, Herbert, 23
market gardening: compared with industrialized farms, 224n2; New York City Greenmarket and, 95–97
Mars trilogy (Robinson), 128–29, 137–41, 152
Marx, Karl, 9–10, 66
mass production, 90–91
McAdam, Thomas, 40
McDonald's, 99
McKay, George, 164
McPhee, John, 99, 123–24; "Giving Good Weight," 95, 109–10, 116, 203. *See also* farmers' markets: New York City Greenmarket
Meals to Come (Belasco), 103
mechanization, 65, 76–77, 87–88
memory, 113–17, 186–92

Messervy, Julie, 202
Mickey, Thomas, 91
mind gardeners, 202
miniaturization, 88–89, 223n31
Miss Tiller's Vegetable Garden and the Money She Made by It (A. B. Warner), 37
monocultures, 82–83, 224n5
Montaigne, Michel de, 24–25
Monticello, 25–28
More, Thomas, 132–35, 161
Morris, William, 135, 141, 158
Morrison, B. Y., 89
Morrison, Toni, 185, 193
Morton, 103
Morton, Margaret, 177–79
"Movement of Wheat, The" (Baker), 63, 69–70, 71
My Ántonia (Cather), 69, 79–81, 84–85
My Garden (Book) (Kincaid), 186–92
My Summer in a Garden (C. D. Warner): bridging chasms and, 42; on economic value of gardening, 48, 51–52; gardener persona, use of, 43–45; gardening as independence, 44–45; on gardening as pleasure, 20–21, 21–22, 47; gardening as pleasure and practical, 44–49; integration of genres, 21–22; legacy of, 56, 201, 213; on nature and cultivation, 52–53; as new literary mode, 16, 53–56; reception of, 43; rewards for labor, 45–47; as serial narrative, 53–55; social attachments, 52

National Education Television, 103
Native American Gardening (Caduto and Bruchac), 196
Native American rights movement, 195–96
Native Americans, 12, 193–200; displacement of, 170–72; excluded from "cultivation," 24–25, 51, 170–72, 193–95, 198; fictionalized accounts of, 187–88, 197–99; Sky Woman, 173
nativism, 169–70, 198–99
nature writing, 206–9
Naylor, Gloria, 225
neoliberalism, 108, 164–67
New Agrarianism, The (Freyfogle), 58
New Agriculture. *See* bonanza farms
New Atlantis (Bacon), 103
New Deal, 224n5

News From Nowhere (Morris), 135, 141, 158
New World, as pastoral, 24–25. *See also* wilderness
Nixon, Richard, 224n5
NOMADgardens, 159–60
nomadic gardens, 159–60, 161–62
non-English-speaking population, 179
Nook Farm, 43
Norris, Frank, 67, 73–77, 85, 87–88
North America (A. Trollope), 87–88
nostalgia, 60, 76–77, 79–88, 113, 170

Obama, Michelle, 28
Observations on Modern Gardening (Whatley), 34
Octopus, The (Norris), 67, 68, 73–77, 85, 87–88
Old Time Gardens (Earle), 84, 90
Olmsted, Frederick Law, 35, 150
Omnivore's Dilemma, The (Pollan), 58–59, 71
On Longing (S. Stewart), 86
Orwell, George, 5
overproduction, 9, 10–13. *See also Grapes of Wrath, The*
Ozeki, Ruth, 75

Parable of the Sower (Butler), 143
Parable of the Talents (Butler), 143
Paradise (Morrison), 185, 193
parks, 208–9
peaches, 108, 114
Pearson, Edmund Lester, 38–39
Perenyi, Eleanor, 14, 109, 114, 206, 223n31; *Green Thoughts*, 169
Pérez, Miguel Angel, 165
Petrescu, Doina, 159–60
Pfannschmidt, Julia, 113
picturesque landscapes, 147–50
Piercy, Marge: *He, She, and It*, 137, 143, 146–47, 153–54, 155; *Woman on the Edge of Time*, 137
Piggly Wiggly, 121
Pike Place Market, 121
Pineapple-Juice Bias, 115
place, definition of, 63–64
Plain and Pleasant Talk about Fruits, Flowers and Farming (Beecher), 39
plantations, 25–28, 187, 188

Pollan, Michael, 58–59, 71. *See also Second Nature*
Pope, Alexander, 29, 30–31
postcolonialism, 186–92
Powers, Richard, 7–8, 20, 209–10
Prescott, William, 190
Principle of Hope, The (Bloch), 2
print technology, 81–82
processed foods, 99–100, 101–6
produce, 105–7, 110–12, 113–17
Production of Space, The (Lefebvre), 136–37
property disputes, 75–76
pushcart markets, 119–20
Pyle, Robert, 229n2

Radical Gardening (McKay), 164
Raíces Latinas, 176
railroads, 68–69, 75–76, 80, 81
reciprocity, 197
Red Alert! (Wildcat), 197
reflexive localism, 226n14
Reynolds, Richard, 162–63
Rion, Hanna, 88–89
Road to Abundance, The (Rosin), 103–4
"roaming" gardens, 159–60, 161–62
Robbins, Mary Caroline, 170
Robinson, Kim Stanley: *Mars* trilogy, 128–29, 137–41, 152; *Three Californias Trilogy*, 143
Rosin, Jacob, 103–4
Ross, Stephanie, 20

saccharin, 103
"sacred ecology," 196
Sargent, Irene, 89–90
school lunch programs, 99
"Scientific Restaurant" (Gernsback), 105
Scott, Frank J., 37
Second Nature (Pollan): garden enclosures and, 84; as gardener, 93; on gardening as "hobby," 129; on lawns, 150–52; self-sufficiency and, 205; Warner, legacy of, and, 56; waste reversal and, 8–9, 15; on weight of produce, 112
self-reliance, 50–51
Sense of Things, A (B. Brown), 112
Seremetakis, Nadia, 80, 108, 113
sharecroppers, 174

Silko, Leslie Marmon, 186, 187–88, 197–99, 200, 216n4
Simpson, Lewis, 216n5
skill, 45, 180–85
Sky Woman, 173
slavery, 25–28, 168–69; farming expertise (in literature), 78. *See also* Kincaid, Jamaica
social privilege, 115
Solnit, Rebecca, 205
Sounder, Clarence, 121
South Central Farm, 162, 164–66
space: defined, 63, 64; technology's effects on, 68
species loneliness, 204
Spectator, The (Addison), 29
Starr, Armory, 163
Steinbeck, John, 9, 174, 206
Stewart, Amy, 210
Stewart, Martha, 202
Stewart, Susan, 88, 89; *On Longing*, 86
Story of Gardening, The (Hoyles), 5
Stourhead, 30
Stout, Ruth, 13, 14, 19–20, 211; *How to Have a Green Thumb*, 10, 223n31
Stowe, Harriet Beecher, 37
subsistence farming, decline of, 66
superfund sites, 229n9
supermarkets, 120–21, 226n16

Tangled Routes (Barndt), 219n2
Taste of America, The (Hess and Hess), 105–6
Taylor, Frederick, 89
Taylor, Laurie, 4–5, 6, 153
telegraph, 68
telephones, 73–75
tenancy, rise of, 220n8
terraformation, 137–41
Thaxter, Celia, 38
This Changes Everything (Klein), 5
Thompson, E. P., 153
Thoreau, Henry David: and sustainable diets, 224n1; *Walden*, 48–51; *A Week on the Concord and Merrimack Rivers*, 50–51; "Wild Apples," 100–101, 112, 117–18, 225n8
Three Californias Trilogy (Robinson), 143
"Three Sisters," 194–96, 197

Thunder Tree, The (Pyle), 229n2
Tobar, Héctor, 151, 180–85
tomatoes, 105–6, 107, 109, 114
Traditional Native American Farmers Association, 195
Treatise on the Theory and Practice of Landscape Gardening (Downing), 34–37
Trollope, Anthony, 87–88
Trollope, Frances, 34
Twain, Mark, 43
Twickenham, 29, 30–31

Uchida, Yoshiko, 177
"Unguarded Gates" (Aldrich), 169–70
United States, as garden, 169–72
urban gardening. *See* community gardens
urban gardening campaigns, 150
Utopia (More), 132–35, 161
utopias: dialectical utopianism, 161–62; as process, 135–41, 161; as static, 132–35

Van Dyke, Henry, 71–73
Van Rensselaer, Mariana Griswold, 170
Vaux, Calvert, 150
Veblen, Thorstein, 151
Versailles, 147
victory gardens, 158–59
Villaraigosa, Antonio, 164
Virgil, 24
vital sympathies, 201–2
Voltaire, 5, 130
von Hassell, Malve, 162

Walden (Thoreau), 48–51
Walker, Alice, 184–85
WALL-E, 15
Walpole, Horace, 29
Wanderlust (Solnit), 205
Warner, Anna Bartlett, 37

Warner, Charles Dudley, 14, 20. See also *My Summer in a Garden*
waste, 13–15
Week on the Concord and Merrimack Rivers, A (Thoreau), 50–51
Weinstein, Jay, 219n2
Wells, Patricia, 123
Whatley, Thomas, 30; *Observations on Modern Gardening*, 34
Wheeler, Candace, 91
White, Katharine, 1–2, 206–7, 215n1
White, William, 73, 87; "The Business of a Wheat Farm," 68
White House garden, 28
Whitman, Alden, 107, 113
Whitman, Walt, 14
Whole Foods, 226n16
"Wild Apples" (Thoreau), 100–101, 112, 117–18, 225n8; on weight of produce, 112
Wildcat, Daniel, 197
Wilder, Louise Beebe, 91
wilderness, 49–50, 140, 169–72
Williams, Raymond, 148; *The Country and the City*, 146, 157
Wilson, Peter Lamborn, 107–8, 114, 130–33, 157
Winthrop, John, 171
Winthrop, John, Jr., 194
Wise, Henry, 217n10
Woman on the Edge of Time (Piercy), 137
women's publications, impracticality of, 37–40
"Workers, The" (Wyckoff), 61, 70
World's Fairs, 104
Wright, Mabel Osgood: *Flowers and Ferns*, 41; *Garden of a Commuter's Wife*, 38
Wright, Richardson, 89
Wyckoff, Walter, 67; "The Workers," 61, 70

Year of the Flood, The (Atwood), 15, 143–46
Your Bread and Your Life (Grant), 95

www.ingramcontent.com/pod-product-compliance
Lightning Source LLC
Chambersburg PA
CBHW011755220426
43672CB00018B/2971